"This book is urgently needed – crucial task of reconnecting hun terconnected with. The book po~~~~~~~ ecological and social commons can tame the destructive forces of capitalism.
— **PAUL CHATTERTON, Professor of Urban Futures, School of Geography, University of Leeds**

"Henri Lefebvre's 'Right to the City' is an important, but nevertheless limited, idea, as Lefebvre himself did not pay due attention to the ecological dimension of social emancipation. *Social Ecology and the Right to the City* is a welcome step in the right direction, as it provides that motto with a powerful framework: Murray Bookchin's neo-anarchist approach to social ecology."
— **MARCELO LOPES DE SOUZA, Professor of Environmental Geography and Political Ecology, Federal University of Rio de Janeiro**

"This book constitutes an important contribution to the elaboration and articulation of the paradigm of social ecology. It could hardly be more timely, with the multiple, interconnected crises of capitalist modernity engulfing the world in ever-expanding, permanent war and ecological catastrophe. This volume provides abundant reason for hope that, as one of the chapters puts it, our calamitous present is pregnant with a more sustainable, social-ecological future."
— **THOMAS JEFFREY MILEY, University of Cambridge**

"With a majority of the world's population now living in urban areas, the city has re-emerged as a definitive focus for popular struggles and contemporary social movements. This book brings us to the epicenter of today's municipal movements, exploring the recent evolution of urban alternatives, together with theoretical perspectives on the changing character of urban space. The book features some of the very best of the current generation of writers and thinkers in the tradition of social ecology, mainly from Europe and the Middle East, to critique capitalist false solutions and rekindle the promise of an urban future rooted in the commons, a moral economy, and visions of a radically different future."
— **BRIAN TOKAR, author of *Toward Climate Justice: Perspectives on the Climate Crisis and Social Change***

"Not only is the book comprehensive but extremely useful for its interdisciplinary and global analyses. The combination of theory and social movements scholarship within general debates on contemporary political and ecological crises, due to the rise of hostile and narcissistic policies, make this book a timely and significant contribution."
— **SUTAPA CHATTOPADHYAY, University of Windsor, Department of Sociology, Anthropology, and Criminology**

Library and Archives Canada Cataloguing in Publication

Title: The right to the city and social ecology : towards democratic and ecological cities / Federico Venturini, Emet Değirmenci, Inés Morales (editors)
Names: Venturini, Federico, editor. | Değirmenci, Emet, editor. | Morales, Inés, 1976- editor.
Description: Includes bibliographical references and index.
Identifiers: Canadiana (print) 20190166010 | Canadiana (ebook) 20190166053 | ISBN 9781551646831 (hardcover) | ISBN 9781551646817 (softcover) | ISBN 9781551646855 (PDF)
Subjects: LCSH: Sociology, Urban. | LCSH: Urban policy. | LCSH: Urban ecology (Sociology) | LCSH: City and town life.
Classification: LCC HT151 .R54 2019 | DDC 307.76—dc23

C.P.35788 Succ. Léo-Pariseau
Montréal, QC, H2X 0A4

Explore our books and subscribe to our newsletter:
www.blackrosebooks.com

Ordering Information

USA/INTERNATIONAL	CANADA	UK/IRELAND
University of Chicago Press	University of Toronto Press	Central Books
Chicago Distribution Center	5201 Dufferin Street	50 Freshwater Road
11030 South Langley Avenue	Toronto, ON	Chadwell Heath, London
Chicago, IL 60628	M3H 5T8	RM8 1RX
(800) 621-2736 (USA)	1-800-565-9523	+44 (0) 20 8525 8800
(773) 702-7000 (International)	utpbooks@utpress.utoronto.ca	contactus@centralbooks.com
orders@press.uchicago.edu		

Cover art by James Mckay "A Dream of a Low Carbon Future"

This publicationis published in collaboration with the Transnational Institute of Social Ecology

Social Ecology and the Right to the City

Towards Ecological and Democratic Cities

Edited by Federico Venturini, Emet Değirmenci, Inés Morales

Montréal/Chicago/London

CONTENTS

Introduction   1
Federico Venturini, Emet Değirmenci, and Inés Morales
     About this Book   1
     Getting Started: Understanding Ecological Disasters   1
     and Inequality
     Changing the World   3
     The Role of the Activist-Researcher   5
     Contributions to this Volume   6
     Acknowledgements   9

Part 1: Discovering Social Ecology   12

The Legacy of Murray Bookchin   12
Brian Morris
     Introduction   12
     The Modern Crisis   13
     Social Ecology   16
     Dialectical Naturalism and Ethics   21
     The Politics of Libertarian Socialism   24

Social Ecology: A Philosophy for the Future   32
Dan Chodorkoff
     Theory and Practice   32
     The Role of Education   33
     Utopian Thinking   34
     The Principles of Social Ecology   36
     Opposition   40
     Reconstruction   40
     Politics   42

A Critique of The Limits to Growth from a Social Ecology   46
Perspective
Emet Değirmenci
     A Green Growth Economy   47
     The Right to the City and Space-Making   48
     Commons for a "Steady-State Economy"   51
     What Sorts of Growth do We Want?   53

Part 2: Engaging with the Right to the City   58

Is the Right to the City a Right or a Revolution?   58
Magali Fricaudet
> The Paradigm of the Urban Miracle, or How Global   58
> Capitalism Has Reached Massive Consent
> Lefebvre and the Philosophy of Urban Revolution   60
> The Emergence of the Right to the City as a Global   62
> Claim for Socio-Spatial Justice
> Municipalities: At the Forefront of the Right to the   64
> City?
> What if Urban Revolution Meant Permanent Insur-   67
> rection?

Moving beyond the Right to the City: Urban Commoning in   71
Greece
Theodoros Karyotis
> The Right to the City   71
> The Urban Commons   74
> Urban Struggles in Greece   76
> The Subject of Social Mobilisation   80

Reconceptualising Rights and Spatial Justice through Social   86
Ecology
Federico Venturini
> Introduction: Critically Exploring the Right to the   86
> City
> Critically Exploring Spatial Justice   88
> A Convergence of Concepts   89
> Reconceptualising Citizenship, Justice, and Freedom   91
> Reconceptualising the Right to the City and Spatial   93
> Justice
> Conclusion   96

Part 3: The Kurdish Answer: Democratic Confederalism   101

The Evolution of the Kurdish Paradigm   101
Havin Guneser with Eleanor Finley
> The Early Years (1970–1989)   101
> Soul-Searching within the PKK (1990–2010)   103

Ocalan's Abduction and Captivity (1999–)   105
The Present: Where Do the Answers Lie?   107

The Democratization of Cities in North Kurdistan   110
Ercan Ayboga and Egit Pale
     The History of Cities in North Kurdistan   110
     Cities Under the Governance of the Kurdish Free-   112
     dom Movement
     Challenges   115
     Urban Warfare and the New Wave of Gentrification   116

Part 4: Transforming Social Theory   118

Do We Need a New Theory of the State?   118
Metin Guven
     The Current Transition of World Leadership   118
     The Heritage of Domination   120
     The Axial Age and Later Developments   122
     China in the Twenty-First Century   124
     The Strength of the Chinese State Model   125
     A New State Theory for the Struggles to Come   126

Direct Democracy, Social Ecology, and Public Time   128
Alexandros Schismenos
     Aspects of the Global Crisis of Significations   129
     The Problems of the Internet Age   132
     The Emergence of New Significations   134
     The Political Significance of Public Time   136

The Present is Pregnant with a New Future   141
Olli Tammilehto
     Gradual versus Abrupt Change in Western Thought   141
     Abrupt Social Changes in the Past and Present   142
     Shadow Society and Abrupt Change   143
     Regime Shift Theory in Biology and its Relevance to   145
     Society
     Societal Phase Shift and Social Movements   147

Part 5: Walking with the Right to the City   155

Squatting as Claiming the Right to the City   155
Diana Bogado, Noel Manzano and Marta Solanas
    Introduction   155
    Methodological Frame   156
    Financial Urban Management and the Right to the   158
    City in Brazil and Spain
    Squats and Occupations   160
    The Struggle for Housing in Spain   162
    The Social Housing Movements in Brazil   163
    A Transnational Comparison between Brazilian and   164
    Spanish Practices of Occupation and Squatting
    Conclusion: Towards an Internationalization of Ur-   165
    ban Social Movements

Rights Begin in the Small Places Closest to Home: A Story   171
from Constitution Street
Jemma Neville

Notes on the Contributors   178

Introduction

Federico Venturini, Emet Değirmenci, and Inés Morales

"We have seen the future—and it doesn't work"
– Jerome Ross, *ROAR Magazine*

"We don't want to manage the inferno, we want to disassemble it and build something new"
– Raquel Gutiérrez Aguilar, *Pikara Magazine*

"The ecological principle of unity in diversity grades into a richly mediated social principle; hence my use of the term social ecology"
– Murray Bookchin, *The Modern Crisis*

About this Book

This volume arose from proceedings of the conference *The Right to the City and Social Ecology—Towards Ecological and Democratic Cities*, held in Thessaloniki 1–3 September, 2017. The conference was organized by the Transnational Institute of Social Ecology (TRISE).

TRISE is an association of activists and intellectuals based in Europe, who are concerned with current socio-ecological crises. It was founded in Greece in 2013 and focuses on research, education, and training. The association initiates, supports and facilitates research on social ecology, urban social movements, and the democratization of society. Historically, its inspiration can be traced to Vermont, US, where the Institute for Social Ecology was co-founded by Murray Bookchin and Dan Chodorkoff in 1974.

At the heart of the organization's mission lies the theory of *social ecology*. Multiple definitions of social ecology exist. However, TRISE largely follows the innovative philosophy of Murray Bookchin, as well as other writers and activists who developed his work. TRISE aims to foster and develop social ecological analysis and practice that can be adopted for the struggles to come.

This book answers this call, exploring the contemporary discourse surrounding urban rights—*the right to the city*—and presents a selection of new essays on social ecology. This volume seeks to bring the ideas of *social ecology* into conversation with the worldwide call for the *right to the city*, thereby challenging and extending existing discussions on both topics in a fruitful cross-fertilization. Theories and practices need to be discovered, engaged with, and transformed in order to build an effective culture of resistance.

Getting Started: Understanding Ecological Disasters and Inequality

Social and ecological crises are intertwined and, as becomes more evident every day, they are exacerbated by the dominant social, economic, and political systems. Human impacts on the planet are so evident and unique that more and more commentators are calling the geological time in which we live the "Anthropocene" era (Crutzen and Stoermer 2000), from "anthropos" (human) and "-cene", from kainos (new or recent). The biosphere and geological time scale have been fundamentally transformed by human activity and researchers have identified many processes that regulate the stability and resilience of the Earth's systems and nine quantitative planetary boundaries (Steffen et al. 2015) that must not be crossed if humanity is to continue thriving. These include such trends as stratospheric ozone depletion, loss of biosphere integrity, chemical pollution and the release of novel entities, climate change, ocean acidification, freshwater consumption and the global hydrological cycle, land system change, nitrogen and phosphorus flows to the biosphere and oceans, and atmospheric aerosol loading. Crossing these boundaries threatens the existence of life on this planet as we know it, potentially bringing deep or even irreparable change. Of these boundaries, two (biodiversity loss and climate change) have already been crossed, while others are in imminent danger of being crossed.

Bookchin expressed his concerns for the future of humanity and warned us that "if we do not do the impossible, we shall be faced with the unthinkable" (2005: 107).

However, more appropriate still is the term "Capitalocene" (Moore 2016). The causes of current changes are determined not just simply by human intervention, but by the current system that permeates all aspects of our societies—capitalism. These pressing planetary environmental problems can be addressed only by facing the problems within society.

Even the United Nations acknowledges that we live in a world of global inequality and poverty (United Nation Development Programme 2005; 2010). Oxfam (see Hardoon 2017: 2) has also collated some alarming statistics on economic inequality:

- "Since 2015, the richest 1% has owned more wealth than the rest of the planet's population.
- Eight men now own the same amount of wealth as the poorest half of the world.
- Over the next 20 years, 500 people will hand over $2.1 trillion to their heirs—a sum larger than the GDP of India, a country of 1.3 billion people.
- The incomes of the poorest 10% increased by less than $3 a year between 1988 and 2011, while the richest 1% increased their incomes by 182 times what they earned in 1988.
- A FTSE 100 CEO earns as much as 10,000 garment factory

workers in Bangladesh.

- In the US new research by economist Thomas Piketty also shows that over the last 30 years income growth for the bottom 50% has been zero, whereas income growth for the top 1% has been 300%.
- In Vietnam the country's richest man earns more in a day than the poorest person earns in 10 years."

Insofar as these data depict a grim picture, economic inequality is just one indicator among many that illustrate a widespread social crisis; we could add unequal access to resources, gender/racial/class discrimination, widespread conflicts, the Global North–South divide, and so on.

Cities today represent both one of the major causes of the aggravation of the ecological and social crises, but also a potential solution to them. Many contemporary authors have dealt with the complexity of cities. Merrifield (2013) argues that we live in an era of global urbanization, where the majority of the world population now live in cities, which are at the forefront of the current environmental and social crises (Harvey 2012). The world's population is expected to reach 9.7 billion by 2050; of this number an astonishing 66% will live in urban areas and almost all of the increase will be concentrated in Asian and African cities (United Nations 2014).

Indeed, cities today represent the main source of ecological and social problems (Low and Gleeson 2005) And 71% of global energy-related carbon emissions are generated in urban areas (Rosenzweig et al. 2010). Moreover, they are also the frontier of the capitalist model of development, being fundamental to the reproduction of capital, as Harvey (2008) points out. Even NATO (2003) recognizes that cities are also likely to be the arenas of highest conflict in the future. In developing countries, cities are growing at an unstoppable pace, making clearer every day the unequal access to, and distribution of, resources and living conditions, as evident in *Planet of Slums* (Davis 2006). The increase in pollution, violence, and marginalization suffered by the urban poor, especially in the Global South (Aguirre 2009), constitute the hidden face of urbanization, and poverty is becoming a distinctly urban problem (Pugh 2000). Thus, by examining cities and urban crises the contradictions of capitalism become increasingly evident (Swyngedouw 2005).

At the same time, other authors (Hern 2010; Evans 2012; Portugali et al. 2012) argue that cities are major sites for re-imagining a more ecologically and socially resilient future, becoming the locus where the future of humanity is discussed and contested. This is why cities are so central to this volume.

Changing the World

By facing the social and environmental crises created by capitalism, social movements are key actors for change. From Cairo to Seattle, from Hong

Kong to Barcelona, millions of people are working under the surface of oppression to build a different world. Sometimes this work surfaces with the eruption of millions of people in the street. However, a resurgence of populism and right-wing politics seeks to oppose them. In this respect, the call for the right to the city is echoing around the world.

The debate around rights gained extreme relevance after the Second World War when, in 1948 the Universal Declaration of Human Rights was adopted by the United Nations General Assembly. The concept of the right to the city was first introduced by Lefebvre in 1968 in his work *Le Droit à la Ville*, and has since been developed and spread, becoming a key phrase within urban social movements (Harvey 2008; Roussopoulos 2017).

The right to the city calls for a re-appropriation of the city in all of its aspects from full and equal access to resources to the possibility of collectively shaping the city environment. Moreover, it calls for a "revolutionary conception of citizenship" (Lefebvre in Merrifield 2017: 23), implying a sea change in society.

Since its first formulation, the importance of the right to the city has grown to the point that it has been introduced into the United Nations agenda (UN Human Settlements Programme 2010) and other international bodies, most notably in city charters and statutes. If we can say that speaking of the right to the city "*has become fashionable these days*" (Souza 2010: 315), this notoriety has come with a price. A plurality of actors now use the term to mean different things for different purposes, causing it to lose the revolutionary charge of Lefebvre's formulation.

In this volume we wish to critically analyse the mobilizing concept of the right to the city, offering new insights and ways forward. To this end, we believe that social ecology offers a powerful analytical tool and a theory of action for strategies, ethics, and a reconstructive vision for a future society based on freedom. To sum up, social ecology understands the relationship between ecological and human exploitation and aims to assess and solve the current social and environmental crises, conceived as the direct consequences of capitalism and all forms of domination.

However, we have to admit that social ecology is often neglected, or dismissed, as political theory. Nevertheless, since Bookchin's death in 2006 this holistic approach remains of inestimable value, leading to its revival, most visible in its vital influence on the Kurdish resistance in Syria and Turkey (Hammy and Finley 2015; Stanchev 2015; Hunt 2017), and the municipalist movement worldwide (Mansilla 2017; Rubio-Pueyo 2017).

We believe that social ecology has much to offer contemporary struggles, both as a theory to analyse reality and as a practice to change reality. However, we see the necessity of advancing social ecology, to open spaces for debate and organically make the discipline grow. In recent years few works have attempted to develop social ecology further; one of the few exceptions is the collection that Eiglad (2015) edited, *Social Ecology and Social Change*. The aim of the present work is to continue in the same spirit, going even further in a critical re-assessment of social ecology, offering ideas and reflections to use for social change, combatting the trend of dehumanizing urbanization, and moving towards active and revolutionary citizenship.

The Role of the Activist-Researcher

This book showcases the work of a vast array of authors with different cultural backgrounds, coming from different disciplines—some with academic experience, others with more activist sensibilities—but all united by a common aim: to change the current system that is based on exploitation and domination.

As people committed to social change, we believe it is important to share some overarching beliefs that have pushed us while working on this book and in our daily efforts. As Conti expresses it, "the goal of research is not the interpretation of the world but the organisation of transformation" (2005: np). We hope that this book will not be simply relegated to academia but will appeal to activists and thinkers interested in social change.

We agree that research and knowledge production is fundamental to the advancement of social and political struggles. But it needs to be free of the interference of capitalist interests in order to help political groups and revolutionary social movements. The distinction between activism[1] and research should be blurred because researchers should, first and foremost, be committed to social change. Research and knowledge production are key for social movements that aim to change social relations in today's dominant capitalist system.

Through research, critical reflection is realized, endowing the aim of specific and general knowledge to understand the society in which we live and at the same time develop mechanisms that help in its transformation. Research organizes and systematizes knowledge and allows the development of methods and analytical tools to support and improve the performance of groups and movements. In addition, research involves the possibility of socializing the knowledge produced. Indeed, knowledge should both be collectively produced and shared. Research should not be restricted to one group; it is not the sole responsibility of some technicians or specialists, despite the importance of technical and specialized study. Social movements themselves should be the subject of knowledge production, geared to the needs of their struggles and addressing societal problems. What we learn in university, in life, in the street, and at work should be used to fight, to help better understand the world, its conflicts and contradictions, and at the same time think through and prepare the most effective strategies for building a new society.

Research is not only for achieving new results, but it is a dynamic process of education, training, and collective growth. The research presented here is based on the principle of active participation, which starts from a collective formulation of objectives, then develops dynamically, involving all participants, and aims to produce useful knowledge to be incorporated into daily revolutionary practice.

From this perspective, we proudly call this volume an *undisciplined production*. As critical scholar Raman wrote:

> The call to be "undisciplined" is both a way of exceeding the limits of disciplinary borders, and a refusal to conform to the requirements of neoliberal academia. It can open up new possibilities for radical research. (Raman 2017: vi)

On the one hand, reality is so complex that we need to engage with multiple knowledge realms. We wish to break down the wall of a compartmentalized knowledge, so often reproduced in universities. Limiting our approach to one discipline or perspective is, indeed, limiting. Society is complex and social change needs a holistic approach in which knowledge production is a collective effort, not just something that emerges from designated researchers.

On the other hand, not only are all the contributors to this volume committed to social change but, given their backgrounds, they have not followed the classical academic/research path. We are undisciplined. We do not exhibit good behaviour—not even self-control. Certainly not regarding this system that is bringing us towards sociological catastrophe and ever-expanding social inequality. We believe in the right to resist tyranny, oppression, and domination. We hope that this work stimulates debates, fosters a culture of resistance, and helps to inspire action. In order to facilitate this knowledge exchange, we have agreed with the contributors and the publisher to publish this book under a Creative Commons license. As St. Columba said in 561 CE:

> The knowledge in books should be available to anybody who wants to read them and has the skills or is worthy to do so; and it is wrong to hide such knowledge away or to attempt to extinguish the divine things that books contain. (Columba in Pollock 2018: 111)

We believe that information and research should be freely shared in order for new ideas and practices to flourish and thrive. This collective book is an example that we hope will be followed.

Contributions to this Volume

The book is comprised of a series of different chapters, grouped into five parts. The wide diversity of contributions is a consequence of the rich and vibrant presentations at the 2017 TRISE conference. We see this as an

6

opportunity to explore our world, giving voice to different actors to portray the complex mosaic of reality. The contributions span from political theory to grassroots experience, from UK-based examples to the Kurdish revolution, from social ecology to the right to the city.

In the first section, *Discovering Social Ecology,* the concept of social ecology is introduced, highlighting the key points.

For over 50 years, American radical scholar and activist Murray Bookchin produced a steady stream of impressive essays, political tracts, and substantive books on the ecological crisis, the culture of cities, libertarian political movements, and social ecology. Brian Morris' essay outlines and re-affirm Bookchin's enduring legacy, focusing on his philosophy of dialectical naturalism and his radical politics with respect to his thoughts on direct democracy within the context of the city.

In the following chapter, Dan Chodorkoff presents an overview of social ecology and explores a political ideology within social ecology called "communalism" or "libertarian municipalism". He argues that we must change the underlying political and economic structures that govern us and create a new sensibility if we are to achieve an ecological society.

In her chapter, Emet Değirmenci analyses the limits to growth from the perspective of critics of social ecology. This contribution underlines that a steady-state economy is possible through de-growth strategies based on libertarian municipalism and revolutionary institutions.

In Part 2, *Engaging with the Right to the City*, authors introduce the concept of the right to the city and problematize it. Magali Fricaudet first explores the actual resonances of the right to the city as an emancipatory narrative and social practice, treating cities as centres of capitalist accumulation processes that commodify life in all its aspects. The right to the city should be based on the use-value of the city, rather than its exchange value, as a way of freeing citizens from private property and space-based class relations. This perspective has influenced a diversity of interpretations and practices that have in common the aim of taking back the city as a common good, a place for collective emancipation and freedom.

Theodoros Karyotis then juxtaposes urban commoning and the right to the city as two different vocabularies for making sense of urban struggles. The two narratives give rise to different conceptualizations of social conflict, different tactics and objectives, and ultimately different antagonistic subjects. The author offers examples from the past decade in Greece to show that commoning is not necessarily an alternative to "rights talk", but rather a way in which rights may be fleshed out, and tethered to contentious politics waged by concrete communities.

In the final paper of Part 2, Federico Venturini explores the relations between the right to the city, spatial justice, and social ecology. He claims that the more general concept of challenging all forms of power that oppress freedom can be developed as a unifying concept to include and amplify the agendas of both the right to the city and spatial justice.

In Part 3, *The Kurdish Answer*, the experiences of the Kurdish movement are introduced. In her piece, Havin Guneser explains the "Molotov cocktail" of historical conditions which drove the Kurdish freedom movement to break with the old orthodoxies. Guneser shows how Abdullah Öcalan and the Kurdistan Worker's Party (PKK) question what is handed down as truth in an ongoing process of self-transformation.

In their contribution, two ecology activists from the Mesopotamia Ecology Movement, Ercan Ayboga and Egit Pale, then analyse the development of cities in North Kurdistan in the twentieth century. However, they focus on the social, cultural, and economic changes that have accompanied the growth of the Kurdish freedom movement and the takeover of municipalities. Against a neoliberal framework and political pressure, the Kurdish freedom movement is challenged to develop a social and ecological city with an emphasis on popular participation in decision-making processes.

In the fourth part, *Transforming Social Theory*, an array of theoretical topics is presented. Metin Güven's analysis includes the transition from a US-dominated world system to a new one, varieties in the evolution of the State, and the cultural differences between states during the Axial Age. The chapter then focuses on state capitalism in China and explains why a new theory of the State is needed to tackle upcoming struggles against domination as China develops its authoritarian capitalism state model.

The purpose of Alexandros Schismenos' work is to correlate central aspects of the crisis of established signification in order to highlight the opportunities for social emancipation that emerge through collective forms of direct democracy. Inspiration is drawn from social ecology, which calls for a "free" public time. The main point of this chapter is that creating a free public time implies the creation of a democratic collective.

In his contribution, Olli Tammilehto attempts to understand how rapid and profound societal change is possible. He develops a theory of a "shadow society" and a "shadow personality" that come to the fore when societies undergo deep structural transformations. This chapter also explores the relevance of this theory for social movements.

The fifth and final section, *Walking with the Right to the City*, presents two different experiences of groups working with the right to the city. Diana Bogado, Noel Manzano, and Marta Solanas focus on the phenomenon of *squatting* and *occupying*, showing how it currently constitutes a global way of resisting the "neoliberal" dynamic of the global metropolis. By comparing experiences in Spain and Brazil, they attempt to explain how cities have menaced the popular classes in both countries, transforming the city to attract speculative financial capital. They observe how local populations reacted to maintain their rights to the city.

Finally, Jemma Neville offers a short story from her street in Edinburgh, Scotland. As much as human rights are universal, indivisible, and interdependent, neighbours living side by side must still negotiate and share common ground. This piece explores how academic theory and social ecology activist practices can be blended in everyday interaction.

As stated in the essay opening this book, building a lasting culture of resistance that can operate within all societies requires discourse that not only explores the negative effects of capitalism, but also offers a reconstructive and revolutionary vision. Contributing to building this vision is the aim of this book. Let us implement it and transform our societies!

Acknowledgements

Federico Venturini:
I wish to thank: my co-editors, Emet and Inés, for their patience and guidance; TRISE and BRB for the opportunity to undertake this project; Josie for being close to me in a dark period of my life; Margherita for having brought back a smile on my face; David Cann for his tireless work copy-editing the text of this book, and the Korov'ev and 3E collectives for continuously helping me to discover, engage, and transform reality.

Emet Değirmenci:
First, I would like to thank Federico for proposing the book project during the conference. Gathering all the contributions required great patience. I wish to thank my other co-editor, Inés, for her academic insights. I am grateful too for guidance from TRISE and BRB. Without their constructive efforts, this project would not have materialized.

Inés Morales:
Thanks to all those who struggle to disassemble the inferno.

References

Aguirre, M. 2009. *Crisis of the State, Violence in the City. In: Koonings, K. and Kruijt, D. eds. Megacities: The Politics of Urban Exclusion and Violence in the Global South. London: Zed Books, pp.141-152.*
Bookchin, M. 2005. *The Ecology of Freedom. Oakland: AK Press.*
Davis, M. 2006. *Planet of Slums. London: Verso.*
Crutzen P.J. and Stoermer, E. F. 2000. *The Anthropocene. International Geosphere-Biosphere Programme Newsletter. (41), 17-18.*
Eiglad, E. ed. 2015 *Social Ecology and Social Change. Porsgrunn: New Compass.*
Evans, J.P. 2011. *Resilience, ecology and adaptation in the experimental city. Transactions of the institute of British Geographers. 36(2), 223-237.*

Hardoon, D. 2017. *An Economy for the 99 per cent. Oxfam Briefing Paper (January 2017). [Accessed 6 September 2017], Available from: https://www-cdn.oxfam.org/s3fs-public/file_attachments/bp-economy-for-99-percent-160117-en.pdf*

Harvey, D. 2008. *The Right to the City. New Left Review. 53, 23-40.*

Harvey, D. 2012. *Rebel Cities: From the Right to the City to the Urban Revolution. London: Verso Books.*

Hern, M. 2010. *Common Ground in a Liquid City: Essays in Defense of an Urban Future. Oakland: AK Press.*

Low, N. and Gleeson, B. 2005. *If Sustainability Is Everything, Maybe It's Nothing? In: Proceedings of the 2005 State of Australian Cities Conference, 30 November–2 December, Brisbane. Brisbane: Griffith University, pp.1-12.*

Mansilla, J.A. ed. 2017. *Nuevos municipalismos y conflicto urbano [special issue]. Quaderns-e, 22(1).*

Merrifield, A. 2013. *The politics of the encounter: Urban theory and protest under planetary urbanization. Athens, Georgia: University of Georgia Press.*

Merrifield, A. 2017. *Fifty Years On: The Right to the City. In: Verso editors, The Right to the City: A Verso Report. [iBooks]. London: Verso, pp.18-32.*

Moore, J.W. ed. 2016. *Anthropocene or capitalocene? Nature, history, and the crisis of capitalism. Oakland: PM Press.*

NATO 2003. *Urban Operations in the Year 2020. Brussels: NATO.*

Pollock, R. 2018. *The Open Revolution. A/E/T Press.*

Portugali, J., Meyer, H., Stolk, E. and Tan, E. eds. 2012. *Complexity theories of cities have come of age: an overview with implications to urban planning and design. Springer Science & Business Media.*

Pugh, C. ed. 2000. *Sustainable Cities in Developing Countries. London: Earthscan.*

Rosenzweig, C., Solecki, W., Hammer, S. A. and Mehrotra S. 2010. *Cities lead the way in climate-change action. Nature. 467, pp.909-911.*

Steffen, W., Richardson, K., Rockström, J., Cornell, S. E., Fetzer, I., Bennett, E. M. et al. 2015. *Planetary boundaries: Guiding human development on a changing planet. Science, 347(6223), p.1259855.*

Raman, P. 2017. *Foreword. In: Patchett, E. and Keenan, S. Spatial Justice and Diaspora. Oxford: Counterpress, pp.v-vii.*

Roussopoulos, D. ed. 2017. *The Rise of Cities. Montreal: Black Rose Books.*

Rubio-Pueyo, V. 2017. *Municipalism in Spain: From Barcelona to Madrid, and Beyond. New York: Rosa Luxemburg Stiftung.*

Swyngedouw, E. 2005. *Introduction to David Harvey. In: Scholar, R. ed. Divided Cities. Oxford: Oxford University Press, pp.79-82.*

United Nation Development Programme. 2005. *Human Development Report 2005. Wellington: United Nation Development Programme.*

UN-Habitat. 2012. *Estado de las Ciudades de América Latina y el Caribe 2012, Rumbo a una Nueva Transición urbana. Nairobi: UN-Habitat.*

United Nation Development Programme. 2010. *Human Development Report 2010. Wellington: United Nation Development Programme.*

United Nations 2014. *World urbanisation prospects, 2014 revision*. New York: United Nations.

Notes:

[1] We use the term "activism" for convenience and for reasons of space. However, we believe that we should go beyond the divide between activists and the rest of the world, building a unifying/plural society working towards social change.

PART 1:
DISCOVERING SOCIAL ECOLOGY

The Legacy of Murray Bookchin
Brian Morris

Introduction
Although Murray Bookchin has been described as one of the most provocative, exciting, and original political thinkers of the twentieth century, it is worth noting that he is singularly ignored by many academic scholars writing on green philosophy or the history of the ecology movement (e.g. Scruton 2012; Radkau 2014), while he is invariably caricatured or reduced to a negative stereotype by anarcho-primitivists and spiritual ecologists (e.g. Black 1997; Curry 2011: 64; cf. Price 2012).

In this essay I aim, therefore, to outline and re-affirm Bookchin's enduring legacy as an important scholar, both in terms of his philosophy of nature—dialectical or evolutionary naturalism, and in terms of his radical politics—libertarian socialism or communalism. For Bookchin's political legacy offers the only real solution to the immense social and ecological problems that now confront us, as neither communing with the spirit world (mysticism), nor the technocratic solutions offered within the current capitalist system will suffice (Roussopoulos 2015).

In a recent widely acclaimed text, *Facing the Anthropocene*, Ian Angus writes, with respect to the present crisis of the earth system, particularly global warming, that it is "a challenge to everyone who cares about human-ity's future to face up to the fact that survival in the Anthropocene requires radical social change, replacing fossil capitalism with an ecological civiliza-tion, eco-socialism" (Angus 2016: 20).

Angus neglects to mention, of course, that this is something that Murray Bookchin extolled over 40 years ago, although, for Bookchin, this did not entail that "we need governments" (op. cit. 197) in order to create an ecological society. Bookchin, following Bakunin and Kropotkin, always felt that Marxist politics, specifically the "conquest" of state power, would lead to either reformism, or, as in Russia and China, to state capitalism and political tyranny.

Both a radical activist and an important radical scholar, for over 50 years Murray Bookchin (1921–2006) produced a steady stream of essays, political tracts, and books on environmental issues, the culture of cities, libertarian political movements, and social ecology that are truly impressive and path-breaking. Yet he remained one of the few key figures in the ecology movement not to succumb either to religious mysticism or to fashionable postmodernism, but remained true to the rationalist tradition of the radical Enlightenment. Throughout his life, Bookchin was an evolutionary naturalist, as well as a libertarian socialist—a leftist and a revolutionary. (For his biography, appropriately titled *Ecology or Catastrophe*, see Biehl 2015.)

The notion that in his last years Bookchin became a "grumpy old man", that he abandoned his earlier ecological vision and attempted to "trash" his own political legacy (Black 1997; McKay 2007; Clark 2013), seems to me highly misleading. Granted, given his polemical writings, Bookchin was assailed on all sides—by deep ecologists, political liberals, technophobes, anarcho-primitivists, spiritual ecologists, neo-Marxists, and Stirnerite egoists, as well as by the acolytes of Nietzsche and Heidegger. In many ways Bookchin became an isolated figure. Yet in an important sense he remained throughout his life a committed and passionate evolutionary naturalist and a revolutionary anarchist—that is, a libertarian socialist. The situationists mockingly described Bookchin as "Smokey the Bear". In many ways this is a fitting depiction—for Bookchin was gruff, solid, down to earth, and enraged at the present state of the world, and committed to doing something about it.

He was a coherent thinker, and all aspects of his work are closely interrelated. I shall focus in this essay on some of his key ideas, and outline his legacy in terms of four themes—namely: the modern crisis, social ecology, dialectical naturalism and ethics, and, finally, Bookchin's libertarian socialism.

The Modern Crisis

Along with Rachel Carson, Barry Commoner, and Rene Dubos, Murray Bookchin was one of the key figures in the rise of the ecology movement around 1970 (Carson 1962; Dubos 1968; Commoner 1972). There is no doubt that when I first became involved in environmental issues in the 1960s ecology was seen as a radical movement. Indeed, the biologist Paul Sears described ecology as "the subversive science". Bookchin's writings, along with the Marxist Barry Commoner's (1972), emphasized that we were confronting a severe ecological crisis unprecedented in human history, and that its roots lay with an economic system—capitalism—that is geared not to human well-being but to the generation of profit, and envisages no limit to industrial progress and technology. Ultimately, Bookchin felt that capitalism was destructive not only to ourselves but to the whole fabric of life on earth. For the underlying ethic of capitalism was indeed the technological domination of nature, an anthropocentric ethic that viewed the biosphere as having no intrinsic value; it was simply a resource to be exploited. In his pioneering ecological study, *Our Synthetic Environment* (1962), and in various other writings, Bookchin graphically outlines the social and ecological crisis that emerged following the expansion of global capitalism at the end of the Second World War (Bookchin 1971; 1980).

Apart from die-hard neo-conservatives, many people now recognize that the world is in a sorry state and that there is a lot to be angry about. Long ago, Bookchin outlined what he described as the "modern crisis", highlighting that both global capitalism and the modern liberal state are in dire straits (Bookchin 1986). This crisis, for Bookchin, was indeed manifold; at once social, economic, political, and ecological. For under global capitalism there has been a growing concentration of economic power, and the continuous expansion of economic inequality. It is now estimated that the 400 richest people in the world have a combined wealth greater than that of 45% of the world's population. No wonder rampant poverty exists throughout the world. Out of a world population of seven billion people, nearly a billion (15%) are estimated to be severely undernourished—that is, unable to obtain the basic conditions of human existence (Tudge 2016: 16). Such poverty is not integral to the human condition but, as Bookchin emphasized, directly related to "development"—to the global expansion of capitalism.

Equally significant is that across the world we find a "dialectic of violence"—reflected in the widespread existence of weapons of mass destruction, both chemical and nuclear, and the stockpiling of conventional weapons. This can hardly be said to have kept the peace, for since the Second World War there have been hundreds of armed conflicts, killing millions of people (Roser 2019). This dialectic has led to the disintegration of local communities, the denial of human rights, widespread genocide and political oppression—usually by governments. Along with Bookchin, many scholars have emphasized that the impact of free-market capitalism has been socially devastating, not only leading to economic inequality and widespread poverty, but also to political instability, religious fundamentalism, racial and ethnic conflict, and family and community breakdown (Ekins 1992; Morris 2004: 15–17). Finally, there is an ecological crisis. As Bookchin outlines, this is clearly manifested in the degradation of the natural environment under industrial capitalism:

- the polluting of the atmosphere and of the seas, lakes, and rivers;
- widespread deforestation;
- the impact of industrial agriculture, which, as Bookchin expresses it, is "simplifying" the landscape, while giving rise to the adverse effects of toxic pesticides and soil erosion;
- the creation of toxic wastelands; the loss of biodiversity with many species now facing extinction; the problem of chemical additives in food; and

- a serious decline in the quality of urban life through over-crowding, poverty, and traffic congestion.

Equally important for Bookchin is that capitalism has ceased to be simply an economic system, for the market economy has come to "penetrate" every aspect of social life and culture. Wealthy celebrities are now extolled by many, and greed and self-aggrandisement has come to seem virtuous.

For Bookchin, of course, it was not simply that there were too many people on earth, or that technology itself (rather than the mechanistic Cartesian world-view) had brought about the "modern crisis" and the degradation of the natural environment. Rather, the roots of the ecological crisis lay firmly with global capitalism, which was continually "plundering the earth" in the search for profit. Bookchin felt that the capitalist market economy had become a "terrifying menace" to the very integrity of life on earth. Industrial capitalism, he argued, was fundamentally *anti-ecological* and—over 40 years ago, long before Al Gore, George Monbiot, and Bruno Latour—he stressed with some prescience that the burning of fossil fuels (specifically coal and oil) had created a "blanket of carbon dioxide" that would lead to destructive storm patterns and eventually the melting of the ice caps and rising sea levels (Bookchin 1971: 60–67; 1982: 19; Morris 2012: 180–187; Kovel 2002; Monbiot 2006; Gore 2009; Latour 2017).

It is important to emphasize that, while Bookchin recognized that humans often degraded the natural environment in which they lived, in the past this had been essentially a local phenomenon and a local problem. But, he argued, since around 1950, with the expansion of global capitalism, humanity had come to place severe ecological burdens on planet earth that were global in extent, with "no precedent in human history". Two issues particularly troubled Bookchin: the possibility of a worldwide thermonuclear war, given the "balance of terror" strategies of Russia and the United States, and the climatic changes that had been induced by the widespread burning of fossil fuels. Both, he felt, could have a *catastrophic negative* impact upon organic life—the biosphere. What concerned Bookchin, therefore, was both "our destiny as a life form and the future of the biosphere itself". Contrary to the opinions of his critics—both the anarcho-primitivists and the mystical (deep) ecologists—Bookchin was concerned not only with the survival and well-being of the human species, but also with the flourishing of other life-forms and the earth itself. We need, he argued, to maintain the "restorative powers" of both nature and humanity, and to "reclaim the planet for life and fecundity" (1986: 100–108).

In response to the "modern crisis", especially regarding the social and ecological challenges it invoked, Bookchin proposed a re-affirmation and re-elaboration of the revolutionary anarchist tradition that essentially stemmed from Michael Bakunin, Peter Kropotkin, and their nineteenth century associates. His tradition emphasized the need to integrate an ecological world-view, a social ecology that Bookchin (1995a) later described as "dialectical naturalism", with the political philosophy offered by anarchism—that is, libertarian socialism.

Ever since I read *Post-Scarcity Anarchism* (1971) some 40 years ago, I have admired Bookchin, in the same way as I have been a fan of Peter Kropotkin, Lewis Mumford, Richard Jefferies, and Ernest Thompson Seton. All were pioneer social ecologists. For in his early writings Bookchin sensed that human social life must be seen in terms of a new unity, that the time had come to integrate an ecological natural philosophy (social ecology) with a social philosophy based on freedom and mutual aid (anarchism or liberal socialism). This unity was essential, he argued, if we were to avoid an ecological catastrophe. What we must therefore do, Bookchin stressed, is to "decentralize, restore bioregional forms of production and food cultivation, diversify our technologies, scale them down to human dimensions, and establish face-to-face forms of democracy", as well as foster a "new sensibility toward the biosphere" (1980: 27).

In later years Bookchin became embroiled in acrimonious debates with deep ecologists, anarcho-primitivists, and bourgeois individualists, in which Bookchin fervently defended his own brand of social ecology and libertarian socialism. He never deviated from the views he expressed in his earlier writings. Bookchin's core ideas about social ecology, libertarian socialism, and libertarian municipalism, which he defended and elaborated throughout his life, can be found in three key early texts, namely *Post-Scarcity Anarchism* (1971), *Toward an Ecological Society* (1980), and his magnum opus *The Ecology of Freedom* (1982). As Tom Cahill (2006) remarks in his generous tribute to Bookchin, these books contain the essence of Bookchin's thoughts. Therefore, Bookchin was not only an important figure in the emergence of the ecology movement, but also played an important role, as Peter Marshall indicates, in the "renewal" of anarchist theory and practice during the 1970s (1992: 622).

Social Ecology

In the Vatican there is a famous painting by Raphael entitled *The School of Athens*. It depicts Plato as a grey-haired older man pointing to the heavens, while the younger Aristotle points to the Earth (Lewis 1962: 50). Plato, of course, while holding mathematics in high regard, was fundamentally a religious mystic, a scholar who expressed a dualistic spiritualist metaphysics and contempt for sensual experience and empirical knowledge. Aristotle, on the other hand, was an empirical naturalist, with a deep interest in biology, He described himself as a *physikos*—one who studies nature. He expressed, as Bookchin recognized, an "organic" way of thinking.

It has often been said that western philosophers either side with Plato or with Aristotle. Bookchin clearly sided with Aristotle, and was vehemently opposed to all mystical or theological interpretations of the natural world. Indeed, Alfred Whitehead famously described western philosophy as merely a series of footnotes to Plato.

All the major figures of the western philosophical tradition—Aquinas, Descartes, Locke, Leibniz, Kant, Hegel, Husserl, Wittgenstein, and Heidegger—were fundamentally religious thinkers, as well as pro-State. Bookchin, therefore, belonged to a minority tradition within western philosophy—that of philosophical naturalism.

But what is significant about Raphael's painting is that it reflects the essential *paradox* at the heart of the human condition. For, as scholars as different as Lewis Mumford, Edmund Husserl, and Erich Fromm insist, humans have, in a sense, a dual existence. On the one hand humans are earthly beings and, as organisms, intrinsically a part of the natural world. But on the other, humans are a unique species, having a high degree of self-consciousness and sociality, highly complex symbolic systems, and forms of technology, leading recent scholars to suggest that, over perhaps the last 50 years, humans have become a "geological force" within the "earth system" itself. (Fromm 1949: 40–41; Mumford 1952: 48; Morris 2014a: 112–113, Crutzen 2002; Angus 2016: 27–37).

What is significant about Bookchin's philosophical naturalism is that he firmly embraced this paradox, emphasizing that humans are a product of, and had roots in, organic evolution, while at the same time they are animals of a "very special kind". As he expressed it:

> Human beings are OF the biotic world as organisms, mammals and primates, yet they are also APART from it as creatures that produce that vast array of cultural artefacts and associations that we call second nature. (1982: xxix; 1995a: xiii)

Bookchin, therefore, expressed, like Michael Bakunin and many other scholars, a triadic ontology of the human subject, recognizing that humans are intrinsically both natural and social beings, as well as having, like other organisms, a special sense of self-identity and personhood. Bookchin found deplorable the notion that humans are "aliens" or "parasites" on earth, as suggested by some deep ecologists and the acolytes of Friedrich Nietzsche. It implies, he argued, the "denaturing" of humanity, and denies the fact that humans are rooted in biology and are the products of organic evolution (Bookchin 2007: 27).

Bookchin's own metaphysics of nature is a form of evolutionary naturalism, akin to that of Darwin, Marx, and Kropotkin. Therefore, he fervently rejected the two dominant world-views that have long characterized western philosophy and culture, namely religion and mechanistic philosophy (Morris 1996: 25–36).

The first of these are the various religious (or mystical) cosmologies; this world-view has taken a variety of forms. These include (with their respective adherents), tribal animism (or polytheism) (Watson 1999), Christian theism and goddess religion (Starhawk 1979; Berry 1988), pantheism (or theosophy)—which conceives of God as both a transcendental creator and manifested in natural phenomena (Nasr 1996) and, finally, various types of mystical pantheism (Naess 1989).

The second form of cosmology that has been dominant in western culture is the mechanistic world-view, invariably identified with René Descartes. This cosmology expresses a dualistic metaphysic—a radical opposition between humans and nature—an atomistic epistemology, an anthropocentric ethic that validates the technological domination of nature, and a conception of nature simply as a resource for human use.

Rejecting *both* ecological *mysticism* and the *mechanistic* approach of Cartesian philosophy, Bookchin, in contrast, advocated an *organic* or evolutionary way of thinking—an ecological world-view that he described as dialectical naturalism (see below).

Although in the broadest sense the term "nature" implies everything that exists, and although this materialist definition may be valid in some respects, Bookchin suggests that the term is too limiting. Nature, from a social ecological perspective, refers to an evolutionary process or development. Bookchin thus defines nature as "a cumulative evolutionary process from the inanimate to the animate and ultimately, the social, however differentiated this process may be" (1982: xx).

There is a widespread tendency within western culture, Bookchin argues, to view nature as a realm that is opposed to human freedom and human well-being, one characterized as "stringy", "intractable", "cruel" and "competitive.". It was an image of nature expressed not only by Cartesian philosophy, social Darwinism, and the ideology of capitalism, (neo-classical economics in particular) but also, Bookchin contends, by Karl Marx. For Marx conceived of nature as a "realm of necessity" which must be subdued in order to engender a "realm of freedom" (Bookchin 1986: 50; 1995a: 72; but cf. Foster 2000 on Marx's ecology).

As an evolutionary naturalist and realist, Bookchin of course found the idea that nature is simply a social construction facile and obscurantist. In contrast, Bookchin conceives of nature not as an inert or recalcitrant material realm, but as a graded, self-developing evolutionary process. Nature, therefore, is not some divine cosmos nor a lifeless machine, nor could it be equated, as deep ecologists have tried, with a pristine wilderness. It is rather an evolutionary process of graded and phased development that indicates increasing fecundity, diversity, and complexity, and is characterized by the developing and ever-expanding activities of self-consciousness, subjectivity, creativity, and freedom. Following important studies by Kropotkin (1902) and Lynn Margulis (1981), Bookchin also contended that nature is characterized not only by conflict and competition, but also by co-operation, mutual aid (mutualism), and symbiosis, even between diverse organisms (such as lichen). Life, therefore, is inter-active, procreative, relational, and contextual (Bookchin 1986: 57).

All life-forms, for Bookchin, even bacteria, exhibit a sense of self-identity and self-maintenance, however germinal and nascent. Therefore, they have in varying degrees, subjectivity (choice), self-consciousness, agency, and freedom, and are active participants in their own evolution (1995a: 81). Bookchin was critical of fashionable neo-Darwinian theories that unduly emphasized the impact of the external environment (adaptation) and advocated a gene-centred approach to biology (e.g. Dawkins 1976). This approach, Bookchin argued, tends to completely bypass the subjectivity and agency of the organism. Like Brian Goodwin (1994), and even Darwin, Bookchin advocated an approach to biology that affirms the organism as the fundamental unit of life (Bookchin 1995b: 137–43).

Bookchin, therefore, concluded that within organic evolution there is a striving for greater complexity and increasing degrees of subjectivity (or selfhood) which constitutes "the immanent impulse of evolution towards growing self-awareness" (1995a: 128).

Bookchin consistently argued that mutualism (co-operation), self-consciousness, subjectivity, and freedom are inherent tendencies in the natural world. They may, therefore, be realized as potentialities in human social life, specifically in the creation of an alternative ecological society (Bookchin 1995a: 127–128).

Following a long tradition going back to the beginnings of western philosophy, and which was well expressed by the Roman scholar Cicero, Bookchin makes a clear distinction (*not* a dichotomy) between "first nature", the realm of non-human nature that pre-exists the emergence of humans, and "second nature", the realm of human artefacts, cultural landscapes, and social and symbolic life (Bookchin 1989: 25). But he insists that human social life is "within the realm of nature", thus always has a naturalistic dimension. The emergence of humans as a life-form and of human socio-cultural and symbolic life is, therefore, for Bookchin, a "natural fact", having its roots in biology. (Bookchin 1989: 26).

Not just an emergent materialist, Bookchin was fundamentally a social ecologist, and he continually emphasized the *integrity* of both nature as an objective reality, and human social life. The relationship between nature and human social life is, therefore, one of *continuity*, a dialectical relationship, not one of opposition. Nature is a realm of potentiality for the emergence of human life—in terms of technics, social labour, language, subjectivity—as well as a precondition for the development of society. Bookchin was fond of describing the relationship between humans and first nature in terms of a concept derived from Hegel, namely that it is a dynamic "unity in diversity" (1982: 24; 1980: 59).

In an important sense, Bookchin, like Mumford and Dubois, was an ecological humanist, offering a creative synthesis of humanism and naturalism. By "humanism", of course, Bookchin meant a shift "in vision from the skies to the earth, from superstition to reason, from deities to people" (1987: 246), thereby emphasizing the agency and cultural creativity of the human subject, both individually and collectively. Equating humanism with Cartesian philosophy and anthropocentrism, as do many deep ecologists and postmodernists. (e.g. Manes 1990; Braidotti 2013), was for Bookchin stultifying and obscurantist. Needless to say, secular humanists from Ludwig Feuerbach to Fromm and Mumford long critiqued Cartesian metaphysics, emphasizing that humans are fundamentally "earthly beings" (Lamont 1949; Morris, 2012).

In contrast to much social theory and ecological thought, Bookchin stressed *both* natural and social evolution, on nature and the integrity of the human species. He was, therefore, opposed to all dualistic theories that tend to radically bifurcate or separate nature from the social (and spiritual) aspects of human life—as reflected in Platonism, Cartesian theism, and other religious cosmologies, as well as much sociological theory and the humanities. Bookchin was especially critical of postmodernism, which tends to ignore biology entirely, although he was mainly concerned with the relativism, misanthropy, ahistoricism, and the ultimate nihilism of the likes of Nietzsche and Heidegger (Bookchin 1995b: 112–201).

But Bookchin was equally critical of all forms of reductionism. He was critical of socio-biology, which tends to reduce social life to biology or even to genetics, and of many mystical deep ecologists who tended to oblate the integrity of the human subject with reference to a universal spiritual "one-ness". This was akin, he felt, to the "night in which all cows are black", Bookchin being fond of quoting Hegel's joke about Schelling's mystical idealism (Bookchin 1982: 22). Bookchin, in fact, became a rather maligned figure among many academic philosophers for his trenchant critique of deep ecology (Bookchin 1987), even though the substance of this critique is quite compelling. For Bookchin was critical not only of the eclecticism of the deep ecologists and their tendency to embrace mystical theology—as expressed in Devall and Session's seminal text (1985)—but also of their neo-Malthusian tendencies and their emphasis on "biospherical equality" (biocentrism) which tended, Bookchin argued, to lapse too easily into mis-anthropy. In fact, Bookchin was particularly critical of two prominent deep ecologists, Dave Foreman of *Earth First* and Christopher Manes who ex-tolled famine in Africa and the AIDS epidemic as acceptable ways of controlling the human population. Such notions deeply disturbed Bookchin, hence the stridency of his polemic. But Bookchin was also critical of the deep ecologists for holding an undifferentiated humanity responsible for the ecological crisis, when the crisis had its roots in social problems—specifically with regard to the capitalist market economy—thus requiring fundamental social changes and the "remaking" of society (Chase 1991: 32). Bookchin's harsh critique of deep ecology (1997) generated a heated debate, although the critical responses to Bookchin's own critique and his advocacy of social ecology tend to verge on caricature (Price 2012: 49–61).

Dialectical Naturalism and Ethics

To understand the natural world as an evolutionary process, and the place of humans in the cosmos, Bookchin argued that we need to develop an organic way of thinking, one that is dialectical and processual rather than instrumental, mechanistic, and analytical. Such a way of thinking avoids the extremes of both *anthropocentrism*, exemplified by Cartesian metaphysics and the ideology of capitalism which radically separates humans from nature, and *biocentrism*, a naïve form of biological reductionism expressed by mystical deep ecologists. Both approaches, Bookchin felt, express a logic of domination, and a hierarchical mind-set.

As a philosophy of social ecology, Bookchin, therefore, advocated a dialectical or evolutionary form of naturalism, one that combined and integrated an ecological world-view (naturalism) as a metaphysic of nature with dialectics as a relational epistemology. To develop a sense of dialectics, Bookchin seems to have immersed himself in three classical texts on dialectics, namely Aristotle's "*Metaphysics*", Hegel's "*Science of Logic*", and Engels' "*Dialectics of Nature*". Bookchin fully embraced their dialectical sensibility, but he rejected the theological and teleological aspects of Aristotle's and Hegel's philosophy, emphasizing that they lacked an evolutionary perspective, while he felt that Engels was still deeply entrenched in mechanistic materialism, Engels emphasizing not development but matter in motion. Bookchin aimed to develop a *dialectical* naturalism by "ecologizing the dialectic", as he put it (Bookchin 1995a: 119–133).

A good deal has been written on dialectics. Some, like Kropotkin, identifying dialectics with Hegel's pantheistic mysticism, found the concept unhelpful; others have dismissed it as mystical mumbo-jumbo. "What have Galileo's laws of motion and the life-history of an insect to do with dialectics?" asked Sidney Hock (1971: 75–76), whose early writing on Hegel appealed to Bookchin. Following Karl Popper, anarcho-primitivist Bob Black dismissed dialectics as "mystical gibberish" and, embracing the nihilism of postmodernist theory, dismisses Bookchin as a naïve positivist (1997: 90–97). Black thus has a rather facile understanding of Bookchin's work, and even less understanding of dialectics, Popper, or positivism.

Neither Popper, a critical rationalist, nor Bookchin, a dialectical naturalist, were positivists. Bookchin emphasized that "reality is not simply what we experience" (1995a: 21). Hardly a positivist sentiment!

What then is dialectics? Following Engels (1940), three aspects of the principles of dialectics may be briefly indicated.

The first principle to understand in dialectics is the idea that both the natural world and human social life are in a constant state of flux, and that the historical sciences have made the "immutable" concepts of Newton, Descartes, and Linnaeus redundant.

The second principle of dialectics emphasizes the notion of totality (holism). This is the idea that all the seemingly disparate entities that make up the material world are interconnected, and that no phenomenon (whether natural or social) can be understood in isolation. As many have expressed it, nature is a complex interactive web.

The final principle of dialectics is expressed by the terms "paradox", "contradiction" and "unity of opposites". Engels and Bookchin contend that ordinary common-sense understandings, traditional logic, conventional (or instrumental) reason, and metaphysical philosophy (especially the kind expressed by Descartes and Kant) tend to think in terms of "oppositions", rather than dialectically in terms of development into a "unity of opposites".

As Engels succinctly described the limitations of metaphysical (non-dialectical) thinking:

> In the contemplation of individual things, it forgets the connection between them; in the contemplation of their existence, it forgets the beginning and end of that existence; of their repose, it forgets their motion. (Engels 1969: 32)

As Bookchin conceived of it, dialectics is not a form of logic, nor is it a method, and it certainly is not "mystical gibberish"; it is rather a "way of reasoning about reality" (1995a: 15). It is a mode of understanding the world that posits an "emergent" rather than a mechanistic form of causality, expressing an organic rather than a religious (mystical) or mechanistic way of thinking, emphasizing process and development—not simply change or motion. And finally, it stresses the unity and agency of organisms, as well as their complex relationships or inter-actions (mutualism) (Bookchin 1995a).

The conception of nature that Bookchin expressed in many contexts focusses around a number of key concepts: holism (complexity); differentiation (diversity); freedom (subjectivity); fecundity (creativity), and participation (mutualism). For Bookchin, nature constitutes "a participatory realm of inter-active life-forms whose outstanding attributes are fecundity, creativity, and directness, marked by a complementarity that renders the natural world the grounding for an ethics of freedom rather than domination" (1986: 55).

As ethics, for Bookchin, is an eminently human creation, in that human beings can derive a sense of meaning and value first from nature by virtue of their interpretive powers, he suggested that humanity is "the very *embodiment* of value in nature as a whole". He goes on to advocate an "ethics of complementarity", which "opposes any claim that human beings have a 'right' to dominate first nature, assuming that they can do so in the first place, much less any claim that first nature has been 'created' to serve human need" (1982: xxxvii).

Following Aristotle, Bookchin sought to promote an ethical naturalism that was consistent with ecological principles and an ecological sensibility.

Arguing against the fact/value of the positivists. Bookchin held that first nature may be reasonably regarded as the *ground* for an ecological ethic. But the natural world itself is not ethical; it is never "cruel" or "kind" or "caring", nor good or bad. Bookchin affirmed that, from our knowledge of the natural world and the place of humans within first nature, humans could thereby derive ethical principles—to guide human conduct and to establish an ecological community based on the values of co-operation, self-organization, freedom, and diversity.

As an ethical naturalist, like Spinoza and Kropotkin, Bookchin explicitly rejected ethical theories that based moral value simply on tradition or custom (cultural relativism), on subjective whims and individual emotions (as per the logical positivists), or on a denatured conception of the human subject (as per Kant). He was equally critical of all transcendental or absolutist forms of ethics, those which derive moral edicts either from the holy scriptures of Oriental religions (Judaism, Christianity, Islam, and Hinduism, mediated, of course, by the clerics), or from the emanations of shamans, charismatic priests, or religious gurus, whether enlightened visionaries or messengers of God.

As Bookchin wrote of humans as "the embodiment of nature rendered self-conscious and self-reflective", and advocated the human "stewardship" of the earth, stressing the need to go beyond the present dichotomy or rift between first and second nature to create a "free nature" (1995a: 131–36), he has been widely denounced by mystical deep ecologists, anarcho-primitivists, and liberal philosophers alike. He has been accused of being "anthropocentric" and "utilitarian", advocating a Faustian domination of nature, and expressing "humanistic arrogance" (e.g. Manes 1990: 160; Marshall 1992: 618; Black 1997: 98; Curry 2011: 64). These critiques seem to wilfully misinterpret the meanings that Bookchin himself gave to these concepts.

By "stewardship" of the earth, Bookchin certainly did not intend to imply that humans should take complete control of nature or steer organic evolution—Bookchin was an ontological realist, holding that first nature has an independence and integrity quite separate from the human species. What he implied by "stewardship" was the development of an ecological sensibility that "respects other forms of life for their own sake and responds actively in the form of creative loving and supportive symbiosis" (Chase 1991: 34).

Likewise, the concept of "free nature" did not imply the "mastery of nature but rather the opposite: the freeing of the natural world from the plundering of the capitalist system, and the creation of an ecological society in which the relationship between humans and the natural world would be one that was co-operative, harmonious and mutualist—a "creative inter-action". It would be a society that enhanced the flourishing and well-being of *both* the human species and other life forms along with the nature itself, a mutuality "between first and second nature that enriched *both* natures" (1995a: 120). Bookchin always advocated and stressed an "ethics of complementarity" that is lost on his numerous critics.

Neither indifference nor the technocratic management of problems within the capitalist system (environmentalism) are viable options to the present social and ecological crisis (Roussopoulus 2015).

The Politics of Libertarian Socialism
In response to the social and ecological crisis, Bookchin not only insisted on the need to develop a philosophy of dialectical naturalism (a form of ecological humanism), and an ecological sensibility or ethic. He also stressed the need to create—as a radical alternative to liberal capitalism—an ecological society. He envisaged a rational society based on anarchist principles—libertarian, socialist, ecological, and democratic.

Around 2002, at the age of 81, Bookchin announced that he had ceased to define himself as an anarchist—leading Ian McKay (2007: 39) to suggest that Bookchin in his final years attempted to "trash his own legacy".

But it is important to recognize that the anarchism that Bookchin abandoned was what he had earlier rejected, in a harsh polemic (1995c), as "life-style" anarchism. This kind of anarchism, otherwise known as "post-Left anarchy", or (by academics) as the "new anarchism", consists of a motley collection of several distinctive strands, among them Stirnerite egoism (Jason McQuinn), Nietzschean aesthetic individualism, otherwise known as poetic terrorism (Hakin Bey), anarcho-primitivism (John Zerzan et al.), postmodernism and, at extremes, the anarcho-capitalism of Ayn Rand and Murray Rothbard (Morris 2014b:133–148).

As a political tradition, anarchism has usually been defined in two ways. The first, well exemplified by Peter Marshall's (1992) history of anarchism, conceives of anarchism in terms of an opposition to coercive authority, specifically as "anti-State". Thus a wide variety of philosophers and individuals have been described as anarchists—Godwin, Stirner, religious mystics such as Tolstoy and Gandhi, radical libertarians (Spencer and Whitman), mutualists, anarcho-capitalists as well as many anarcho-communists (Kropotkin, Malatesta, Goldman, Rocker, et al.). Even Margaret Thatcher and the authoritarian-Marxist Che Guevara, an icon in the 1960s, find a place in Marshall's important survey of anarchism. This has enabled liberal and Marxist scholars to dismiss anarchism as a completely incoherent philosophy.

But it is not. There is another way of understanding anarchism. That is, to view it as a fundamentally historical social movement and political tradition that emerged around 1870, mainly among working class members of the First International. This form of anarchism, as many scholars have emphasized, combined the best of both radical liberalism, with its emphasis on liberty and individual freedom, and socialism (or communism), with its emphasis on equality, voluntary associations, mutual aid, and direct action. This unity, which defines anarchism as libertarian socialism, was most succinctly expressed in the well-known adage of Michael Bakunin that "liberty without socialism is privilege and injustice; and that socialism without liberty is slavery and brutality" (Lehning 1973: 110; Morris 2014b: 204–207).

In his polemic *Listen, Marxist!* Bookchin critiqued Marxism for its lack of a *libertarian* perspective, while in his later polemic *Social Anarchism or Lifestyle Anarchism* he criticised a wide variety of contemporary anarchists for their bourgeois individualism and lack of a *socialist* perspective (Bookchin 1971: 173–220; 1995c). Thus anarcho-communism, social anarchism, libertarian socialism, and communalism are virtual synonyms. That is, different expressions of Bookchin's political philosophy of anarchism. Thus it is important to recognize that, throughout his life and even in his last years, Bookchin remained true to the legacy of St. Imier—a committed and strident libertarian socialist.

Lifestyle anarchists, as Bookchin described them—Nietzschean aesthetes, Stirnerite egoists, and, especially, anarcho-primitivists—not only rejected socialism (and society) but went to extremes and rejected civilization (even agriculture and human language), technology and city life. What is important about Bookchin was that he attempted to avoid these extremes, and, like Mumford, was never anti-civilization, anti-technology, or anti-urban. On the contrary, he affirmed all three as vital creative aspects of the human spirit.

Alive to the achievement of human civilization, Bookchin rejected anarcho-primitivism.

In *Ecology of Freedom*, Bookchin devotes a chapter to what he described as "organic society", the early hunter-gatherers and tribal societies. He ascribes the following features to such tribal societies: a primordial equality and an absence of coercive and domineering values; a feeling of unity between the individual and the kin community; a sense of communal property with an emphasis on mutual aid and usufruct rights and, finally, an ecological sensibility, involving a relationship with the world that was one of "reciprocal harmony, not of domination" (Bookchin 1982: 43–61).

But like Kropotkin, Bookchin was only too aware of the limitations of tribal life, and concerned that we draw inspiration and lessons from the past and from tribal cultures, rather than romanticizing them. Still less should we try to emulate them. Given the present human population, the "future primitive" of John Zerzan is simply not a political option (Morris 2014b: 141–42).

While Bookchin was always a harsh critic of anarcho-primitivism, he was not an obsessive technocrat as David Watson (1996) portrays him. Nor was he besotted with civilization. He certainly emphasized the importance of city life, especially given its introducing the idea of a common humanity, a universal *humanitas* (2007: 61), but like Kropotkin and Mumford, both important influences on Bookchin—and unlike the anarcho-primitivists—Bookchin had a much more nuanced approach to technology and civilization. As he put it in defending his pro-technology stand:

> [This] is not to deny that many technologies are inherently domineering and ecologically dangerous or to assert that civilization has been an unmitigated blessing. Nuclear reactors, huge dams, highly centralized industrial complexes, the factory system, and the arms industry—like bureaucracy urban blight and contemporary media—have been pernicious almost from their conception. (1995c: 34).

Technology, Bookchin felt, had to become "liberatory", and to be reduced to a "human scale" and, through the Institute of Social Ecology cofounded with Dan Chodorkoff, he pioneered the use of renewable energy sources and promoted organic farming (Biehl 2015: 159).

Following Kropotkin, Bookchin emphasized two sides of human history—the legacy of domination reflected in the emergence of hierarchy, state power, and capitalism, and the legacy of freedom, reflected in the history of ever-expanding struggles for emancipation (1999: 278).

Eager to develop libertarian municipalism as an integral part or strategy of anarchism (communalism), Bookchin detailed the many forms of popular assembly that have emerged in the course of European history, particularly during times of social revolution. Bookchin was particularly enthusiastic with respect to the Athenian polis and the system of direct democracy, while recognizing its historical context and limitations. But forms of popular democracy have occurred throughout history: popular assembles in medieval towns; neighbourhood sections during the French Revolution; the Paris Commune of 1871; workers' soviets during the

Russian Revolution; New England town meetings; and anarchist collectives during the Spanish Civil War. Bookchin refers to them all (1992; 2007: 49).

In his later essays Bookchin came to explicitly distinguish between four radical political traditions, namely Marxism, anarcho-syndicalism, anarchism (equated with lifestyle anarchism), and communalism or libertarian socialism.

Always critical of Marxism, or what is termed "proletarian socialism", Bookchin rejected the notion that the individual proletariat could any longer be conceived as the "hegemonic historical agent" in the struggle against capitalism, given the fundamental social and technological changes that were taking place within global capitalism during the second half of the twentieth century. He was equally critical of the Marxist emphasis on the State, whether this implied the bourgeois democratic State or Bolshevik strategies of state control during the Russian Revolution (2007: 88–89; 2015: 155–160).

Bookchin was also critical of revolutionary zeal, with its strategic focus on the industrial worker and the factory system. While acknowledging their libertarian bias, Bookchin rejects the "workerist" (*ouvrierist*) emphasis of the anarcho-syndicalists, and laments their lack of a coherent theory—especially evident in the summer of 1936 during the Spanish Civil War (2007: 93).

It has been suggested by many scholars that Bookchin ignored the importance of class, and that the concept of labour virtually disappears from his social ecology, even though the workplace still remains a critical site of capitalist exploitation. But Bookchin never repudiated the concept of class, nor the importance of class analysis. As a fervent anti-capitalist, he always acknowledged the crucial importance of the working class in achieving any form of social revolution, and categorically affirmed the importance of the class struggle (1999: 264). But given the emphasis on advancing the "communalist project" as the socialism of the twenty-first century, class issues nevertheless seem to be side-tracked in his writings.

As indicated earlier, Bookchin's polemical essay *Social Anarchism or Lifestyle Anarchism* (1995c) was essentially a defence of libertarian socialism, offering a trenchant critique of several anarchist tendencies that were prominent in the 1990s, specifically so-called Nietzschean poetic terrorism, anarcho-primitivism, and Stirnerite egoism. Labelling them together as "life-style anarchism", what linked these various tendencies for Bookchin was their affirmation of a radical individualism that gives absolute priority to the unfettered, autonomous ego (Bookchin 2007: 91; 2015: 160–61).

For Bookchin, none of these currents of thought—Marxism, anarcho-syndicalism, and lifestyle anarchism—articulated an authentic political theory that was based on democratic self-management of the municipality.

Unlike Nietzschean "free spirits" and Stirnerite individualists, who, in elitist fashion, rely on other mortals to provide them with the basic necessities of life, Bookchin recognizes that throughout human history some form of social organization has always been evident. For humans are intrinsically social beings, not autonomous possessive egos. Some kind of organization has, therefore, always been essential not only in terms of human survival, but specifically in terms of child care (kinship), food production and distribution, shelter, clothing, the basic necessities of social life (the social economy), and the management of human affairs as they relate to community decisions and the resolution of conflicts (politics). Bookchin, therefore, was always keen to distinguish between ordinary *social* life—focussed around family life and kinship, affinity groups, various cultural associations, and productive activities—and the *political* life of a community, focussed around local assemblies.

Bookchin equally insisted on distinguishing between *politics*, which he defined as a theory relating to the public realm and those social institutions by which people democratically manage their community affairs, and what he called "*statecraft*". The latter focuses on the State as a form of government that also serves as an instrument for class exploitation, oppression, and control.

Thus Bookchin came to emphasise the need to establish popular democratic assemblies based on the municipality, on neighbourhoods, towns, or villages. Such local assemblies rely on face-to-face democracy to make policy decisions relating to the management of community affairs. He argued consistently that such decisions should be made by majority vote, although Bookchin does not advocate majority *rule*, and emphasized that a free society could only be one that fosters the fullest degree of dissent and liberty. Municipalities would be linked through a confederate political system. He warned, however, of the dangers of the assembly becoming an "incipient state" (Bookchin 1971: 168; 2007: 101–110).

Bookchin summed up his own conception of anarchist politics in terms of four basic tenets: (1) a confederation of decentralized municipalities; (2) an unwavering opposition to Statism; (3) a belief in direct democracy; and (4) a vision of a libertarian communist society (1995c: 60; see also Biehl 1998 and Eiglad 2014).

Of course, Bookchin did not provide us with all the answers to our current problems. On the contrary, he left us with many unresolved issues. Exactly what kind of technology do we need to sustain or develop? What exactly is involved in decentralizing the urban landscape? And what precisely is the relationship between community politics and class struggle focussed on the workplace? These are all unresolved issues for contemporary radicals.

But, alongside his focus on nature, what is truly significant about Bookchin is his critique of urbanization, especially given the fact that roughly half of the human population now live in cities. He had a vision of greening and decentralizing the city and, by establishing truly democratic institutions to manage the municipality, restoring people's "right to the city."

References

Angus, I. 2016. *Facing the Anthropocene.* New York: Monthly Review Press.

Berry, T. 1988. *The Dream of the Earth.* San Francisco: Sierra Book Club.

Biehl, J. 1998. *The Politics of Social Ecology: Libertarian Municipalism.* Montreal: Black Rose Books.

Biehl, J. 2015. *Ecology or Catastrophe: The Life of Murray Bookchin.* Oxford: Oxford University Press.

Black, B. 1997. *Anarchy After Leftism.* Columbia, Mo: Cal Press.

Bookchin, M. 1971. *Post-Scarcity Anarchism.* London: wildwood House.

Bookchin, M. 1980. *Toward an Ecological Society.* Montreal: Black Rose Books.

Bookchin, M. 1982. *The Ecology of Freedom.* Montreal Black Rose Books.

Bookchin, M. 1986. *The Modern Crisis.* Philadelphia: New Society Publishers.

Bookchin, M. 1987. *Social Ecology versus Deep Ecology.* The Raven: 1/3, pp.219-250.

Bookchin, M. 1989. *Remaking Society.* Boston, Ma: Southend Press.

Bookchin, M. 1992 (1987). *Urbanization Without Cities: The Rise and Decline of Citizenship.* Montreal: Black Rose Books.

Bookchin, M. 1995a. *The Philosophy of Social Ecology: Essays in Dialectical Naturalism.* Montreal: Black Rose Books.

Bookchin, M. 1995b. *Re-Enchanting Humanity.* London: Cassell.

Bookchin, M. 1995c. *Social Anarchism or Lifestyle Anarchism: An Unbridgeable Chasm.* Edinburgh: AK Press.

Bookchin, M. 1999. *Anarchism, Marxism and the Future of the Left.* Edinburgh: AK Press.

Bookchin, M. 2007. *Social Ecology and Communalism.* Eiglad, E. ed., Edinburgh: AK Press.

Bookchin, M. 2015. *The Next Revolution.* ed. D. Bookchin and B. Taylor London: Verso.

Braidotti, R. 2013. *The Posthuman.* Cambridge: Polity Press.

Cahill, T. 2006. Murray Bookchin (1921–2006). *Anarchist Studies,* 14(2), pp.163-66.

Carson, R. 1962. *Silent Spring.* Boston: Houghton Muttlin.

Chase, S. ed. 1991. *Defending the Earth.* Boston Ma.: Southend Press.

Clark, J.P. 2013. *The Impossible Community: Realizing Communitarian Anarchism.* London: Bloomsbury.

Commoner, B. 1972. *The Closing Circle.* London: Cape.

Crutzen, P. 2002. Geology of Mankind. *Nature,* 415(3): p.23.

Currey, P. 2011. *Ecological Ethics: An Introduction.* Cambridge: Polity Press.

Dawkins, R. 1976. *The Selfish Gene.* Oxford: Oxford University Press.

Devall, B. 1985. *Deep Ecology.* and C. Sessions Salt Lake City: Peregrine Press.

Dubos, R. 1968. *So Human an Animal.* London: Sphere Books.

Eiglad, E. 2014. *Communalism as Alternative.* Porsgrunn: New Compass Press.

Elkins, P. 1992. *The New World Order.* London: Routledge.

Engels, F. 1940. *The Dialectics of Nature.* London: Lawrence and Wishart.

Foster, J.B. 2000. *Marx's Ecology: Materialism and Nature.* New York: Monthly Review Press.

Fromm, E. 1949. *Man for Himself.* London: Routledge and Kegan Paul.

Goodwin, B. 1994. *How the Leopard Changed its Spots.* London: Orion Books.

Gore, A. 2009. *Our Choice: A Plan to Solve the Ultimate Crisis.* New York: Melcher Media.

Kovel, J. 2002. *The Enemy of Nature.* London: Zed Books.

Kropotkin, P. 1902. *Mutual Aid.* London: Heinemann.

Lamont, C. 1949. *The Philosophy of Humanism.* New York: Philosophical Library.

Latour, B. 2017. *Facing Gaia.* Cambridge: Polity Press.

Lehning, A. ed. 1973. *Michael Bakunin: Selected Writings.* London: Cape.

Lewis, J. 1962. *History of Philosophy.* London: English Universities Press.

Manes, C. 1990. *Green Rage.* Boston: Little Brown.

Margulis, P. 1981. *Symbiosis in Cell Evolution.* San Francisco: C and H Freeman.

Marshall, P. 1992. *Demanding the Impossible.* London: Harper Collins.

McKay, I. 2007. Murray Bookchin (1921–2006). *Anarcho-Syndicalist Review,* 46, p.39.

Monbiot, G. 2006. *Heat: How to Stop the Planet Burning.* London: Allen Lane.

Morris, B. 1996. *Ecology and Anarchism.* Malvern Wells: Images.

Morris, B. 2004. *Kropotkin: The Politics of Community.* Amherst NY: Humanity Press.

Morris, B. 2012. *Pioneers of Ecological Humanism.* Brighton: Book Guild.

Morris, B. 2014a. *Anthropology and the Human Subject.* Bloomington: Trafford.

Morris, B. 2014b. *Anthropology and Anarchism: A Reader.* Oakland, Ca: PM Press.

Mumford, L. 1952. *The Conduct of Life.* London: Secker and Warberg.

Naess, A. 1989. *Ecology, Community and Lifestyle.* Cambridge: Cambridge University Press.

Nasr, S.H. 1996. *Religion and the Order of Nature.* Oxford: Oxford University Press.

Price, A. 2012. *Recovering Bookchin.* Porsgrunn: new Compass Press.

Radkau, J. 2014. *The Age of Ecology: A Global History.* Cambridge: Polity Press.

Roser, M. 2019. War and Peace. *OurWorldInData.org.* [Online]. [Accessed 9 June 2018]. Available from: https://ourworldindata.org/war-and-peace

Roussopoulos, D. 2015. *Political Ecology: Beyond Environmentalism.* Porsgrunn: New Compass Press.

Scruton, R. 2012. *Green Philosophy.* London: Atlanta.

Sears, P. 1964. Ecology: A Subversive Science. *Biosciences,* 14: pp.11-13.

Starhawk 1979. *The Spiral Dance.* New York: Harper Collins.

Tudge, C. 2015. *Six Steps Back to the Land.* Cambridge: Green Books.

Watson, D. 1996. *Beyond Bookchin.* New York: Automedia.

Watson, D. 1999. *Against the Megamachine.* New York: Automedia.

Social Ecology: A Philosophy for the Future

Dan Chodorkoff

Theory and Practice

I am going to try to offer some thoughts on how we might move forward from here. I think this is an important discussion. I will refer to familiar themes that we have raised this weekend. Overall, I believe the connection between theory and practice has been an essential part of social ecology and certainly of Bookchin's thought. Although he was a scholar and did incredible research and produced very important works, he was at heart an activist. For Bookchin, the real soul of social ecology is praxis—an ongoing process of putting our ideas into practice, analyzing our experience of putting them into practice, revising our ideas in relation to that analysis, and taking those revised ideas and applying them again in the real world. That is an overall framework that we should keep in mind. It is very easy, given the sense of urgency that I am sure we all share, considering the time of crisis we are experiencing, to believe that it is time to act. And it *is* time to act, certainly, but the action that we take has to be informed, thoughtful, considered, and I believe should be taken within a framework of ideas that are developed and consequently examined and re-examined. What I am going to try to do today is lay out some broad ideas that I think will help us moving forward and enable us to develop effective praxis.

I wish I could offer a prescription or a mathematical formula or mantra that we can all chant that will get us to where we need to go, but I cannot. I will offer some concepts and ideas but I think each of us in our own particular community are going to have to determine how these ideas are applied in the world because the conditions in our communities differ. Cultural traditions and histories, the ecological areas in which we live, and the particular issues that we are facing vary. Certainly, there is an urgency here in Greece, that may not be felt in other parts of Europe or the US; the economic crisis is a particular concern here. But there is a crisis that is universal—the climate crisis and it is unprecedented. The threat is evident to us all. It has transcended issues of local pollution or development and has taken on a truly global nature, something that Bookchin was aware of in the 1960s but most people chose to ignore, and certain segments of society are still choosing to ignore. Furthermore, we are now seeing a resurgence of fascism, which I personally find terrifying, and there is no question that we may not in the future have an opportunity to act. So now is the time for action but, once again, let us make sure that our actions are actually informed by ideas.

The Role of Education

I offer a quote from Murray Bookchin: "Every revolutionary project is an educational project." I believe this is a crucial insight. We need to educate ourselves no matter who we are, no matter how widely we have read. There is an awful lot that we need to learn and think through. And I want to emphasize that education happens on many different levels and in many ways. I am not simply talking about education in a classroom or education through conferences such as this, as important as that kind of learning is. But education also occurs by acting on ideas. Education occurs when you learn how to act with others in a democratic fashion, when you begin to reshape your understanding and relationships between yourself and others and the environment in which you live. Education occurs when you organize a cooperative, when you organize a demonstration. We have to acknowledge this and we accept too that people learn in different ways, that some people will be reached by an academic treatise, some will be touched by a polemic, others may be reached by a novel or a song or a work of art; these all need to be incorporated into our educational process. We have to be holistic and multi-dimensional in the way that we approach the issue of education. And perhaps we must abandon our preconceptions about what constitutes education. We have a role to educate ourselves and then educate others, to take these ideas out into the world, to not be cautious about proposing what we believe, and be able to do so in a coherent and convincing fashion so as to allow others to enter into this new world that we are beginning to conceptualize and actualize. I think this is a really critical moment and an educational process has to progress.

I say this because what I envision in order to bring about the kinds of change I think are necessary is a process which is analogous to the Enlightenment. We need a new Enlightenment, not necessarily in terms of the content but in terms of the process. We have to remember that the Enlightenment began with just a tiny handful of radical thinkers who challenged all the beliefs of their day—the idea that a king had divine rights, the idea that the masses were incapable of learning or incapable of governing themselves. All of this flew in the face of history and tradition. And it took about 100 years for those ideas to percolate throughout the population. Bear in mind that levels of literacy were much lower than we have today, no radio, social media, no TV, so these ideas were popularized by those who read. People passed books and pamphlets hand-to-hand and discussed ideas over kitchen tables and in taverns. The process took 100 years but these ideas did spread and resulted in the democratic revolutions which set the stage for today. So it is an analogous process, except we don't have 100 years because our crisis is in fact so dire and compelling that we need to act now, we need to act soon. But it will not take 100 years because in fact these ideas, the ideas that we've been discussing this weekend, are already shared by millions of people around the world and it is important for us to keep that in mind, to not feel isolated, to not feel marginalized, because in fact these ideas are at the center of the kind of change that has to occur if we are going to create a new world. I contend that the notion of education, both self-education and the education of others, is critical. It is not going to take 100 years; we are already partway there. We need to take advantage of our access to technology and our literacy. We need to educate using all of these media and means, re-conceptualize education as something that occurs not only in formal settings like this, but also in informal settings.

Utopian Thinking

The second idea that I want to emphasize is that I used the term "revolution" earlier. I am surprised that I have not heard that word used much here this weekend. The kind of change that we are seeking really is revolutionary change. I am not talking about the classic notion of revolution—insurrection, going to the barricades with guns—although there may be settings in which that is necessary and appropriate to defend these ideas. Rather, I am talking about a revolution which transforms the underlying structures of our society, the economic and political structures that govern our lives. In order for us to achieve that, we need to develop not just revolutionary movements, but a revolutionary sensibility. The Italian anarchist Errico Malatesta said, "Everything depends on what people are capable of wanting." I have to agree with this. If we cannot develop the imagination to conceptualize a qualitatively different world, we are doomed. The situation we are in is taking us down the path of destruction. Bookchin used to wear a button with a quote from Bakunin: "I will continue to be an impossible person as long as those who are now possible remain possible". I think that is worth thinking about. We need this new sensibility to reconceptualize our relationships with each other and our relationship with the natural world. And this is not a simple task. It is not simply an intellectual exercise. We need to incorporate this new understanding and this new sense of self and relationship to others into our very being. We need to transform ourselves, and this is a process that will only occur through practice. In the crucible of thought and action we can begin to see the outlines of the new world that we want to create. I would also suggest that this new sensibility needs to stem from a utopian perspective. One of the problems I see facing movements today is the lack of a truly revolutionary imaginary. Certainly, we are facing pressing issues in the here and now which require our attention (e.g. in the US, the Black Lives Matter impulse). It is crucial, because black people, particularly young men, are killed by the police on a regular basis. Civil rights have been denied to a whole segment of the population who are subjected to all kinds of degradation and their struggle is crucial. It is absolutely necessary and it is not sufficient.

We cannot simply stop at civil rights—the core concern for Black Lives Matter, for people in the black community, or in any other community. That struggle needs to be incorporated into a larger transformative struggle that recognizes the need to transform underlying structures. I know that intersectionality is a very popular concept today. We have used the term a "holistic" movement or a "revolutionary" movement, but we did not really talk about intersectionality back in the 1960s, 1970s, and 1980s. Nevertheless, I believe we can recognize that all of the issues that people are dealing with, be they Black Lives Matter or stopping pipelines, or stopping the development of a gold mine here in Greece, are really one struggle. They are struggles against the dominant culture which has no respect for human life, which puts profits before people, and is responsible for the kind of rapacious treatment of the earth which will ultimately lead to the decline of the human species and our ability to inhabit this planet. Bookchin thought about this back in the 1960s, wrote about global warming in 1964 and was ridiculed, and at that point he said maybe in 200 years we will begin to see the greenhouse effect take shape and influence our environment. He was prescient in understanding this issue, as in so many others.

We need to be utopian and think beyond the given and understand that there are, within our current situation, potentialities that can be actualized that will take us to a qualitatively different place. So when I use the term "utopian", I mean it in the positive sense. I do not think I have to lecture the Greeks here about the roots of the word "utopia" but it was coined in 1515 by Sir Thomas More and he indicated it had two roots, both from ancient Greek. One was the word οὐτόπος (comprised of οὐ (*ou*, "no") + τόπος (*tópos*, "place, region")), and the other word was "u-topia", which means *the good place*. It is in this second sense that I use the term. Unfortunately, utopian thinking has largely fallen by the wayside. We are dismissively told, "Oh, that's utopian", or as a pejorative; "that's cloud cuckoo-land; it's unachievable; it can never happen." But from our understanding of anthropology and history we know that, in fact, what is defined *for us* as a very narrow human nature—greedy, competitive, violent, and acquisitive— seems to define humanity in a way that fits beautifully as the rationale for capitalism. We know that previous cultures existed in very different ways with qualitatively different relationships with each other and with the natural world. Not that we can return to these cultures, but rather they represent certain principles that are part of our legacy as human beings. Rather than talking about a narrowly defined human nature, anthropologists discuss a continuum of human possibilities. Among these possibilities, and we know they exist because they have been actualized in other cultures, are the ability to function through mutual aid, to live and create an economic system that does not depend on the market, to make decisions in non-hierarchical ways, to live an egalitarian life, and to achieve a degree of self-reliance in humanly scaled communities in which relationships are based on face-to-face ties rather than the bureaucratized, atomized, and alienated forms of social life that predominate today. In short, the re-harmonization of people with nature and people with people.

I think it is very important that we begin to articulate our utopian vision and once again there is no universal here. It is going to vary from community to community, to grow out of our own cultures and experiences, be located in a particular environment, but nonetheless it needs to be based on a set of broad principles on which we find agreement. We began the weekend by talking about the idea of rights or a constitution or a set of ethical principles on which we can find broad agreement, even ultimately a global agreement. Such principles will be actualized in different ways in different places and this is how we find that elusive balance between the universal and the particular that was one of the themes that we addressed in our first conference.

The Principles of Social Ecology

Now where do we find those principles? Social ecology has some concrete suggestions. Brian Morris did a marvelous job describing Bookchin's concept of dialectical naturalism and I think dialectical naturalism gives us insight into what those principles might be. I would like to lay them out briefly here. First, I would emphasize that these are tendencies in nature, not immutable natural laws but possibilities that find expression at various times in various places and they are crucial to the whole process of evolution, a model which unfortunately has been misinterpreted and abused. We know the concept of natural law was one of the axioms that the social Darwinists used to classify people and cultures into various levels and hierarchical schemas. Herbert Spencer wrote of the primitive savage and the civilized, a schema which provided a marvelous rationale for colonialism and materialism, because, of course, the West "brought civilization" to these benighted savages, the "primitives" who could barely speak, according to the western view, who were barely human. We also saw the abuse of the theory of natural law in Nazi Germany. So I will talk about certain tendencies and principles of nature. Undeniably, competition plays a role, mutations occur through a process that sorts out winners and losers in terms of species, not individuals, but there are other aspects of natural evolution that have not been emphasized but, in fact, have been largely ignored. I would also add that Bookchin tried to elucidate these principles because he believed we must incorporate them into society if we are to re-harmonize humanity and nature, which is ultimately the goal of social ecology—the integration of first nature and second nature, which leads to a third nature. So if we are going to do that we have to understand how these principles that are at work in natural evolution can be transformed and applied in society.

First among them is the understanding that in nature there is no hierarchy. When we talk of the lion, king of beasts, or the lowly ant, we are anthropomorphizing. We are taking our particular social structure and looking at the rest of nature and saying that is what it is. But this thesis is not correct. Ecologists know that; they understand that in fact there is not a food chain in which the big carnivores sit on top, but rather a food web in which interdependency is the rule. The ant, of which there are 40 or so species on the floor of the rainforest, plays a crucial role in decomposing the organic matter, which then feeds the plants, which feed the herbivores, which feed the carnivores. Without the carnivores the herbivores would destroy the plant matter. The carnivores help keep that population in check, and without the herbivores the carnivores could not exist, and the lowly ant provides the nutrition that allows all of those relationships to exist, and the micro-organisms in the soil play a crucial role as well. So nature is not hierarchical and, by extension, society should not be. Once again, the anthropological record shows us that for the most of human history people existed without formal hierarchies. And here I am using "hierarchy" in the technical sense—as a system of command and control that ultimately has recourse to physical coercion. A hierarchical society is a fairly recent invention. To use the old anthropological saw in which the whole of human history becomes a clock, for about 95% of our time on the planet, it is only the last five minutes or so that hierarchies emerge. We lived without hierarchies before that, which indicates that we have the capacity to live without hierarchies in the present. Social relations are shaped by our sensibility and the kinds of social structure under which we choose to live or under which we are forced to live.

We can decide how to organize our own society and we must. According to Bookchin, people are part of nature. There is first nature which is non-human nature and then there is second nature and we are organic beings, an outgrowth of the process of natural evolution and the same principles that have carried us through that process need to be applied in human society. If our goal is to achieve a re-harmonization of first and second nature, that is a project of social ecology. In relation to hierarchies within species, bear in mind the technical definition I offer of hierarchy, an institutionalized relationship of command and control that ultimately has recourse to physical coercion. People often ask, "Well, what about the alpha males in the gorilla troops?" What you see there is not a hierarchy but a form of situational dominance and, in fact, ethologists who have observed the gorilla troops in the wild have noted that the silverback gorilla alpha male beats his chest to scare off the other males and gain exclusive access to the females of the troop for breeding purposes, while a younger male will sneak into the woods with a female, so it is not even an effective form of situational dominance. I would maintain that there truly is no hierarchy in the technical sense in first nature.

I look at anthropology to understand what qualitatively different forms of leadership look like. When Western society encountered, say, Native Americans they immediately looked for the chief. And they could not find the chief, so often they would assume someone was a chief, or they appointed a chief. In fact, what happened in those societies was that leadership existed but it was also situational. There was no permanent leader and situational leaders could not coerce others to follow their will. Leaders depended on their ability to persuade others through logic or rhetoric. They were admired because of their experience, their knowledge, their insight. One would lead a hunt because of their proven ability to find the game that was necessary for the survival of the group. But they could not force anyone to follow their instructions. They suggested or they exhorted, they tried to inspire, maybe they manipulated sometimes. But they lacked that coercive ability that the kind of leadership in our societies entails. Virtually every individual in a hunting and gathering band eventually plays a leadership role in one activity or another. One individual may lead the hunt, another give the dance, another makes gathering activities. Even the gender division of labor between men and women was very fluid. We are told that men are the hunters and women are the gatherers, but the Marshals, who lived among the San people, observed that when women were out gathering they sought game, and they would hunt it. And if the men saw something that could be gathered in the wild they gathered it. Women were even observed hunting with the men. So these hard and fast categories that have emerged in our time are not really an essential part of our humanity. There are alternative arrangements that have existed for millennia, for most of our time on the planet. We have lost sight of that. Once again, I am not a primitivist. I am not suggesting going back to hunting and gathering, but I am suggesting that the relationships that existed in those societies represent certain principles that we can extract and dialectically transform and apply in our own society. We have a lot to learn from these people.

The second principle that I would suggest we need to derive from our understanding of the natural world, which may inform our actions, our movements, and our utopian vision, is the fact that nature is mutualistic. Mutual aid plays a crucial role in natural evolution. This was brought up by Kropotkin and re-emphasized by Bookchin and others thinkers. In first nature life is interdependent, just as individuals are interdependent, which is why humanity created societies. So mutualism also has to be incorporated into our utopian vision and into the vision of the new society that we wish to create.

Another principle is the notion of unity and diversity. When we look at natural history in ecosystems, we see that the most stable ecosystems, those which last, are those that have the greatest number of species interacting at various trophic levels. Hence, even though there may be great fluctuations in individual species, even the elimination or extinction of a particular species, there are other species to fill that niche and as a result the ecosystem derives some stability. It is not static, it is homeostatic. It is a dynamic balance, but a balance nevertheless. And this balance is dependent on diversity. Unity is only achieved through diversity, and clearly this is another principle that needs to inform our thinking and our action, our vision, and our movements. We need to strive for diversity and find within such diversity strength, resilience, and unity.

Another principle that we derive from our understanding of the natural world is the idea of homeostasis. Bookchin understood, as biologists understand, that nature is not static; it is constantly changing. Yet in the midst of that constant change, healthy ecosystems are able to maintain a dynamic balance. This is the very definition of sustainability, the ability to maintain balance in the midst of constant change.

Finally, natural history is the process of evolution and in that process we see a development. It is not a steady process of ascension, there are peaks and valleys, there is fluorescence and extinction but over time the process of natural evolution has moved towards ever greater diversity, complexity, and degrees of freedom. It is undeniable because, if you agree with Darwin, life on earth began as single-celled organisms and those organisms became more and more complex: they came together to form various species and, as a result, we moved from single-celled organisms to a multitude of highly complex life forms. Over that process we have seen greater and greater degrees of consciousness and self-consciousness—the ability to make choices and, ultimately, the ability to choose freedom.

So, once again, we see principles that we can extract from the natural world and apply in the specific situations in which we find ourselves to move towards ever greater degrees of freedom. Regarding freedom and utopia, we will never achieve them. They will always hover on the horizon and, as we approach them, will recede into the distance. But that is as it should be, because natural evolution is dynamic, constantly changing, constantly moving, constantly developing, and we have to acknowledge that, learn to live with it and embrace it. And we have to learn how to live with ambiguity. For me, paradox, ambiguity, and ambivalence is inherent in the human condition, and we need to accept that. Nevertheless, we need to embrace our freedom to make choices so I suggest that these are some basic principles on which we need to find agreement, whether this takes the form of some kind of a constitution or a set of ethics on which we can agree. It has to be a basis on which we can begin to create our free communities because these communities cannot exist in isolation. We live in a global world, globalization of course in its current form is an extremely destructive process, but there is the opportunity to create an alternative form of globalization in which free self-reliant communities confederate, offer each other mutual support and exchange, and create a richer and fuller life for all of us. And I believe that has to be our goal.

Opposition

This is all very abstract and theoretical and I realize that ideas are most important when they arise from the theoretical and move to the concrete. I am not going to be prescriptive, I am not going offer easy answers or solutions, but I do want to suggest some arenas in which I think we need to begin to work effectively. The first would be to recognize the need for oppositional movements. Let us not fool ourselves. We are in the midst of a deep crisis, something unprecedented in human history, and I do not believe it is overly dramatic to suggest that the future of humanity on the planet is at stake today. The decisions that we make and the actions that we take over the next few years are going to determine the course of human life. This is a big responsibility and what we are seeing is an increasing pace of exploitation and domination, as expressed in capitalism, a system which is rationalizing control of every aspect of our lives, which has expanded dramatically and functions not only in the economic sphere, but has actually colonized our consciousness—so these are pressing problems. And we need to oppose it; we need to protest, we need to stop the goldmine, stop the pipeline, stop the murder of black people, stop the imprisonment of people, and so on. We need to do all of these things, and protest is a very powerful weapon in that process. Protest and opposition is absolutely necessary, but not sufficient. It will not get us to where we need to go because protest is about negation. We do need to stop those who are now in power; we need to remain impossible as long as those who are possible remain possible. But it is not enough. I think those of us who have been active have seen the limitations of protest. We have been able to gain certain rights for certain groups, we have been able to prevent a dam from being built here or there, but we are fighting a holding action. While it is necessary to stop these exploitative moments from destroying the things that we hold dear, we also need to move beyond protest.

Reconstruction

We need to move beyond opposition to reconstruction. Once again, this is not something new and I am sure many of you are actively engaged. By "reconstruction", I refer to the *Wobbly* slogan. The IWW (International

Workers of the World) was an American anarcho-syndicalist movement at the turn of the twentieth century, whose slogan was "we have to build the new world in the shell of the old". I refer to it because we need to begin to create new relationships, new ways of being together, and we need to institutionalize them. This means creating cooperatives, creating community gardens, creating community housing, moving towards the forms of mutual aid and cooperation that this society tends to ignore. And we need to propose such measures as a way of showing people that another world is possible, that we can build a new world in the shell of the old. These experiences, these reconstructive projects, also serve as a form of education because through them we learn how to come together and make decisions democratically—horizontally. We learn how to accept and create new forms of leadership. When I talk about a non-hierarchical society, I am not suggesting there is a lack of influential, experienced, wise, knowledgeable, or brilliant people who can offer us insights and lead us forward. But it will be a process in which leadership is redefined. It is no longer defined hierarchically—it is not power over, it is power with. We need to educate ourselves and others and learn how to function in these horizontal and democratic ways.

I think that this reconstructive process begins to show us ways that we can begin to actualize our utopian vision. I had incredible experiences in the 1970s working in the Puerto Rican community in New York City where people were living in a ghetto consisting of 40% city-owned property, abandoned buildings, vacant lots. Through direct action, I saw that neighborhood act and claim as their own the abandoned properties and reshape them according to a very concrete utopian vision which emerged through a series of community planning fora, where everyone in the neighborhood came together and developed the blueprint for their neighborhood. They planned how to use the buildings: some for elder housing; some for artists; a vacant lot to become a garden, and another a park. Block by block, building by building, lot by lot, they put together a plan. And then they began to implement it through direct action, initially squatting in abandoned buildings and reclaiming vacant lots without any legal recourse, but through their own will and the development of particular kinds of political pressure, through protest with direct action, they were able to begin to transform the neighborhood. We became involved because, at that time, the Institute for Social Ecology was doing a lot of work where we were looking at alternative technologies.

In the early 1970s we were working with solar and wind power, which we saw as crucial to the development of an ecological society, although of course we applied these technologies in communities that are human-scaled, where people democratically control them, far from the kind of corporatization of alternative technologies that has occurred today. The point being that this kind of direct action is as important as the type that we use in our opposition and we need to begin to actualize and create models for what society might look like and within those physical changes we can begin to make social changes. That is, organize the community to enable participation in this transformative process. Controlled by the people on the block, people can begin to take actions where they live today. I find it very heartening that people have talked about this over the weekend. We must recognize that different people have different skills and aptitudes and some people may be very effective at organizing street demonstrations, while others may be more effective organizing a community garden. The crisis is so dire and so compelling, and is occurring on so many levels that there are many different ways in which we can enter into this process of opposition and reconstruction.

However, I think we have to recognize that, as important and necessary as these reconstructive actions are, they are not sufficient. It is very easy for cooperatives to be co-opted right into the capitalist system, for our community gardens to fall prey to the developer's bulldozer, so we need to develop within our communities and ourselves the sensibilities I argue for, and we need to be very conscious of the ambiguities inherent in human life. The best intentions can be turned against us, so we constantly need to be aware of how powerful and insidious the forces arrayed against us are, in the sense that we have internalized so many of the basic frameworks that capitalism presents to us because we have all been acculturated by that same system. It is a question of purging ourselves of these old beliefs and creating new ways of living together, and new ways of organizing.

Politics

Finally, the political realm, the realm of political action, is all-important. By this I mean a redefinition of politics, not politics as statecraft, not politics of Washington or London, but rather politics on the most basic level—developed and applied where we live, right outside our doors in our neighborhoods, and our towns and our villages. And in order to realize this we need to create fora for directly democratic decision-making and institutionalize them. I have a big problem with anarchism as it developed in the late twentieth century because there is so much emphasis on individualism, so much misunderstanding of the very nature of society, and politics was rejected. Ultimately, anarchists say, "we don't want power, we want to do away with power." But you cannot do away with power. Power exists, and the question is how we structure it. Are we going to accept *power over* or are we going to create *power with*? And in order to exercise power with, we need to develop politics. And this means we need to create neighborhood assemblies, town meetings, all kinds of fora, a kind of democratic confederalism. Rojava is the most inspiring example that I have seen and it proves that it is possible. My personal experience also proves that it is possible.

I come from the State of Vermont. It is a small rural state. I live in a tiny town of 1,300 people, but for the past 200 years the town has been governed through a direct democracy, through town meetings. We get together as citizens face-to-face, we discuss the issues, and we make decisions as to how we intend to carry out our business over the next year. It works, and this is not a town made up of anarchists or hippies. This is a town with a progressive element, but also a very conservative element. And yet, we are able to come together as neighbors, not as Democrats or Republicans, and find a common interest through respectful dialogue. We disagree. We even get angry at each other but we walk into that room as neighbors and we leave as neighbors. In the process of making these decisions, we work through a whole series of issues and you might say, "Well, that's easy because it's a town of 1,300, it's tiny, it's humanly scaled, that's no problem." However, I had a similar experience working on the Lower East Side of New York, with 30,000 people, where people have town meetings as well. They come together and they go through this whole planning process. They have created a vision for the neighborhoods in their community, they have contested the official plans of the city, and achieved a degree of success. So I have seen it happen in larger urban settings as well.

But it is not enough to simply create these small-scale face-to-face democratic fora. We need to use them as a vehicle to contest for power with the State. We need to use them to redefine politics, create situations in which there is true accountability, in which everyone has a voice about decisions that will affect them—a direct voice, not a mediated voice. And, in order to do this we need the flip side of decentralization, the idea of confederation. We need to create a confederation between our local democracies based on a set of common principles or ethics. I believe this is the ethics that social ecology endorses.

This is the framework in which we need to move forward in these three interrelated areas, and no single one area, as necessary as it may be, is sufficient. If we can holistically bring together these different levels of action and coordination and institutionalize them, we can achieve an ecological society. Anarchists tend to be anti-institution, but human society is based on institutions. There are institutions. The question is what is the quality of the institution. I have been frustrated because I see many people embrace the idea that a new society will form spontaneously. I saw this in Occupy Wall Street, for example—this notion of temporary autonomous zones. It is as if that is the best we can do: a temporary autonomous zone—a "festival of the oppressed", as Marx called them. These festivals may last weeks, they may last months, but ultimately they dissipate because we are unable to institutionalize them. We want permanent autonomous zones, not temporary autonomous zones.

Clearly, there is an urgency to our situation and there is a very strong tendency to look to the existing means of power in order to ameliorate the immediate suffering and destruction that is taking place today, and I think that has a certain value. But it has to be framed within a much more radical program. Bookchin proposed beginning with minimum demands which might be something that would express itself through existing political channels and then you move to transitional demands. You are constantly pushing, and from there you move to your maximum demands. And in terms of where to begin, each of us has to determine where we can work most effectively, and enter into this with whatever energy we can bring to it and whatever generosity of spirit, and we just need to keep pushing and working and recognizing. That it is not going to happen overnight, although there are moments where these ideas come to the fore. Then we have to be ready to act and institutionalize; we cannot allow them to be temporary. It is really a matter of where people feel they can contribute the most, and where they can work most efficiently. This is where we begin.

Thanks to Donald Trump we are facing the same problems in the US today as in many European countries: the rise of fascism. I don't know if people in Europe followed the events in Charlottesville last week or the week before, but the media reported only the fascists marching with torches, but there were right-wing militias that had automatic weapons and they out-gunned the police, which is why the police stood down. This is serious and I cannot offer an answer, but we have to oppose it on every level. We have to confront them; we have to be oppositional; we have to shut down the fascists. I believe this can be done non-violently, and we need to be ready to propose real solutions that address the root cause, systems based on hierarchy and domination. However, I must caution that moving to implement direct democracy in the US tomorrow would be a disaster because the consciousness is not there to support the kind of humanistic direct democracy that I think we all want to see. Therefore, education in various forms is the key. We need to change consciousness, we need to develop a new sensibility, and we will do that in different ways, by working in different groups.

Clearly, deep divisions exist. However, my experience has been that when decisions are being made in a considered way by a community, some of those distinctions and identities begin to break down and people find common ground. I think we need distance, we need to look for that common ground and at the same time we have to recognize that there will be those who oppose it. Then we need to create counter power, counter institutions. At the same time, we need to work to mitigate the worst excesses of what is. So it happens on many different levels simultaneously.

It is only by moving forward in a self-conscious fashion informed by the kind of theoretical framework I propose that we can begin to learn our way out of this crisis together.

A Critique of *The Limits of Growth* from a Social Ecology Perspective

Emet Değirmenci

"Simplicity is the ultimate form of sophistication" – Leonardo da Vinci

The Limits to Growth was commissioned by the Club of Rome and published in 1972. The cautionary message of the report (Meadows et al., 1972) was intended to signal the need for reforms that would ensure the survival of capitalism. We are now already seeing the greening of capitalism through the supply of so-called environmentally friendly products and the "sustainable growth" agenda as pushed by the United Nations. But is long-term sustainability compatible with Capitalism's need for growth and accumulation? The report did not address the question of the fundamentally political nature of these limits, and how they challenge capitalistic notions of quality of life and development. In response to the gap, the degrowth movement has sought to politicize these limits in order to fundamentally challenge capitalist assumptions of a "good life" and economic growth, as degrowth is based on creating and implementing a culture that prevents unnecessary consumption and production. This is possible through an open, connected local economy and real democratic participation through striving for a convivial quality of life. To do this it is obvious that human needs and wants should be reviewed radically in this so-called Anthropocene epoch.

Today, not only is the decline in biodiversity an issue owing to global climate change, but many types of ecosystem are declining and even collapsing. Climate statistics show that 71% of greenhouse emissions are due to fossil fuel companies and their investors (Riley, 2017: 39). I am considering that if we take into account that 60–70% of the world's population live in cities that are dependent on fossil fuels, then the problem becomes more visible in urban settings due to their dependence and modern consumption patterns. At the same time, cities are where the accumulation of money, assets, and investment occurs. And yet, despite this, Murray Bookchin, the founder of the philosophy of social ecology, emphasizes that cities have also been sites of culture and "liberatory" politics (Bookchin 1996). That is why cities (ideally with socially and ecologically responsible citizens) also exhibit the potential to bring the degrowth issue into focus in the context of the "right to the city" (Harvey, 2008).

Social ecology provides us with a framework to understand how an ecological crisis is closely linked to social crises. As Bookchin explores, unequal power relationships in society are based on human domination of nature and humanity itself (Bookchin, 2005).

The aim of this paper is to explore limits to growth and degrowth from a social ecological standpoint. I will first look at how sustainability has been framed in terms of green growth. Second, I will discuss one of my own initiatives as a case study about space-making in the context of the right to the city in Wellington, Aotearoa (New Zealand). Third, I link the concept of the commons to the proposal for a steady-state moral economy. In conclusion, I will focus on what sort of growth would be appropriate from a social ecological perspective. As an ecofeminist, I also tie in issues of gender throughout the paper.

A Green Growth Economy

Many terms in the language of sustainable development and green growth continue to frame nature in terms of ownership. For instance, "natural capital", "carbon trading", and "polluters pay" all have materialistic and opportunistic meanings that serve capitalist ideologies. If we view nature as capital, it does not matter how many wind turbines or solar panels are placed on green roofs. Putting a price on nature through "carbon trading" also has a false meaning. For example, pine trees are toxic to Australia's environment. But when mining companies cease activities, they prefer to plant pine trees because they grow fast and their seedlings are cheap. Carbon offsetting assumes the replicability and commensurability of totally different forms of natural value and services. "Polluters pay" is another arguable term. First, it gives the rich the power and opportunity to pollute. Second, it is difficult to identify who the polluters are and how much damage they have done. How would you calculate, for example, the damage to large and widely accessed rivers such as the Nile, the Rhine, or the Mekong?

The growth economy also fosters polarization, as well as scarcity. Bookchin emphasized hierarchies and polarization in this context: "Material scarcity provided the historic rationale for the development of the patriarchal family, private property, class domination and the state; it nourished the great divisions in hierarchical society that pitted town against country, mind against sensuousness, work against play, individual against society, and, finally, the individual against himself" (Bookchin 2004: 182).

All the disparities serve to generate insecurity in individuals and promote further consumption. A consumer society based on scarcity tactics aims to sell a variety of products rather than looking at the issues from a holistic perspective.

Sustainable development does not seem to bring any solutions at the grassroots level either. The Club of Rome's influential text emphasizes that the state of global equilibrium could be designed so that the basic material needs of each person on earth are satisfied and each person has an equal opportunity to realize his individual human potential (Meadows, 1972: 24). However, this raises the question: how can the individual's basic material needs be measured when living standards such as access to land and ownership are different from North to South? In this way, proposed avenues of action remain technical and do not address the political and ideological nature of the limits to growth outlined in the report.

This presents a deep contrast to indigenous approaches to the natural world, since indigenous communities see themselves as belonging to nature as a whole, not in anthropocentric terms. Since 1998, I have observed and worked with some indigenous and local communities in Australia, Aotearoa (New Zealand), and North America through environmental campaigns and ecological restoration projects. These cultures do not view nature as a separate entity. Even so-called "non-living" features such as rocks, mountains, and rivers are important components in everyday life. They believe all living and non-living beings feed each other in a mutual way. Rivers, mountains, and minerals are seen as quotidian experience. They value the ecosystem as a whole. Furthermore, many indigenous cultures pass on ethics of guardianship, not stewardship, from generation to generation. We should learn from them and implement their practices accordingly. This is the only way to reconnect with nature and repair the damage done in Anthropocene times.

In the next section, I move on from the debate on "limits" to reflect on what a different vision of grassroots politics may look like, inspired by my own experiences.

The Right to the City and Space-Making

The World Charter for the Right to the City highlights the rights that inhabitants of cities can claim, including democratic management of a city and equality. The UNESCO UN-HABITAT project lists five themes: inclusion, governance, human rights/rights-based approaches, participation and urban planning (Brown and Kristiansen, 2009). However, almost all cities feature injustice. According to current city zoning requirements, it seems that the need for land to build housing and grow food are the top priorities among various class, race, ethnic, and sexual orientation groups. The lower classes live on the peripheries or are pushed out of the city through gentrification, because they cannot afford to live close to the city centre. The authorities often do not want marginalized people, such as ethnic minorities, people of colour, LGBTQI communities, or the homeless, to be visible.

I witnessed this when I sought to initiate a social ecological food justice project through women's leadership for refugees and new migrants in Wellington, in 2006. We claimed a piece of public land and education space for our multicultural group, which was made up of people from eleven different nationalities in the central part of the city. The city of Wellington, however, insisted that we accept land at least one hour away from the city centre. That neighbourhood was not only far, it was also predominantly inhabited by poor and marginalized communities—suggesting that the city seemed more comfortable if our project appeared in more peripheral, marginalized areas than in the economic and cultural centre. And yet, a perfect spot with a building was available for us in the middle of the city on a brownfield site. It was a sort of abandoned site about two acres in size with an existing building. Also the soil was contaminated with DDT since it was an old bowling club. We were happy to clean it up. It took us three years to convince the city council and the predominantly white residents who opposed us that the project was worthwhile. Some of them even asked us if we were going to bring seeds from our home countries to invade the native environment. It was sad to hear that sort of prejudice, despite the fact that we were working with the Maoris and some academics. It required energy to explain our genuine desire to help restore the natural environment, as well as enriching and contributing to the city's social diversity. We were persistent in bringing the various groups into the city and meeting with the city council. After struggling with the council and the dominant white culture, our *Innermost Gardens* project was able to put its roots down in the fourth year. Now, the project has become one of the most respected regenerative edible landscape projects in the Green Belt section of Wellington.

This experience highlighted to me the relevance of the right to the city concept, as first defined by Henri Lefebvre and David Harvey. If we consider the right to the city in the context of space-making, Grégory Busquet elaborates Lefebvre's work on space and justice:

> Space is a crucial dimension of human societies and reflects social facts and influences social relations. Consequently, both justice and injustice become visible in space. Therefore, the analysis of the interactions between space and society is necessary to understand social injustices and to formulate territorial policies aiming at tackling them. Planning policies that aims to reduce them. …However, the diversity of definitions of "Justice" (and of the possible "social contracts" that legitimate them), is high and the political objectives of regional planning or urban planning can be quite different and even contradictory. (Busquet, 2012: 2)

Busquet here points out that planning and policy-making regarding public spaces can be either inclusive or exclusive for different disadvantaged groups. If we recall the *Innermost Gardens* project, unless Wellington city drafts a policy to offer a diversity of cultural, ecological, and social spaces in the city, new groups like us will have similar difficulties in future.

Historian and city planner Lewis Mumford emphasized the city as a community in which everyone is responsible for their everyday activity

(Mumford, 1970: 89). As shown by Bookchin, this requires active citizenship. In *The Limits of The City* Bookchin wrote:

> For all its collectivism and strong bonds of solidarity, tribal society was surprisingly patriarchal. Based on kinship, however fictitious its reality, the tribe rooted its affiliations in lineage ties or what I call the "blood oath". (Bookchin, 1986: 52)

Since there are not many matrilineal communities in the world, tribal roots often pass through male links. Men maintain authority for the sake of the tribe. Hence Bookchin's term "blood oath" recalls violence and exclusion. Bookchin envisions a city with its cosmopolitan potential where people can mingle:

> The city corresponded to the creation of spaces where "insiders" and "outsiders" met and decided their affairs together, spaces where citizenship was a constantly reworked, dynamic and organic process. In this way, at best, political decision-making in cities was independent of ties of kinship or ethnicity. Accordingly, "the city" is a type of settlement where "people advance beyond the kinship bond to share, create, and develop the means for life, culturally as well as economically, as human beings". (Bookchin, 1992: 173)

In a city, citizenship extends beyond kinship ties to create spaces of social justice that go beyond kinship. It can be based on citizenship and responsibilities of space to create a shared justice concept like in Portland city in Oregon, US, where it is easy for all citizens to intermingle regardless of ethnicity, class, race, and sexual orientation. The project is called *City Repair*[1]. The project not only encourages conversation and connection between neighbours via the circular street intersections, but it is also building a lively living space with ecological and social principles for hundreds of homeless people as well. If there was any blood-related or ethno-centric agenda during the city-wide transformation, the project would not have been possible. Rigid boundaries, such as defining insiders as blood-related, can create fragile situations that can easily lead to conflict.

Finally, Harvey claims that transforming cities towards social justice is a common process: "The *right* to the city is far more than the individual liberty to access urban resources: it is a *right* to change ourselves by changing the city. It is, moreover, a *common rather than* an *individual right since* this *transformation inevitably depends upon* the *exercise* of a *collective power* to *reshape* the *processes* of *urbanization*" (Harvey, 2008: 25). In the *Innermost Gardens* project, for instance, we have attempted to change our concept of multiculturalism instead of integration, which is a false tabloid concept. Multiculturalism is not only food, music, and dancing girls. Multiculturalism can use actual voices and ideas to contribute to a city's biodiversity, as well as its cultural diversity. This makes a local culture resilient and strong, as though it was a kind of ecosystem. I believe that an edible landscape project such as *Innermost Gardens* has the potential to contribute to local transformation in a positive way socially and culturally. There is no need to be afraid of the sort of complexity that is recognizable in healthy ecological systems.

Commons for a "Steady-State Economy"
Although it's root can be traced to Herman Daly (1973), the phrase "steady-state economy" brought to our attention the concept of sustainable economics from an ecological point of view. According to the Center for the Advancement of the Steady-State Economy (CASSE) site:

> The term typically refers to a national economy, but it can also be applied to a local, regional, or global economy. An economy can reach a steady state after a period of growth or after a period of downsizing or degrowth. To be sustainable, a steady-state economy may not exceed ecological limits. (CASSE, 2019)

Gathering resources in a common pool and sharing them in a village-sized community is not a transformative practice in itself. Before the advent of capitalism in the eighteenth century, it was the most common form of land management. Let us explore how commoning may help to transform a society. The commons are spaces of social reproduction accessed equally by all, without intervention by the State or the market. Production takes place under collective labour and equal access to resources of production. The idea of the commons also refers to collective activities of production and reproduction. It means inclusiveness, belonging, and sharing the outcome together as a group or as a community.

Commons may fail when privately owned. This is called the "tragedy of the commons", a term coined by Garrett Hardin (1968) to define the eighteenth century land-grabbing and enclosure movement in England. Hardin emphasized that commons can fail from over-exhaustion caused by taking too many resources. Elinor Ostrom, on the other side, analysed tragedy of the commons from a political economy point of view, particularly self-organizing and self-governing institutions. She pointed out that mutuality and reciprocity are essential for the success of common pool resources (CPRs). Individuals using CPRs are viewed as if they are capable of short-term maximization, but not of long-term reflection about joint strategies to improve joint outcomes (Ostrom, 1990: 216). It is true that, a commons may fail if the community does not bring a continuous reinvigorating energy and joy to the common space for the common good, or the commons is not managed in a self-governing way. The exhaustion of ecosystems can be seen in any former commons. I observed such a tragedy in my own village in the Aegean region of Turkey during the 1970s. A parcel of common land was allocated for grazing village animals. The herd was comprised of animals from every household with one person taking care of the herd every day. Even the job did not invoke gender politics. Villagers were flexible in giving the responsibility to a different man or a woman every day. While a mature woman's appearance was not acceptable in public spaces, this job of sharing for the commons made them free in public spaces. The problem began when people decided to keep a number of animals in their own individual pastures. The common lands gave them extra benefits without putting any effort or minimum effort in. When individual plot pastures were exhausted the people took advantage of the common lands. This brought about exhaustion in both common land and in the community's capacity to organize the common property. After a couple of years, the common lands were privatized. However, Hardin's view and my example may not be valid in some cases, because there are many successful examples of surviving commons around the world. Traditional communities are creating local commons by tracing their ecological practices back in time. For example, there is a successful example in Rajasthan, India. They recharged groundwater and restored a large irrigation system by creating small dams through women's leadership in 1989. Even the engineering and fundraising was done through women's leadership. They are known as "Rajasthan's water warriors". Thousands of old earthen dams called *johads* were replenished with underground water as well. This was a 10-year effort led by village committees. They practiced direct democracy. This is a good example of the struggle against drought: "Close to 10,000 *johad* systems and other water collecting and conserving structures [were created] in approximately 1,200 villages and 19 districts of Rajasthan during the past 28 years" (Suutari and Marten, 2005: np). Since the irrigation issue was resolved, their well-being increased and crime and violence reduced significantly, because some progressive cooperatives were built. This also helped economic justice, and collective abundance is the result. Another example is from Rojava, in northern Syria, where a women's cooperative called *Jinwar* lays mud bricks. They have engineered an ecovillage project, and say "this will be the first women's village and the most radical response to the male-dominant mindset in the Middle East" (Cooperative Economy, 2017).

In a degrowth strategy, a moral economy is the answer for a self-governing institution. Let us bear in mind that degrowth requires voluntary simplicity to reduce consumption for material needs. Rather than GDP as measurement of growth, ecological economics becomes the implementation of regenerative and restorative practices.

Commoning is an alternative to the growth economy because it means voluntarily limiting the extraction of natural resources. It helps reduce carbon emissions by saving energy and water. However, the examples above show that commoning is a dynamic collective activity, which requires continuous attention to keep going in the right direction. There is still a risk of reversal through privatization. Any community trying to recreate the commons should be careful about the potential for this to occur.

In a degrowth strategy, a stable-state moral economy would fit well with this commoning process. Degrowth strategy should be based on a moral economy with ecological restoration, rather than extraction from nature, and have a social and economic justice dimension. Recall that degrowth requires voluntary simplicity to reduce consumption for material needs. Rather than GDP as a measurement of growth, the *Index of Sustainable Welfare* can be used as the indication of a stable-state moral economy.

This is why the moral economy embodies norms and sentiments regarding the responsibilities and rights of individuals and institutions with respect to others. These norms and sentiments go beyond matters of justice and equality to conceptions of the good, for example, regarding the needs and ends of economic activity. They might also be extended further to include treatment of the environment (Sayer, 2004: 6).

For a steady-state moral economy in the context of ecological economics, biophysical and social indicators seem appropriate for a regenerative and restorative transition, as opposed to the "extractivist" behaviour of the capitalist growth economy: "The great challenge of degrowth is how to maintain (or even enhance) the well-being of the planet's citizens while global resource use and waste production are being reduced to within ecological limits. Social indicators are needed to ensure that quality of life is maintained or improved by degrowth and not diminished by it" (O'Neill, 2011). Indeed, waste reduction for a healthy environment must be the main focus since the growth economy produces an enormous amount of waste, including toxic types. Quality of life could be measured from many different perspectives, such as happiness. When a system reaches a stable stage, that point could indicate the achievement of stability. While society should have a new way of living, it is possible to keep the equilibrium at a stable state at a global level.

What Sorts of Growth do We Want?

There is no doubt that *Limits to Growth* brought us green consumerist literature. In other words, *Limits to Growth* neither helps to create a vocabulary to limit consumption nor does it prevent the declining natural resources which, we all agree, are limited. This is because most green developments are, in the end, based on growth in capitalist society. It means that consumerism is just replacing so-called "green" products—recall the shopping bags that are made of GMO corn which are coming into vogue.

The reality of nature's limits requires clear ethics to reassess human needs, wants, and desires. As ecofeminist and social ecologist Chaia Heller underlines, "Our new ways of desiring nature entail changes not only in personal life-style and outlook, but changes in social institutions as well" (Heller, 1999: 102). The feminist movement contributed an important phrase to social movements: "the personal is political". Hence, personal lifestyles are interconnected with social life. This applies to institutions as well. We can follow a path in which our needs, wants, and desires serve to regenerate nature and repair the social relations that help to revolutionize social institutions.

Bookchin distinguished human evolution in regards to the relationship with nature as "first nature" and "second nature". He named nature as "first nature", which becomes "second nature" through human intervention (Bookchin, 2005). Through the relationship between these two arise dynamics of domination over nature and domination over human (and between genders). As human beings, we have created social ecosystems and many sorts of hierarchy, such as men's domination of woman, the boss's domination of labour, white people's domination of people of colour, dominant cultures' domination of ethnics, and so on. However, all these hierarchies can be resolved by learning from nature. Nature cooperates rather than competes. For instance, from my long-term observation during my landscape management practices, most trees cooperate to reach sunlight and share the minerals in the root system. Of course, there are also some opportunistic invasive plants that are not native to the local environments. This process makes them a part of natural evolution. That is why from second nature evolution comes third nature which brings social diversity and ecological complexity. Democratic and participatory technological development plays a vital role in the social ecological realization of an emancipated society. Bookchin emphasizes the hierarchical concept: "Organic societies are not yet divided into the classes and bureaucracies based on exploitation that we find in hierarchical society" (Bookchin, 2004: 167).

From a true ecological design perspective, if a city is designed in an ecological way it does not generate waste. Of course, municipal education, voluntary practices and incorporation of citizens are significant components here. In this way, a city is considered a big ecosystem. I can draw on my ecological design experience, in which every element is linked to serve not only mutual support, but also to provide multiple functions at the neighbourhood level. Since all human activities are supposed to be circulated in the closed system, one system's output can be an input for the following system. This is how chickens gain protein from a compost pile, and produce eggs and feathers as well as resolving the compost problem.

Transformation in everyday life through genuine ecological society is necessary by consuming less and by building radical commons. Environmental scientist, degrowth activist, and writer Giorgos Kallis, who is critical to utilitarianism, explains how degrowth and welfare is possible through alternative economics:

> First, reconstructing the commons; second, reclaiming state decoupling well-being such as basic income, public money, work-sharing, carbon caps and taxes; third, political organizing (Kallis 2015: 31'40").

I agree that adjusting the economy to cap carbon, rather than allowing carbon trading, is important for the reasons outlined above in the section on green development. The carbon economy only assists the greening of capitalism. The point is how to reorganize society in a non-hierarchical way. Also I prefer to say government instead of the State as a criticism to Kallis. I believe that we need to reorganize institutions in a degrowth economy, but not through the State. If we want to transform cities into organic eco-communities, as Lefebvre and Bookchin proposed, reorganizing institutions accordingly will bring a lot of chaos. For social ecologists, challenging political and economic power and creating alternatives through municipalism is strategically important. Chaia Heller explains Bookchin's municipalism concept with a community spirit:

> We must develop a new understanding of citizenship that is not defined in relation to capital or the nation-state but instead, defined in opposition to capital and the nation-state. We may become revolutionary citizens defined in relation to local communities that are part of a larger confederation of self-governing bodies. We may become "a community of communities". This new way of thinking about political regeneration is called libertarian municipalism. (Heller, 1999: 12)

Heller here also criticises the Nation-State, which we do not need. Instead, we need to revolutioneer the institutions that create and serve equity and well-being.

Democratic and participatory technological development plays a vital role in the social ecological realization of an emancipated society. Furthermore, a socially and ecologically diverse society keeps its roots strong. A decentralized city requires a municipal level of non-hierarchical governance. This can be applied to degrowth for self-determination and active citizenship as social ecology brings self-determination by opposing any form of domination. When people begin to enjoy helping to resolve their problems through direct democracy, as happened in the autonomous Syrian region of Rojava, it is possible to create alternatives in a social ecological way—even in a war zone.

In the end, yes, we need to limit growth, re-assess our real needs, and simplify life, as well as restore natural so-called "resources" because it has gone beyond saving resources now. We need to concentrate on how to clean up the soil, air, and recharge underground water. Here is my view of utopia. I dream of a city that is more regenerative and self-reliant via its local resources and self-sufficiency through direct democracy principles. I dream of a city, that is connected to surrounding towns at a bioregional level and resources locally managed. I dream of engaging public spaces such as community gardens, urban agricultural sites, wildlife zones, spaces for art and craft activities—also to share stories. I also dream of an inclusive city—along ethical, racial, economic, and gender lines. I dream of a city economy no longer subservient to capitalism's "grow or die" dilemma. Material accumulation will no longer hold as much social kudos, since the radical commons will play vital roles. I want a city of conviviality and frugality, a harmonious place for its own citizens. I want a "convivial" (Ilych 1973) city which is continuously evolving with its commons through the joy of politics in everyday life. I want a city that serves its citizens with the value of *simplicity*—the ultimate goal of sophistication, as indicated in Leonardo's statement.

References

Bookchin, M. 1986. *The Limits of the City* Revised Edition. Montreal: Black Rose Books.

Bookchin, M. 1992. *Urbanization Without Cities: The Rise and Decline of Citizenship*. Montreal: Black Rose Books.

Bookchin, M. 1996. *Toward an Ecological Society*. Montreal: Black Rose Books.

Bookchin, M. 2004. *Post-Scarcity Anarchism*. Oakland: AK Press.

Bookchin, M. 2005. *The Ecology of Freedom*. Oakland: AK Press.

Brown, A. and Annali, K. 2009. Urban Policies and the Right to the City Rights, responsibilities and citizenship. *UN-Habitat Report March 2009*. [Online]. [Accessed 9 June 2018]. Available from: http://unesdoc.unesco.org/images/0017/001780/178090e.pdf#page=21&zoom=auto,-14,831

Busquet, G. 2012. Political Space in the Work of Henri Lefebvre: Ideology and Utopia. *JSSJ*, 5(13).[Online]. [Accessed 9 June 2018]. Available from: https://www.jssj.org/wp-content/uploads/2013/09/JSSJ5-3.en_1.pdf

Casey, R. 2019. *Advancement of the Steady State Economy*. [Online]. [Accessed 9 October 2018]. Available from: https://steadystate.org/discover/definition/

Cooperative Economy 2017. [Online]. [Accessed 9 June 2018]. Available from: https://cooperativeeconomy.info/co-ops/economy-rojava-bakur/economy-rojava/

Harding, G. 1968. "A Short History of Enclosure in Britain. *Science*, 162(3859), pp.1243-1248.

Harvey, D. 2008. The Right to the City. *New Left Review*. (53), pp.23-40.

Heller, C. 1999. *The Ecology of Everyday Life: Rethinking the Desire for Nature.* Montreal: Black Rose Books.

Ilych, I. 1973. *Tools for Conviviality.* London: Calder & Boyars.

Kallis, G., Kothari A., and Baviskar, A. 2015. *Degrowth: A vocabulary for a new era.* [Online]. [Accessed 19 August 2019]. Available from: https://www.youtube.com/watch?v=PHXxXWSJT98

Meadows D.H., Meadows D.L., Randers J., Behrens III W.W. 1972. *The Limits to growth: A report for the Club of Rome's Project on the Predicament of Mankind.* Washington: POTOMAC ASSOCIATES.

Ostrom, E. 1990. *Governing the Commons.* Cambridge: Cambridge University Press.

Daniel, W., O'Neill 2011. Measuring progress in the degrowth transition to a steady state economy. *Ecological Economics,* 84, pp.221-231.

Riley, T. 2017. *Just 100 companies responsible for 71 per cent of global emissions, study says.* [Online]. [Accessed 19 August 2019]. Available from: https://www.theguardian.com/sustainable-business/2017/jul/10/100-fossil-fuel-companies-investors-responsible-71-global-emissions-cdp-study-climate-change.

Sayer, A. 2004. *Moral economic and economic institutions: Polanyi, embeddedness and framing.* [Online]. [Accessed 19 August 2019]. Available from: http://www.lancaster.ac.uk/fass/resources/sociology-online-papers/papers/sayer-moral-economy.pdf

Suutari, A. and Marten, G. 2005. *Water Warriors: Rainwater Harvesting to Replenish Underground Water (Rajasthan, India).* [Online]. [Accessed 19 August 2018]. Available from: http://www.ecotippingpoints.org/our-stories/indepth/india-rajasthan-rainwater-harvest-restoration-groundwater-johad.html#sub

Notes:

1 More information about The City Repair Project available from http://www.cityrepair.org/

Is the Right to the City a Right or a Revolution?
Magali Fricaudet

From a catastrophist point of view, we could probably say that the unprecedented rate of urbanization that the world is currently experiencing is a realization of the more destructive tendencies of capitalism, where life is at serious stake. Indeed, urbanization seems to have no end, as the ideology of growth predominates. In 1920, urban centres represented just 30 per cent of the world population; the proportion of urban dwellers over rural ones will be inverted around 2030—rising to 66 per cent according to the UN Human Settlement Programme, UN-Habitat.[1] In that context, since the late 1990s, Henri Lefebvre's "right to the city" has appeared as a claim among a diversity of voices—from neighbourhood struggles to local government calls for local democracy—that denounces the "competitive city model".

As cities increasingly represent centres of capital accumulation, and the commodification of life in all its aspects, Lefebvre's *The Right to the City* is all the more poignant as an inspiration for the "urban revolution" that he called for as a social practice. Conceiving the right to the city based on its use value, instead of its exchange value, as a way to free citizens from private property and spatialized class relations, has influenced a diversity of interpretations and practices that share the goal to take back the city as a common good—a place for collective emancipation and freedom. At the same time, the exercise of municipal power inspired by the right to the city, in the case of municipalist experiences in Spain since 2014, have also shown the limits of realizing such rights at the local level, as well as the contradictions in exercising institutional power in the hegemonic capitalist city model.

The Paradigm of the Urban Miracle, or How Global Capitalism Has Reached Massive Consent
The preamble of the "New Urban Agenda", adopted by UN-Habitat member States at Quito in October 2016, enshrines the blindness of the so-called "international community" through describing urbanization as an *unprecedented opportunity* for humanity, and cities as *great engines of growth*.

58

The current hegemonic view of cities corresponds to what Bookchin denounced as a poor "spatial and demographic" conception, "viewing the city as an area occupied by a closely interlocked, densely populated human community"—a definition in "quantitative terms". That is, totally in contradiction with his view on the city, which he considered to be a "uniquely human, ethical and ecological community whose members often lived in balance with nature and created institutional forms that sharpened human self-awareness, fostered rationality, created a secularized culture, enhanced individuality and established institutional forms of freedom" (Bookchin, *Urbanization against Cities*, Black Rose Books, 1992, Introduction, p. XIV). In Bookchin's perception, citification does not mean an opposition between nature and human beings. Referring to what Cicero called a "second nature", that is "a *humanly* made nature that exists in balance with the first nature" (ibid, Introduction, p. X), citification is a realization of the natural mutualist tendency of humans to gather and form freely consenting communities. This is why Bookchin denounced urbanization as a result of the accumulation of power by some elites, based on individualism and endless consumption as a "cancerous phenomenon".

Today, cities are where 80 per cent of global GDP is produced and, although cities are responsible for 70 per cent of greenhouse gas emissions and inequalities at city levels have grown faster than at national levels in the past two decades,[2] UN-Habitat affirms that "good management and planning processes" could counter these negative externalities.

Megacities have grown at an unprecedented rate; in 2015, there were 503 cities of more than one million inhabitants, compared with 162 in 1975. Large metropolitan areas are key hubs of value in the international economy, representing huge markets and extremely rapid flows of capital. They are strategic places of specialization within the international division of work, as some cities in the global south, such as Dhaka, Bangladesh, host a very cheap workforce with limited labour rights, while others, such as London, New York or Tokyo, compete to be centres of high-level decision-making within the markets and where elites are concentrated. Cities are central to the capitalist economy as they also represent huge markets, where "consumption" patterns belie high levels of inequality. Most of the time, the mass of "urban poor" settled in the "informal neighbourhoods" of peripheral areas are compelled to pay higher prices for basic services, which the public sector does not provide.

With 1 billion people living in slums among over 3 billion urban dwellers, cities have become the only viable option for a large number of internal and external migrants, pushed around by global climate change, and free trade agreements imposed by the European Union, Canada and United States on their countries, devastating their agriculture. Most people move to urban areas with the hope of accessing the kinds of services and opportunities concentrated in cities.

As David Harvey (2003) writes, city economies are also largely based on a process of "accumulation by dispossession", meaning that in front of the high demand for urban land and housing, the unregulated real estate market is realizing huge profits on people's homes, creating massive segregation processes. Indeed, the real estate market was so high in the global markets during the subprime crisis of 2008 that it marked the beginning of a global financial and economic crisis, unprecedented since the 1930s. According to Saskia Sassen (2016), the huge flows of international capital onto real estate markets in some metropolises, such as London, are now provoking much further consequences than gentrification: they replace traditional elites with international ones (Sassen, 2016)—the famous 1 per cent that controls 82 per cent of the wealth (Oxfam, 2018). The UN Special Rapporteur on housing rights, in her report of February 2017, commented:

> The value of global real estate is about US$ 217 trillion, nearly 60 per cent of the value of all global assets, with residential real estate comprising 75 per cent of the total. … Housing is at the centre of an historic structural transformation in global investment and the economies of the industrialized world with profound consequences for those in need of adequate housing. (*Report of the Special Rapporteur on adequate housing as a component of the right to an adequate standard of living, and on the right to non-discrimination in this context* A/HRC/34/51, p. 3)

At the same time, fierce urbanization has led to a progressive concentration of power in some decentralized metropolitan areas, and resistance movements have developed locally and globally.

Lefebvre and the Philosophy of Urban Revolution

In the late 1960s, from the radical urban sociologist, the "Marxian" Henri Lefebvre, *The Right to the City* called for "the right to urban life, to a renewed centrality, to places of meetings and exchanges, to a rhythm of life that allows the full and entire *use* of these moments and places". [3] For Lefebvre, the right to the city refers both to a social practice of the working class that defends the use value of the city, instead of its exchange value, and to a narrative that he calls "urban revolution". Lefebvre refers to a post-modern acceptation of the working class as the "dispossessed of the city". Lefebvre writes, "As one hundred years ago,[4] although in new conditions, the working class gather the interests (beyond time and superficiality) of the whole society and first of all, of those who inhabit" (Ibid, p. 108).[5]

He refers to the inhabitants as suffering the misery of "everydayness", as managed by the bureaucratic bourgeoisie leading the city. The everydayness of the students, of the intellectuals, of the workers, of the colonized who go every day from their house to the station to take a crowded train or bus to go to the office and go back home to begin again the day after. He pictures the generalized misery of the masses that escape or dissimulate the poorness of everyday life through the satisfactions of urban society, such as commodified culture, hobbies and even nature.

Lefebvre denounces urbanism and the functionalist approach of cities as a political process that underpins the financial sector, which together produces space and alienated time, thus producing power. The technocratic approach of capitalist power to produce the city and space separates the functions of life originally gathered in cities in order to produce and reproduce class relations.

In Marxist theory, social classes are defined as a function of their position in the relations of production between capital and work in industrial society. The modern urbanization phenomenon makes this frame of analysis burst. Lefebvre introduces space and the production of space as the centre of the production of social relations and of the reproduction of the relations of production, because of the increasing exchange value of space. In that regard, western cities, from the political cities of antiquity and the commercial cities of the middle ages have suffered from the increase of exchange relations created by capitalist elites. The critical turning point of the city is the process of industrialization–urbanization at the end of the eighteenth century, which made the city burst, leading to its expansion in a dialectic phenomenon of explosion–implosion. So space and inertia explains the survival of capitalism and the eternally renewed expectation of the final crisis.

Rational planning of the production, organization of the territory, industrialization and urbanization are essential features of the "socialization of society", which fix predetermined functions in the space of the city and allow it to maintain order. In that regard, urban struggles, through re-owning the city, are strategic in the struggle against capital (Claire Revol, 2017).

Thus the space of cities depends on class strategies that produce a segregation of urban spaces, demolishing the idea of cities as shared common spaces, and of the centrality of the notion of the social form of the city—one of gathering and coexistence. In that sense, as Bookchin does, Lefebvre shows that throughout history, cities have been the work of societies, spaces that relate to usage and urban life instead of the product of an exchange value. The right to the city is a claim for transforming life through transforming cities, creating them as collective pieces of work. Hence, the praxis of the right to the city refers to the ideas of struggle and celebration at the same time. Lefebvre used to refer to the creative dimension of the Commune of Paris as a way for the working classes to take back the city that Haussman's work had spoilt from people. Against the functionalist city that separates the diverse dimensions of life in the space, he invites us to take back citizenship through creativity, spontaneity and self-organization processes of re-owning the city. In that sense, he is in tune with the May 68 movement.

Indeed, Lefebvre was a researcher and teacher at the University of Nanterre, a newly built campus located between the slums of the Parisian working class periphery. The May 68 movement really began on 22 March 1968 in the University of Nanterre when a group of students occupied the administration tower of the campus, denouncing the arbitrary authority of the so-called "Mandarin", the omnipotent administrative council of the university led by professors. His group of researchers from the philosophy department of Nanterre inspired the 68 movement. When referring to the idea of celebration and enjoyment of the city, his thought is situated in an insurrectional and creative movement, strongly marked by leftist ideals that demand freedom and new models against the class domination of work and consumption.

The Emergence of the Right to the City as a Global Claim for Socio-Spatial Justice

Since the 1970s, Lefebvre's ideas have acted as a reference for diverse forms of insurgent citizenship that claims ownership of the city—in front of massive investments that evict people from cities, in front of gentrification processes. They also constitute a theoretical basis for movements that occupy public space against its privatization. The South African movement Abahlali baseMjondolo,[6] inspired by Lefebvre, defends the legitimacy of squatters to occupy urban space. They argue against the interpretation by the government of the World Bank's slogan "cities without slums", which has led to evictions through entitling the owners of shacks (but not dwellers) as land tenants and through privatizing the management of services in renewed neighbourhoods. In Durban, 2006, this movement assembled 50,000 shack dwellers from across the country to fight for land reforms and dignity. They occupy land as a way of reclaiming the dispossession–urbanization process, and denounce the accumulation of land by elites, as well as the inaction of the South African State to fulfil social housing programmes. The anti-State[7] process approach of this movement clearly fits within Lefebvre's vision (Marianne Morange, 2017).

At the same time, Lefebvre insisted that the most revolutionary principles of the right to the city would include land reform, as this would have occurred during revolutions of the agrarian age, where the tenancy of land was key to freeing peasants and agrarian workers from landlords. For Lefebvre, the collective tenure of land in cities against private property, which maintains the monopoly of production of space under financial interests, is one of the key issues of the urban revolution.[8]

The social function of land and the city as a strong feature of the right to the city has inspired the claim of many unentitled occupants, mainly in Latin America where urban rights and human rights have a long common history. Supported by NGOs such as Habitat International Coalition (HIC) in their struggle to stay in the city and be recognized as city producers, the right to the city became a more holistic claim than the right to housing in the late 1990s. Promoted through the World Inhabitants Assembly during the Earth Summit of Rio in 1992 under the banner "cities for life, not for profit", HIC developed a "World Charter for the Right to the City", later adopted by social movements in the World Social Forum in 2005. The Charter was developed as an instrument to promote the recognition and legislation of human rights in an urban context and to change the narrative around the "urban poor" as beneficiaries of tiny neighbourhood improvement programmes. In the context of the Charter, the right to the city is defined as:

> the equitable usufruct of cities within the principles of sustainability, democracy, equity, and social justice. It is the collective right of the inhabitants of cities, in particular of the vulnerable and marginalized groups, that confers upon them legitimacy of action and organization, based on their uses and customs, with the objective to achieve full exercise of the right to free *self-determination and an adequate standard of living*. The Right to the City is *interdependent of all internationally recognized and integrally conceived human rights*, and therefore includes all the civil, political, economic, social, cultural and environmental rights which are already regulated in the international human rights treaties. (World Charter for the Right to the City, Art. 2)

The World Charter is a compromise, the result of its institutional purpose to serve as an advocacy tool aimed at introducing the right to the city in international, national and local legislation as an urban component of the "right to development" and as a way to protect people from the arbitrary power of city developers. This claim has received strong opposition from governments, mainly in international negotiations around the so-called "New Urban Agenda", The Declaration of Quito (2016) where the inclusion of the right to the city and some of its principles, such as the social value of land and the city or the prevention of forced evictions, in the international document crystallized tense discussions between the richest countries (led by the US and the EU) and some Latin American countries, such as Mexico, Chile, and Ecuador.

In the meantime, by the end of the twentieth century, Lefebvre's *The Right to the City* had inspired local and national legislations trying to counterbalance the commodification of land, housing and, most generally, the city. One of the most famous examples is the Brazilian Constitution of 1988, translated into the City Statute of 2001. The City Statute refers to the "social function of property", introducing tools to control the land, facilitating the regularization of occupying people and establishing financial mechanisms to correct socio-spatial inequalities. In 2008, the Constitution of Ecuador enshrines the right to the city in the following words:

> Persons have the right to fully enjoy the city and its public spaces, on the basis of principles of sustainability, social justice, respect for different urban cultures and a balance between the urban and rural sectors. Exercising the right to the city is based on the democratic management of the city, with respect to the social and environmental function of property and the city and with the full exercise of citizenship. (Art.11).

This institutionalization of the right to the city also questions the polysemiotic notion of rights that Lefebvre used. A right is essentially attached to all human beings as a *guarantee against arbitrariness* (civil and political rights) and a *guarantee of decent life* (economic, cultural and environmental rights). Rights are instruments protected and guaranteed by nation-states and aim at protecting people against the arbitrary power of those same states. Lefebvre's initial conception was probably more performative in the sense of affirming a right as a social practice and a perspective for urban revolution. For Lefebvre, who was a dialectical thinker, "in difficult conditions, within this society that cannot totally oppose them but at the same time block them, rights are finding their way, defining civilization (rights are at the same time *in* and *against* society, *through* but often *against* culture.)",[9] he writes. At the same time, the polysemiotic nature of the word *right* intrinsically connects the right to the city with a diversity of interpretations and that is perhaps the more powerful meaning of the right to the city, although it could also be its main weakness as this makes it vulnerable to possible misunderstandings.

In a rough capitalist urbanization context, the right to the city is an inspiration for an approach that protects the use value against the voracious appetites of the markets. Are the experiences of municipalism relevant for the process of taking back the city against the long-lasting process of capitalist dispossession that the people of cities have suffered?

Municipalities: At the Forefront of the Right to the City?

From the beginning of the 2000s, under the lead of Porto Alegre and Barcelona City Hall, the locally elected Left took their place in parallel with the World Social Forum as a place to renew political views after the collapse of the Soviet bloc.

In that framework, locally elected representatives of urban social movements and NGOs enabled a dialogue that led to discussions around the narrative of the right to the city as an alternative to the "competitive and smart city" model. As a result of this process, the "Global Charter Agenda for Human Rights in the City", adopted in 2011 in the framework of the organization United Cities and Local Governments,[10] refers to the right to the city.

Later, in 2016, the right to the city became a common claim around the preparation of the Habitat III Summit. Through the Global Platform for the Right to the City,[11] created by the HIC and Polis Institute (a Brazilian NGO that has supported the Brazilian movements of occupants in the city and pushed for the adoption of the City Statute), NGOs, searchers and local governments gathered to advocate for the inclusion of the right to the city in the New Urban Agenda.

In 2010, the Charter for the Right to the City of the city of Mexico, driven by social movements, represented a further step in the institutionalization of the right to the city. Without enough binding processes to translate it into concrete actions, it defines a framework of shared responsibility between the various actors within the city. The right to the city rests upon six principles:

1) respect, protection and realisation of all human rights (civic, political, economic, social, cultural and environmental);
2) the social function of property, land and the city;
3) the democratic governance of villages, towns and metropolitan areas, which supposes a strong decentralization framework;
4) recognition of the social production of habitat and of the social and solidarity-based nature of the economy, as supported by the social production of habitat;
5) democratic and collective management of common goods— environmental and cultural—through a global vision that is not limited by administrative boundaries;
6) the protection and improvement of public spaces, including infrastructure and community facilities, through supporting inhabitants' initiatives and precluding privatization.

This reformist view of the right to the city has influenced the creation of community-based district improvement programmes, initiated by civil society organizations and then included as public policy. For example, Mexico City is often used as a reference against the World Bank doctrine of "cities without slums". The translation of the right to the city into local public policies underlines the tensions that constitute the city, resulting in a very contradictory exercise of power by so-called progressive local governments.

Since the 2015 municipal elections in Spain, it seems that other narratives have appeared that affirm the centrality of the right to the city and the ownership of people before capitalist interests. After the occupations of places in 2011, the "indignados" rooted the movement into neighbourhood assemblies. In the Spanish municipal elections of 2014, in 60 towns and cities, local coalitions comprised of diverse struggles and movements and supported by leftist and ecological parties structured themselves to take the city back. Their organization was based on strong ethical codes to prevent corruption and to guarantee accountability of locally elected representatives, and on participatory programmes based on feminized politics in contrast to the conception of a concentrated and competitive exercise of power. Cities meant the possibility of changing everyday life, implementing mutualist and community-based solutions, which nation-states (with their promiscuous relationships with private interests) are incapable of. Spanish municipalism relies on the commons as a necessary alternative to the market. It organizes programmes that articulate movements and heterogeneous spaces of struggle, which have thus far acted in parallel (ecologists, activists for water as a common good, activists for the right to health and education, feminist groups, anti-racist movements, hackers, and supporters of free culture and of the neutrality of networks, defenders of social and solidarity economy, etc.) (Subirats, 2018).

Nevertheless, in more than three years of exercising power—sometimes based on weak majorities in the councils—their impact on the disastrous effects of the financialized economy have been limited. The structure of the administration based on rigid hierarchies and limited decentralization strongly limits their capacity for action. In Barcelona, for instance, the team of Ada Colau (the mayor elected on a municipalist agenda who came from a housing rights movement) made strong efforts to take back empty buildings and spaces to create housing cooperatives, to negotiate with banks to create social housing in the flats left empty by mortgage-related evictions, to fine Airbnb and landlords who rent flats without authorisation, to count and tax vacant housing, to stop touristic flats and hotel in the city centre, to purchase property for social housing, to impose restrictions that every new construction or rehabilitation project includes a minimum of 30 per cent of affordable housing. Yet, despite all of these measures, the rental market housing speculation process is at a climax in Barcelona. The exercise of power in cities, which is intrinsically marked by a diversity of interests, is always inherently contradictory.

For instance, one of the more paradoxical aspects of governing is that Barcelona's administration, in order to fight real estate companies operating in connivance with drug dealers, is now closing empty flats and installing anti-squatter doors in the popular central neighbourhood of the Raval. Indeed, after the mortgage crisis of 2008, leading to the eviction of thousands of dwellers from their flats in Barcelona, a high quantity of housing was reclaimed by banks and remained vacant. Now that the prices of housing are increasing again under the pressure of tourism and few rental properties are available, real estate companies have been accused of collaborating with drug dealers to despoil the district of the Raval. In 2016, a wave of flat occupations by drug dealers led to the mobilization of their neighbours, denouncing their occupation, and the violence associated with drug dealing and the speculative goal of these occupations. Organizing through WhatsApp, and gathering to denounce traffickers in the streets, neighbourhood groups prompted the end of speculative "narco-flats". In front of the inaction of international banks and investment funds to evict occupying dealers from their properties—despite City Hall demands—the elected team had no alternative other than to use police intervention to evict dealers from the flats and close them with anti-squatter doors.

Another contradictory action of Barcelona's municipality was also be the way that City Hall acted towards the Senegalese street vendors, who survive by selling counterfeit goods. Indeed, under pressure from local merchants to denounce the unfair competition from street vendors, in the summer 2016, Barcelona City Hall launched an anti-counterfeit campaign in multiple languages—inviting people not to buy from illegal street vendors but to buy from local shops instead.

Cities are intersected by a diversity of interests, where certain interests clearly predominate. In that context, the pressure to act in favour of the most powerful is high. Although governing according to "the people's wishes" is a commitment, this is somehow difficult to respect. Governance *as action* is a complex exercise. Barcelona's government asserts that it tries to do its best within a very hostile political and media context, and for this they need people to stay in the streets and attempt to find a "conflictual collaboration" between the street and the institution.

What if Urban Revolution Meant Permanent Insurrection?

Fifty years after Lefebvre wrote *The Right to the City*, where he denounced the total absurdity of the dominant alliance of bureaucratic and private interests, which led the city to fulfil the interests of elites, neoliberalism has increasingly foisted the totalities of the economic system upon city life. Is it possible then, within the current financialized economy, to guarantee the right to the city from a municipalist perspective when cities are places where so much wealth is generated and which have served the interests of production and consumption since times of industrialization?

Referring to the progressive concentration of land into fewer hands, Lefebvre spoke about the ruralisation of cities. From that view, perhaps it is time to look to occupying rural areas to prevent their urbanization, and then try to citify the rural world—in the sense of Bookchin's city as an ecosociety, far away from the necrotic metropolitan way of life. Worldwide mobilizations against megaprojects in the last decades have carved a new path for creating ecosocieties.

In its resistance against Nantes' new airport in Notre-Dame-des-Landes in France, the ZAD movement is a clear example of this. In French law, Zone d'Aménagement Différé (ZAD) means an area owned by public authorities to make a project in partnership with business companies. In Notre-Dames-des-Landes, a ZAD was created in the 1960s to build a new airport in Nantes. Farmers and local residents have resisted this project since that time. In 2009, when the project was relaunched by public authorities, ecologists and libertarian activists from the Climate Camp occupied this land. They renamed the territory ZAD for Zone d'Autonomie et de Defense (Zone of Defence and Autonomy), creating a self-organized area based on autonomy from capitalism, radical ecology and de-growth. Fighting a high degree of repression, the movement received support from a large part of leftist and ecologist movements, leading to the cancellation of the project by the French government in 2018. Since the airport project was halted, Zadists have continued to fight to live in autonomy in the area, free from the capitalist system. The State is denying this, declaring it a "no rights zone".

Finally, urbanization is probably the last step of industrial civilization based on the exploitation of nature. Beyond climate change, scientists from different disciplines agree that a process of collapsing ecosystems and civilization is in march, threatening entire species. The end of fossil-based energy and the scarcity of resources that are currently essential to maintain the urbanized way of life of an increasing number of human beings has put the natural, economic, political and social balance at serious stake. As Pablo Servigne writes, "It's true that the possibility of collapse closes futures that are valuable for us, and this is violent, but it opens some futures that could be really happy. What's at stake is to approach these new futures and make them liveable".[12]

In that context, from the perspectives of both the right to the city and of social ecology, citifying the rural and reaching harmony between the first and second natures, building autonomous communities with a real possibility of creating a face-to-face democracy, and preparing ourselves for the inevitable end of the collapse of the capitalist system is probably the kind of permanent insurrection that we have to make real.

References

Barcelona en comú 2014. *Why do we want to win back Barcelona*, 2014. [Online]. [Accessed 19 August 2019]. Available from: https://guanyembarcelona.cat/wp-content/uploads/2014/06/priciples.pdf.

Bookchin, M. 1992. *Urbanization against Cities.* Montreal: Black Rose Books.

Farha, L. 2017. *Report of the Special Rapporteur on adequate housing as a component of the right to an adequate standard of living, and on the right to non-discrimination in this context* A/HRC/34/51. [Online]. [Accessed 19 August 2019]. Available from: http://ap.ohchr.org/documents/alldocs.aspx?doc_id=27600

Harvey, D. 2011. *Le Capitalisme contre le Droit à la ville. Néolibéralisme, urbanisation et résistances.* Amsterdam: Editions Amsterdam.

Lefebvre, H. 1967. *Le Droit à la Ville.* Economica.

OXFAM 2018. *Reward work, not wealth. To end the inequality crisis, we must build an economy for ordinary working people, not the rich and powerfu.* [Online]. [Accessed 19 August 2019]. Available from: https://www-cdn.oxfam.org/s3fs-public/file_attachments/bp-reward-work-not-wealth-220118-en.pdf

Polis Institute 2015. *The City Statute, New Tool for ensuring right to the city in Brazil.* [Online]. [Accessed 19 August 2019]. Available from: http://www.polis.org.br/uploads/916/916.pdf. Servigne, P. and Stevens, R. 2015. *Comment tout peut s'effondrer: Petit manuel de collapsologie à l'usage des générations présentes.* Paris: Seuil.

Revol, C. 2017, *Le Droit à la ville, Quelques éclairages sur le texte et l'auteur, in Le Droit à la ville*, Cahier des 2èmes rencontres de géopolitique critique, sous la direction de Claske Dijkema et Morgane Cohen, Mars.

Sassen, S. 2016. *Expulsions.* Cambridge, MA: Harvard University Press.

Subirats, J. 2018. Les villes au cœur de la redistribution? Le nouveau municipalisme, antidote à l'Europe de l'austérité et des États dans l'impasse. *Mouvements,* 2(94), pp.11-23.

Charter for the Right to the City of the city of Mexico 2010. [Online]. [Accessed 19 August 2019]. Available from: http://www.hic-gs.org/content/Mexico_Charter_R2C_2010.pdf

UCLG 2011. *Global Charter Agenda for Human Rights in the City.* [Online]. [Accessed 19 August 2019]. Available from: https://www.uclg-cisdp.org/en/right-to-the-city/world-charter-agenda

World Charter for the Right to the City 2005. [Online]. [Accessed 19 August 2019]. Available from: http://hic-gs.org/document.php?pid=2422

UN World Cities Report 2016. [Online]. [Accessed 19 August 2019]. Available from: http://wcr.unhabitat.org/main-report/

Notes:

1 UN-Habitat is based in Nairobi and addresses the impacts of human settlement. The agency executes the UN General Assembly agenda on human settlement and habitat adopted at the Habitat international conference. The first conference, Habi-

tat I, took place in Vancouver in 1976 and the most recent, Habitat III, led to the adoption of the New Urban Agenda, in Quito in October 2016.

2 According to UN *World Cities Report 2016*, inequalities increased in 75 per cent of cities between 1996 and 2016.

3 Translation by the author. Originally: "le droit à la vie urbaine, à la centralité rénovée, aux lieux de rencontres et d'échanges, aux rythmes de vie et emplois du temps permettant l'usage plein et entier de ces moments et lieux", Henri Lefebvre, *Le Droit à la ville Economica*, 1967, p.133.

4 Lefebvre wrote *The Right to the City* in 1967, 100 years after *Capital*.

5 Translation by the author. Originally: "Comme il y a un siècle, la classe ouvrière rassemble les intérêts (dépassant l'immédiat et le superficiel), de la société entière et d'abord de tous ceux qui habitent."

6 See http://abahlali.org/.

7 Lefebvre denounced the State and the companies that were grabbing the city. But we cannot say that he was an anarchist, as he believes that the urban revolution has to be based on an economic revolution (planning oriented towards the satisfaction of social needs) and political (democratic control of the state apparatus and self-organization) and also on a permanent cultural one where arts play a key role (Henri Lefebvre, *Le Droit à la ville, Economica*, 1967, p. 134).

8 Interview with Henri Lefebvre, Urbanose, Office National du film du Canada, https://www.youtube.com/watch?v=0kyLooKv6mU.

9 Translation by the author. Originally: "...dans mais souvent contre la société, par mais souvent contre la culture" (Henri Lefebvre, *Le Droit à la ville, Economica*, 1967, p.134).

10 https://www.uclg.org/ United Cities and Local Government is the International Organization of Local Governments funded in 2001 and recognized by the UN. Its headquarters is in Barcelona.

11 http://www.righttothecityplatform.org.br.

12 Translation by the author. Originally: "Certes, la possibilité d'un effondrement ferme des avenirs qui nous sont chers, et c'est violent, mais il en ouvre une infinité d'autres, dont certains étonnamment rieurs. Tout l'enjeu est donc d'apprivoiser ces nouveaux avenirs, et de les rendre vivables" (in *Comment tout peut s'effondrer: Petit manuel de collapsologie à l'usage des générations présentes*, Pablo Servigne, Raphael Stevens, Seuil, 2015).

Moving Beyond the Right to the City: Urban Commoning in Greece

Theodoros Karyotis

The urban space is the epicentre of social antagonism. At any historical moment, it represents a crystallisation of power relations. While political and economic powers incessantly reform it to better isolate, control and exploit its inhabitants, the latter inevitably seek empowerment through collective mobilisation. After all, this is the space in which people see their social lives unfold, where they form family and community bonds, where they seek self-realisation. Resistance, then, is not the prerogative of radicals or the underprivileged. Most city dwellers are called to confront the neoliberal carving up of urban space if they are to lead fulfilling lives in ecologically sound surroundings.

It is not a coincidence, then, that modern social struggles erupt as urban phenomena with a strong spatial component. While some people may lament the concurrent demise of the workers' movement, it could be argued that the workplace is but one—albeit crucial—of the domains in which capital exploits human labour. The city is common wealth created by the collective efforts of generations; capitalism tries to appropriate this wealth, turning the city into a terrain of accumulation. Capitalization of human energies has expanded to all spheres of social life. Processes of "accumulation by dispossession" (Harvey 2009) are underway in most urban contexts: land grabbing, gentrification, privatisation of shared space, cultural appropriation, commodification of basic human needs such as housing, food, water and healthcare, evictions and displacement, not to mention increasing racism, militarisation and surveillance. Accordingly, the circulation of struggles extends to all fields of life where capital imposes its logic. Many thinkers have tried to conceptualise this shift by examining the relationship between capitalism, urbanism and ecology.[1]

City dwellers may define their desire for full participation in the city's socio-political life as a *right to the city* to be reclaimed against authorities, or they may dive right in and self-manage the urban space as a *commons*, or they may do both. In turn, these urban struggles—along with the frameworks used to make sense of them—will constitute them as *collective subjects*.

These are, then, some of the issues this text seeks to raise, exemplified in the context of Greek urban struggles over the past decade.

The Right to the City

Since its inception by philosopher Henri Lefebvre in the 1960s, the discourse of the *right to the city* has pervaded struggles against urban exclusion, commodification and privatisation. Even when Lefebvre is not overtly referenced, an intuitive grasp of the right to the city underlies many discussions and conflicts over what kind of cities we desire.

Lefebvre's take on the right to the city was a radical one. He never conceived the right to the city simply as a legal notion, a juridical defence of specific human needs. Rather, he envisioned an active subject that would enact and materialise those rights, rather than merely demand their implementation. Being a Marxist, he identified this collective subject as the working class (Lefebvre 1996a:154). Not the uniform, industrial working class of the Marxian oeuvre, consolidated in the capitalist workplace, but "a very different kind of class formation—fragmented and divided, multiple in its aims and needs, more often itinerant, disorganized and fluid rather than solidly implanted" (Harvey 2012: xiii). That is to say, a class formed around the everyday production and reproduction of life in the urban space.

As Harvey (ibid: xvi) suggests, the task of this collective subject would be "to imagine and reconstitute a totally different kind of city out of the disgusting mess of a globalising, urbanising capital run amok". Under this light, the idea of a right to the city becomes genuinely revolutionary, as the question of what kind of city we desire cannot be separated from questions of what kind of social relations, what kind of political organisation or what kind of relationship with nature we desire.

Lefebvre's "right to the city" is not reducible to access of individual citizens to urban resources (housing, public spaces, services, facilities, etc.); rather, he envisioned the city as *managed* by its very inhabitants. The radical edge of Lefebvre's right to the city lies precisely in the implicit conflict between the right to the *use value* of the city against the right to its *exchange value*. In other words, it is a concept that empowers the users of the city against the proprietors of the city, who are in most cases not the same people.

Lefebvre's aim was to rework Marx's idea of revolutionary change by expanding and enriching the collective subject of this change, and moving the locus of revolution from the capitalist workplace to the field of everyday life. Marx and Marxists, however, had notoriously rejected the notion of "rights" as a limited concept that was too intimately tied to capitalist liberalism to be of any use for revolution. Why, then, did Lefebvre employ this concept in his attempt to refashion revolutionary action? It is important to note that Lefebvre was writing in the late 1960s, when doctrinaire Marxism was coming under fire from many directions. In the following years, many Marxists renounced Bolshevism as totalising and authoritarian, and some even sought refuge in liberalism. By the late 1970s, revolutionary politics was in decline, and the discourse of "human rights" had become dominant in progressive circles as a supposedly "apolitical" mechanism of ensuring for populations a minimum of protection from exclusion and domination, in the absence of a meaningful plan of profound structural change (McLoughlin 2016). The ensuing collapse of the Soviet bloc and the ideological prevalence of capitalism and liberal democracy only served to consolidate "rights talk" as the horizon of progressive politics. Lefebvre's, then, was one of many attempts at navigating that adverse conjuncture without renouncing the prospect of revolutionary change.

However, the "rights" discourse does not come without its complications. With the resurgence of radical thought in the 1990s and 2000s, the concept of rights was overwhelmingly criticised by post-Marxist and radical thinkers as part and parcel of a post-political consensus in which political spaces are closing, giving way to technocratic solutions to social conflicts and demands (ibid.). Most notably, Giorgio Agamben (1998: 126–135) criticised human rights as a concept by which state sovereignty extends to non-political forms of life. In this respect, rights legitimise state intervention rather than limiting it. Moreover, since the concept of rights rests on a distinction between the political and the social sphere, it aids in the de-politicisation of subjects. As De Souza Santos (2014) argues, a "majority of the world's inhabitants are not the subjects of human rights [but] rather the objects of human rights discourses".

Often, "the right to the city" takes the form of a mini-charter of human rights—that is to say, a list of "commitments" of municipal authorities towards residents, who are entitled to social and economic goods. While there is great "propaganda value and mobilising potential" in such tactics, in that accusing political opponents of "violating rights" is a powerful rhetorical device (Bond 2018), the mere invocation of "commitments" of authorities towards citizens may lend itself to assistencialist policies. These have been historically shown to perpetuate inequality, as they tend to disempower rights holders in front of rights-granting bodies by treating them as passive recipients instead of active subjects (Freire 2005: 12).

Undoubtedly, rights can be—and have been—used as a bulwark against exploitation and exclusion. However, when social needs are expressed in legalese and enter the juridical sphere, they come to form part of a legal system where they are always subordinate to other legal concepts and other rights. That is to say, when the "social need as a right" is not anymore an instrument of struggle but a commitment of a liberal democracy towards its subjects, it becomes part of a hierarchy of rights, on the top of which lies the right to property. Often, the sanctity of the *rule of law* is little more than a fig leaf to conceal systematic exploitation and plunder (Mattei and Nader 2008). The experience of South Africa (Bond 2018) seems to confirm that courts systematically fail to enforce officially sanctioned rights to the city when they clash with entrenched interests and property rights. A similar situation was experienced in Greece, under the state of exception imposed by austerity policies.

It comes as no surprise, then, that the right to the city has been adopted wholeheartedly by a host of organisations, from local NGOs to UN-Habitat, that not only lack an anti-capitalist orientation but are even an accessory to neoliberal expansion (Souza 2010). The right to the city, in this sense, loses Lefebvre's radical edge and is interpreted as the right of individual citizens/consumers to a better urban life in the context of liberal democracy. At best, it is translated into rights of citizen input—so-called "participation"—in consultations with predefined agendas. At worst, it is used as a pretext for urban segregation policies, as when the authorities repress marginalised populations and exclude them from public space in the name of the citizen's "right to a cleaner and safer environment".

"The right to the city", writes Harvey (2012: xv), "is an empty signifier. Everything depends on who gets to fill it with meaning." However, the question we have to ask here is whether this is simply yet another case of successful appropriation and reabsorption of a radical discourse into dominant capitalist practices, or whether the concept of "rights", by resting on a distinction between rights-holders and rights-granters, is inherently disempowering. Of course, whether movements opt for restoring Lefebvre's revolutionary content of the right to the city or for moving beyond it should be entirely up to them. In any case, being aware of the limits and pitfalls of "rights-talk" is essential.

The Urban Commons

In recent years we observe the emergence of a new explanatory framework, that of the commons. The movement of the urban commons has forcefully entered the global spotlight, especially through the practice of occupation of common space (Tsavdaroglou 2016).

The concept of the commons was popularised by the institutional school of Elinor Ostrom, who studied hundreds of communities forming around natural resources (fisheries, irrigation systems, forests, etc.) to self-regulate extraction and thus prevent the infamous "tragedy of the commons", i.e. the depletion of the resource (Ostrom 2015). While critical of Ostrom's resource-centrism, autonomist Marxist thinkers[2] have taken up the commons discourse, as it allows them to describe empowered communities of struggle that are self-instituted to defend themselves against processes of dispossession, commodification and exclusion.

The commons is an eminently political concept, as its definition includes not only a common "resource", which may be natural (e.g. water) or immaterial (e.g. knowledge or any aspect of social life), but also an active community that organises horizontally and decides upon a set of rules of coexistence. A commons, then, consists necessarily of an active community self-instituted around a shared "resource". This political dimension has made the commons a prominent discourse in explaining the activity of the

urban social movements of the last decade.[3] Rather than relying on traditional tactics of agitprop or forming around concrete identities or demands,
urban social movements in recent years tend to erupt as reappropriations of
public space by horizontal collectives. Participants in the 2011 wave of protest around the world occupied public squares to form impromptu
settlements with their own collectively-run facilities and assembleary decision-making processes. The "square commons" did not dissipate after the
protest ended but became the blueprint for the creation of antagonistic
social structures to promote popular self-sufficiency and resilience, fuelled
by the conviction that capitalism is unable to ensure the reproduction of
societies and the planet itself. In recent years, movements have a growing
propensity to view the urban space as a commons and to propose solutions
to social ills that favour collective forms of ownership, direct participation
and self-management, thus questioning existing forms of integration in city
life.

Of course, the discourse of the commons is not immune to
appropriation. Critics point out that the idea of the commons is appealing
to organisations that promote neoliberal globalisation, as the social self-
initiative is compatible with the neoliberal renunciation of state welfare
provision, which leaves society to fend for itself. Moreover, commons
thinkers have repeatedly warned against "distorted" (De Angelis 2009) or
"pro-capitalist" (Caffentzis 2010) commons, which serve to promote the
circulation of capital.

However, appropriation by capital is not the only problem the commons
faces. What is the degree of openness required of each commons to
maintain its character without becoming exclusionary? How are effective
commons practices at the city level transferred to the management of more
complex systems, such as entire bio-regions? How can the commons
become materially self-sustaining without creating dependencies on the
capitalist market? What are the effective structures through which different
commons can coordinate their actions towards common goals? These
issues—*access, scalability, viability* and *coordination*—are central in the
discussion over the commons. The commons, therefore, should not be
viewed as a set of structures or processes, but rather as a disposition of a
number of people to define themselves as a group, question their existing
circumstances, identify their collective and individual needs, and negotiate
their rules of coexistence through mutual respect and recognition. That is
to say, the commons become politics par excellence.

In any case, my intention here is not to explore the potential of the
commons in tracing socio-political alternatives to capitalism, since I have
done this elsewhere (Karyotis 2018). Here I approach the commons as a
discourse to make sense of, but also shape, urban struggles. The assumption
of initiative by organised society rarely means the renunciation of

negotiated rights to healthcare, education, welfare or basic services. The commons is not an alternative to "rights talk", but rather a way in which rights may be fleshed out, and tethered to contentious politics waged by concrete communities.

In this light, the right to the city and the urban commons are not mutually exclusive strategies of contestation but rather two different vocabularies, two different "grammars of human dignity"(De Sousa Santos 2014), for making sense of urban struggles. The combined use of both discourses brings to mind what Harvey (2012: 87), describes as a "double-pronged political attack, through which the state is forced to supply more and more in the way of public goods for public purposes, along with the self-organization of whole populations to appropriate, use, and supplement those goods in ways that extend and enhance the qualities of the non-commodified reproductive and environmental commons".

Yet, the two vocabularies give rise to different conceptualisations of social conflict, different tactics and objectives, and ultimately different antagonistic subjects. While it is very common for movements to engage in both *rights talk* and *commons talk*, the coexistence of the two discourses is not always as harmonious as Harvey would have us believe. The interplay between the two discourses will be made explicit in the ensuing analysis of resistance against austerity policies in contemporary Greece.

Urban Struggles in Greece

Developments in Greece exemplify the concept of *accumulation by dispossession*, and specifically the tactic of *austerity* as an instrument of wealth extraction and upwards redistribution. Austerity is a recipe systematically being prescribed to ailing economies. It is ostensibly intended to do away with sovereign debt by reducing public expenditure, selling off public assets, raising taxes and slashing labour rights, welfare provision and public-sector jobs. In effect, it represents a radical reshuffling of the cards at the expense of the lower and middle classes.

Other than the fact that for the first time such an ambitious structural adjustment program has been implemented in a "developed" country, the case of Greece is nothing new as far as austerity and counter-austerity tactics go. I have, therefore, repeatedly argued that the idea of Greek *exceptionalism*—both in its "corrupt and lazy" version and in its "heroic and revolutionary" version—is an orientalist fallacy. Nevertheless, it is true that the violent shakeup of day-to-day normality destabilised established identities and thus pushed great parts of the population to a state of *liminality* (Varvarousis and Kallis 2017; Varvarousis 2018). Liminality is an anthropological concept that denotes an intermediate stage in a transition (between life stages, between groups or between seasons), where subjects have shed their previous identities but have not yet assumed new ones. This state of uncertainty and fluidity has certainly given rise to resignation, depression or regression to reactionary identities, but it has also created creative resistances and admirable experiments in social self-organisation.

To understand modern urban struggles in Greece, we have to look into the history of the urban space. Greek cities were built overnight. In the 1950s, rural populations started to urbanise. In the 1960s and 1970s, constructors took advantage of lax planning laws—drafted by their political patrons—to create densely populated high-rise cities without any provision for public space and infrastructure (Makrygianni and Tsavdaroglou 2011). That was the initial process of enclosure that eroded traditional communities, commodified housing, and promoted a peculiar sense of isolation among the crowd of others. A manifest absence of public facilities, open spaces, and community centres characterises Greek cities to this day.

In the 1990s and 2000s, the prevalent social imaginary was one of individual social mobility and consumerism. The debt-fuelled affluence drove the newly-formed middle classes away from inner-city neighbourhoods, which were occupied by working class migrants and natives. Throughout this era, urban renewal projects were underway, culminating in a construction frenzy leading up to the 2004 Athens Olympic Games.

In December 2008, the murder of a teenager by the police sparked the first wave of struggles to reclaim the urban space on the part of students, immigrants and the disenfranchised urban youth. The protests served to shed light on the urban alienation, exploitation and exclusion hidden behind the veil of ostensible prosperity. Participants in the protests were fused in an anonymous collective subject that actively transformed the city through decentralised acts of re-appropriation of urban space: public building occupations, barricades, marches, spontaneous artistic events, disruption of traffic and commerce. Interestingly, there was a complete absence of formal demands; protesters were not struggling for *rights* or *reforms*, but were actively projecting their collective aspirations onto the urban space.

That collective "scream"[4] was a wake-up call for a dormant and complacent society, and has left a legacy of social cooperation and a redefined public sphere. Thousands of collectives were born, ranging from political groups to art ensembles to grassroots trade unions. A whole new generation of youth was schooled in horizontalism, solidarity and direct action tactics, and new spatial practices were adopted by social movements, culminating in the propagation of self-managed squats and social centres.

Navarinou Park is part of "December's" legacy. Only a few months after the revolt, an abandoned urban parking lot was occupied by neighbours and collectives in Exarcheia; the asphalt was dug up, trees and flowers were planted, paths were laid out, benches were installed. The park has since been self-managed by an open assembly and has been the site of political, cultural and social events. Despite attempts at eviction, the park retains its character to this day. Even if the vocabulary of the commons was not widespread at that moment, we have an early instance of the substitution of "public" space with "common" space; of rigid, aseptic space that serves as a neutral ground between isolated individuals with organic space where individuals can connect and intertwine their desires in the context of community, where they can negotiate the terms of their co-existence. This kind of urban commoning would go on to become a blueprint for urban struggles in the following years.

The debt crisis that broke out in 2010 and the concomitant structural adjustment served to intensify social antagonism and exacerbate conflicts over urban space. A defining moment for grassroots spatial practices and organisational forms was the 2011 "movement of the squares". A multitude of individuals with different origins and agendas participated in the mobilisations. This diversity was certainly an advantage as it enabled osmosis between different groups and individuals and the emergence of innovative practices. While there was extensive *rights talk*, since the austerity program was perceived as a rupture of the social contract that threatened social, labour and human rights, the squares themselves were organised as urban commons, with a self-instituted community grouping around the occupied common space. Probably, they can be considered an instance of "liminal commons" (Varvarousis 2018), as the encampments were fluid institutions populated by destabilised identities; the aim of the squares was not long-term resilience as per Ostrom, but experimentation with new spatial practices that could lead to a multiplication of struggles.

Indeed, in the wake of the squares, a multitude of urban commons emerged. It was no longer just youthful protesters who occupied public spaces to turn them into commons, but mixed collectives of young and old, men and women, families and individuals, immigrants and natives. Two examples of such commons were the urban farming at PERKA ("Peri-urban Farming") on the grounds of an abandoned military base in Thessaloniki and the Self-Managed Urban Gardens of Elliniko in Athens, on the site of the former Athens airport. Both sites were earmarked to be privatised and developed into luxury housing and commercial infrastructure. In both cases, instead of demanding that their right of access to urban space was respected, citizens' movements self-enacted this right through commoning.

This "performative"—rather than juridical—reclamation of rights through urban commoning became widespread. The *state of exception* brought about by the crisis meant that most rights of the population were subordinated to the task of "salvation" of the country from debt. Regressive legislation was passed, existing juridical guarantees of human rights remained unenforced, and courts ruled consistently against those trying to judicially defend common wealth against appropriation and privatisation. The urgency of the situation made the abstract invocation of rights seem futile and called for direct, often extra-legal, action.

Local community self-defence initiatives multiplied when the government imposed an indiscriminate land ownership tax—mockingly called *haratsi* for its reminiscence of a despised Ottoman poll tax—arbitrarily charged through the electricity bill. Homeowners who failed to pay had their power cut; meanwhile, wages had been slashed, and one-third of the workforce was out of a job. This extortionate measure would have created a situation verging on humanitarian catastrophe were it not for the self-organised anti-*haratsi* neighbourhood committees, which were on call to extra-legally reconnect the power for families that could not afford the tax.

Food provision was another critical area of self-defence. In the previous decade, oligopolistic, price-fixing intermediaries had come to dominate food distribution, making everyday staples unaffordable for the popular classes, while squeezing the livelihood of farmers. The movement to cut out the middlemen started with truckloads of potatoes arriving in central city squares to be sold directly to end consumers. The *potato movement* soon evolved into a decentralised *guerrilla farmers' market* movement, which occupied urban land without permits, trying to bring together farmers and consumers despite the threat of eviction, arrests and confrontation with entrenched interests.

The creation of *urban commons* extended to other *rights*: the right to healthcare, with the creation of an extended network of self-managed solidarity clinics; the right to a livelihood, with the establishment of alternative currencies[5] and a multitude of egalitarian workers' cooperatives; or the right to affordable food, through the operation of consumer cooperatives[6] and solidarity kitchens.

However, the coexistence of the *rights discourse* and the *commons discourse* has not always been peaceful. A case in point was the movement against water privatisation. Under the terms of a memorandum, the water company of Thessaloniki—among others—was due to be privatised. Small citizens' initiatives organised an opposition to privatisation by effectively mobilising civil society. Within the anti-privatisation block, those conceiving *water as a right* defended state management of the water company; those conceiving *water as a commons* promoted an alternative model of social ownership based on self-management and citizens' participation[7]. Due to diverging conceptualisations and tactics, the rift developed into a bitter ideological conflict. This was reflected in practical issues, as the first group favoured centralised leadership through a committee composed of politicians and trade unionists—unsurprisingly aligned with the Syriza party, which was expected to win the upcoming elections—while the second group favoured assembleary and participatory organising processes. Despite the inner schism,

Thessaloniki's water movement mobilised thousands of volunteers to organise an unofficial referendum, in which 97 per cent of the 220,000 citizens who voted rejected the privatisation. A fragile and defeated right-wing government was obliged to put the privatisation on hold, until the next government (led by Syriza) brought the privatisation back on the table a few years later.

Another field where an unexamined *right to the city* discourse may prove counter-productive is the organisation of visibility events such as the Gay Pride March. To be sure, in a country as pious as Greece, the importance of pride marches in reclaiming public space for the full spectrum of identities and practices cannot be overstated; in effect, such events regularly become sites of confrontation with the Orthodox Church and the extreme right. Such events, however, face an additional risk. To the extent that they promote an individualistic conception of the right to the city and fail to adopt an intersectional view of social oppression, they may involuntarily turn themselves into *niche markets* in the context of urban renewal, under which diversity is prized as long as the overriding social principle remains that of market exchange. Indeed, *diversity*, *creativity* and *innovation* are core concepts of gentrification processes underway in European cities. These exclusionary processes presuppose an individualised recipient of rights, rather than active collectives that affirm their right to self-determine everyday life in the city.

To address the growing commercialisation and co-optation of Gay Pride Marches (see also Ashley Wong 2018; No justice no pride 2018), Radical Pride,[8] an "alternative" gay pride event that safeguards its autonomy from public institutions and corporate sponsors, takes place yearly in Thessaloniki since 2017. Radical Pride offers a rich framework to understand how gender, race, class, sexual orientation, ethnicity, age or ability intersect in the production of oppression and exclusion. It thus seeks to affirm collective action and connect the struggle of the LGBTQ movement with other urban struggles.

The Subject of Social Mobilisation

Social change is not just about the transformation of political and economic structures. Most importantly, it is about the transformation of subjects, of humans as social agents. The smooth operation of capitalism presupposes a specific anthropological type—mockingly dubbed *homo economicus* by critics—and thus the dominant structures of education, family, the mass media, public discourse etc. are geared towards the creation of this mindset. Accordingly, social struggles aim to create subjects of change, an anthropological type that questions dominant values to become the social agents of a future liberated society.

Struggles are constituted precisely as formative experiences that can bring about such subjectifications. The liberated subject is not only a pre-requisite of contestation, but also a product of it, in a dialectic movement. Often, sectarian leftists and anarchists disregard the transformative potential of struggle per se, and thus tend to dismiss diverse and multitudinous mobilisations, such as the squares movement, as "interclass", "reformist", etc. Of course, we cannot deny that the occupied squares have been as much spaces of divergence as they have been of convergence (Simiti 2015). In any case, social mobilisation should not be viewed as a closed club reserved only for the initiated, but rather as a contradictory breeding ground for militant subjectivities.

Indeed, in the liminal period of destabilisation in Greece previous individualistic identities based on consumption, economic rationality, and social mobility were dissolved at a grand scale, giving rise to precarious and transitory collective identities geared towards social change.

A certain degree of abstraction is inevitable when trying to imagine this new subject that will spring from a process of destabilisation to wage the struggle for social justice. Different conceptions of the collective subject have been proposed as part of different liberatory projects: the *working class* as the unitary subject of Marxian class struggle; the *proletariat* as a non-identity, as a class against itself (Holloway 2009; Nasioka 2018); the *multitude* as a diverse, contradictory, fragmented class of everyone who contributes to the material, affective and cultural reproduction of society under the rule of capital (Hardt and Negri 2004); the *citizen* as an inclusive territorial identity of those who jointly manage their common affairs in a face-to-face democracy (Bookchin 1999, 2002); and *the people* as a common identity constructed out of a plurality of demands in the context of a hegemonic project to capture the State (Laclau 2005).

Even if they are nothing more than strategic abstractions in the context of specific schemes of social transformation, all of the above conceptualisations of the collective subject have had their day in the tumultuous years of crisis in Greece. Each of the above abstractions presents specific challenges and problems. Analysing the ramifications of each conception is beyond the scope of the present text; what is of interest is that each presents a different relation of the subject with the political sphere, and thus a different avenue of socio-political transformation. Some envision the abolition of the distinction between the political and the social sphere, either through the implosion of the political or through its expansion to include all areas of life. Others wish to maintain the distinction but offer a fuller definition of the political by bringing disempowered identities to the forefront.

Similarly, the *urban commons* and the *right to the city* as two discourses that try to shape urban struggles lead to contrasting conceptions of the political.

While both are prone to be appropriated by capitalist forces, the former stresses the formation of a political community, while the latter emphasises certain commitments of the authorities. Hence, while the former favours autonomous political organisation, the latter tends to call for top-down and state-centric solutions to social ills.

The above conclusion does not imply that social movements should cease demanding the enforcement of negotiated rights and the expansion of legally recognised rights. After all, "rights" is the way by which social conquests of the past—for inclusion, against exploitation, domination, racism or sexism—have been consecrated in the legal system and given juridical substance and continuity in the context of the State. Rights are thus a progressive force that is here to stay, and the demand for legal reforms that safeguard the commons is an indispensable aspect of urban struggles.[9]

Rather, in this text I have tried to point out that when a technical juridical conception of rights becomes the centrepiece and horizon of progressive politics, the discourse of rights tends to ratify existing systems of domination by subordinating lived, contentious politics to impersonal juridical constructs, thus legitimising state power rather than curbing it. Despite their weaknesses and ambiguities, commoning practices serve to empower subjects and revitalise democratic practice beyond the confines of liberal parliamentary democracy.

References

Agamben, G. 1998. *Homo Sacer: Sovereign Power and Bare Life*. Stanford, Calif: Stanford University Press.

Ashley, W. 2018. "Pride Parades: An Excuse for Straight Kids to Party?" *USA Today*, June 25. [Online]. [Accessed 19 August 2019]. Available from: http://www.usatoday.com/story/news/LGBT-issues/2018/06/22/pride-parades-excuse-straight-kids-party/712068002/

Bond, P. 2018. Limits to South Africa's 'Right to the City': Prospects for and beyond Urban Commoning. In: Hall, S. and Burdett, R. eds. *The SAGE Handbook of the 21st Century City*, pp.236-2555

Bookchin, M. 1999. *The Murray Bookchin Reader*. Montréal; New York: Black Rose Books.

Bookchin, M. 2002. The Communalist Project. *Harbinger*, 3(1). [Online]. [Accessed 19 August 2019]. Available from: http://social-ecology.org/wp/2002/09/harbinger-vol-3-no-1-the-communalist-project/

Caffentzis, G. 2010. The Future of 'The Commons': Neoliberalism's 'Plan B' or the Original Disaccumulation of Capital? *New Formations*, 69, pp.23-41.

Fritjof, C. and Mattei, U. 2015. *The Ecology of Law: Toward a Legal System in Tune with Nature and Community*. Berrett-Koehler Publishers.

De Angelis, M. 2009. The Tragedy of Capitalist Commons. *Turbulence*, 5, 32-33.

De Angelis, M. 2017. *Omnia Sunt Communia: On the Commons and the Transformation to Postcapitalism*. London: Zed Books.

De Sousa Santos, B. 2014. Human Rights: A Fragile Hegemony. *Stanford University Press Blog*. [Online]. [Accessed 19 August 2019]. Available from: http://stanfordpress.typepad.com/blog/2014/12/human-rights-a-fragile-hegemony.html

Freire, Paulo. 2005. *Education for Critical Consciousness*. London   ; New York: Continuum.

Hardt, M., and Negri. A. 2004. *Multitude: War and Democracy in the Age of Empire*. New York: Penguin Press.

Hardt, M., and Negri. A. 2009. *Commonwealth*. Cambridge, Mass: Belknap Press of Harvard University Press.

Harvey, D. 2009. The 'New' Imperialism: Accumulation by Dispossession. *Socialist Register,* 40(40), pp.63-87.

Harvey, D. 2012. *Rebel Cities: From the Right to the City to the Urban Revolution*. New York: Verso.

Holloway, J. 2002. *Change the World without Taking Power*. London   ; Ann Arbor, MI: Pluto Press.

Holloway, J. 2009. Why Adorno? In: Holloway, J., Matamoros, F. and Tischler, S. eds. *Negativity and Revolution: Adorno and Political Activism*, pp.12-17.

Karyotis, T. 2018. Beyond Hope: Prospects for the Commons in Crisis-Stricken Greece. In: Holloway, J., Nasioka, K. and Doulos, P. eds. *Beyond Crisis: After the Collapse of Institutional Hope in Greece, What?* Oakland, CA: PM Press.

Laclau, E. 2005. *On Populist Reason*. London; New York: Verso.

Lefebvre, H. 1996. The Right to the City. In: Kofman, E. and Lebas, E. *Writings on Cities* Cambridge, MA: Blackwell Publishers.

Souza, M. L. de 2010. Which Right to which City? In Defence of Political-Strategic Clarity. *Interface*. 2(1), pp.315-333.

Vaso, M. and Tsavdaroglou H. 2011. Urban Planning and Revolt: A Spatial Analysis of the December 2008 Uprising in Athens. In Vradis, A. and Dalakoglou, D. eds. *Revolt and Crisis in Greece: Between a Present Yet to Pass and a Future Still to Come*. Oakland: AK Press.

Mattei, U. 2015. The Valle Theater Commons Foundation: How to Deploy the Law in Current and Future Struggles. In: Weibel, P.ed. *Global Activism: Art and Conflict in the 21st Century*. Karlsruhe: The MIT Press.

Mattei, U. and de Morpurgo, M. 2009. *Global Law and Plunder: The Dark Side of the Rule of Law*. [Online]. [Accessed 19 August 2018]. Available from: https://works.bepress.com/ugo_mattei/35/

Mattei, U. and Nader, L. 2008. *Plunder: When the Rule of Law Is Illegal.* Malden, Mass: Blackwell.

McLoughlin, D. 2016. Post-Marxism and the Politics of Human Rights: Lefort, Badiou, Agamben, Rancière. *Law and Critique,* 27(3), pp.303-21.

Nasioka, K. 2018. Crisis and Negativity: On the Revolutionary Subject in Crisis. In: Holloway, J., Nasioka, K. and Doulos, P. eds. *Beyond Crisis: After the Collapse of Institutional Hope in Greece, What?* Oakland: PM Press.

No justice no pride. 2018. Reclaim Pride. *No Justice, No Pride.* [Online]. [Accessed 19 August 2018]. Available from: http://nojusticenopride.org/pride-back-roots/

Ostrom, E. 2015. *Governing the Commons: The Evolution of Institutions for Collective Action.* Cambridge: Cambridge University Press.

Simiti, M. 2015. Rage and Protest: The Case of the Greek Indignant Movement. *Contention,* 3(2), pp.33-50.

Stavridis, S. 2013. Re-Inventing Spaces of Commoning: Occupied Squares in Movement. *Quaderns-e del'Institut Català d'Antropologia,* 18(2), pp.22-39.

Tsavdaroglou, C. 2016. "Θεωρητικά Περάσματα Από Τα Κινήματα Για Το «Δικαίωμα Στην Πόλη» Στα Κινήματα Κατάληψης Του «Κοινού Χώρου»: Παγκόσμια Παραδείγματα Και η Περίπτωση Της Ελλάδας Την Εποχή Της Κρίσης." In: Petropoulou, C., Vitopoulou, A. and Tsavdaroglou, C. eds. *Urban and Regional Social Movements,* pp.105-42.

Varvarousis, Angelos, and G. Kallis. 2017. Commoning against the Crisis. In: Manuel C. ed. *Another Economy Is Possible. Culture and Economy in a Time of Crisis.* Cambridge: Polity Press.

Varvarousis, A. 2018. *Crisis, Commons & Liminality: Modern Rituals of Transition in Greece.* Ph.D. Thesis. Universidad Autonoma de Barcelona.

Notes

1. Notably Bookchin 1999; Lefebvre 1996; Harvey 2012.
2. See, e.g., De Angelis 2017; Hardt and Negri 2009.
3. See, e.g., Stavridis 2013.
4. As per Holloway 2002.
5. Notably, TEM in Volos, Syntagma Time Bank in Athens, Koino in Thessaloniki, Faircoin internationally, and a dozen more.
6. A noteworthy case is Bios Coop in Thessaloniki (http://www.bioscoop.gr), which unites some 500 families in "taking food in their own hands".
7. In particular, Initiative 136 (http://www.136.gr/) promoted a citizen-funded bid in the public tender, with the aim of managing Thessaloniki's water company through a socially controlled non-profit cooperative that would integrate all water and sanitation users through 16 local chapters. The bid was controversially rejected by the tender

authorities, but mobilisation proved sufficient to freeze the tender process altogether.

8. http://ourpride.gr/
9. In this respect the work of Italian legal scholar Ugo Mattei is invaluable (e.g. Capra and Mattei 2015, Ch. 9; Mattei 2015).

Reconceptualising the Right to the City and Spatial Justice Through Social Ecology

Federico Venturini

Introduction: Critically Exploring the Right to the City

The aim of this work is to discuss the right to the city, spatial justice and social ecology in order to create new tools and understandings at the service of urban social movements aiming towards ecological and democratic cities.[1]

This work is divided in five sections. In the first and second sections the concepts of the right[2] to the city and spatial justice are introduced, while the third highlights a convergence between the two concepts. In the fourth, social ecology is used in order to explore key concepts such as citizenship, justice and freedom. Building on the previous section, in the fifth the right to the city and spatial justice are finally reconceptualised through social ecology. The main aim of this work, in light of the holistic social change approach, is to reframe the concepts of the right to the city and spatial justice in order to strengthen them and make them more complete.

Since Lefebvre introduced the concept in 1968, the right to the city has been used by different actors for different agendas. In this chapter, however, I focus on the academic and political discussions around the right to the city, avoiding those debates with more institutionalized formulations of the concept. The political philosophy of the right to the city shares many common traits with social ecology, starting with the centrality of the city in discussions of the urban crisis.

Attoh (2011: 670) explores the broadness and difficulty of precisely defining the right to the city: the concept is still "vague and radically open" and this makes it possible for different actors to use it for different purposes. For Lefebvre, the right to the city is "like a cry and a demand" (1996: 158). At the same time, it is a necessity to surpass current inequalities and fulfil basic needs, and an aspiration for change (Marcuse 2012).

However, Lefebvre never fully defined the term (Souza 2010; Attoh 2011). In one of the more articulated expressions he says that "the right to the city, complemented by the right to difference and the right to information, should modify, concretize and make more practical the rights of the citizen as a urban dweller (*cidatin*) and user of multiple services" (Lefebvre 1996: 34). The right to the city is the right to full and equal enjoyment of the resources and services concentrated in cities, something that would only be fully possible in another, non-capitalist society (Souza 2012b). Lefebvre underlines that the right to the city moves towards a "transformed and renewed right to urban life" (Lefebvre 1996: 158), defined as the possibility for people to shape their own city, where the concept of "autogestion" (self-management) is crucial. In Lefebvre's work there is a critique of state power that also resonates with the social ecology approach to direct action. Today state policies are blocking the building of a city shaped on citizenship: "The incompatibility between the state and the urban is radical in nature. The state can only prevent the urban from taking shape" (Lefebvre 2003: 180). This effect of the State is rooted in its nature, which "has to control the urban phenomenon…to retard its development, to push it in the direction of institutions that extend to society as a whole, through exchange and the market" (Lefebvre 2003: 180). Self-management is thus crucial. Harvey stresses that the right to the city is "the freedom to make and remake our cities and ourselves" (Harvey 2008: 23), putting the emphasis on the collective aspect of this right. From a Marxist perspective, the right to the city helps in understanding "the necessary connection between urbanization and surplus production and use" (Harvey 2008: 40). The call for a "real" right to the city comes from the oppressed. As Marcuse (2012: 32) points out, from an economic point of view it comes from the "most marginalized and the most underpaid and insecure members of the working class" and from a cultural expression it comes from the directly oppressed and alienated. It is thus a unifying call for all who have not.

With this radical (and matching the original Lefebvrian formulation) interpretation of the right to the city, urban social movements around the world have started to claim the idea in order to gain access to needs and services and to re-shape the city (Hamel, Lustiger-Thaler and Mayer 2000). At the same time, they have gained strength from it. As Soja (2010: 109) affirms, the right to the city "can help to *unite diverse and particularized struggle into larger and more powerful movements*". Indeed, as Harvey and Potter (2009: 48) point out, the right to the city is a process, continuously shaped by our desire and new challenges and built around "social solidarities". In this, urban social movements play a crucial role, affirming the right to the city in different spatial and social forms:

> The inalienable right to the city rests upon the capacity to force open spaces of the city to protest and contention, to create unmediated public spaces, so that the cauldron of urban life can become a catalytic site from which new conceptions and configurations of urban living can be devised and out of which new and less damaging conceptions of rights can be constructed. (Harvey and Potter 2009: 49)

Thus, in this radical interpretation, the right to the city is a protest call to enable the opening of new social paths towards a better kind of urban living.

However, NGOs, international bodies, and municipal authorities all around the globe have assumed a different perspective on the right to the city. Activist-scholar D'Souza (2016: 7) pointed out "the rights discourse today is a cacophony of discordant voices". This plurality of actors and institutions invoke the notion of rights, yet adopt different ideological orientations that suit other agendas. For example, Kuymulu (2013: 93) found that "UN agencies have not only attempted to co-opt the content of the notion as established by the existing right to the city movements, but have also attempted to rewrite the history of this concept". One of the main activities of NGOs, international bodies and city authorities—under the slogan of the right to the city—is thus based around the development and implementation of charters of the right to the city. As Mayer (2012; 2013) points out, this approach presents several issues: (1) it excludes what is not in the list; (2) in contrast to the class reference of the Lefebvrian right to the city, it does not acknowledge class and power divisions; and (3) "the demands for rights as enumerated merely target particular aspects of neoliberal policy" (2012: pp. 74–75), watering down the radical call to transform the city.

Souza (2010: 317) holds a similar position, asserting that the right to the city for NGOs and official agencies (as well for some social movements) can be summarized as "the right to a better, more 'human' life in the context of the capitalist city, the capitalist society and on the basis of a ('reformed' and 'improved') representative 'democracy'", with the aim of fixing the current political and economic system, not challenging it.

Critically Exploring Spatial Justice

Spatial justice is another key concept for current urban social movements. Justice is a concept that has been always invoked by social movements, especially from the spatial perspective. For example the following quote, referring to an American city, dramatically captures the experience of the urban poor:

> People in the ghetto know perfectly well it is different in other neighbourhoods that are whiter and wealthier. They know that this is not accidental. They might be fuzzy on the history and the exact actors, and might even have bought into the sizeable efforts to blame the poor for their own poverty, but the culpability of banks, city officials, employers, corporations and absentee landlords is widely, if rather intuitively, understood. Which means that people understand that they live in a space that is socially produced, and could even tell you how that works though they would never articulate it using this kind of language. (Gibbon 2010: 619)

The poor have a clear understanding of the spatial dimension of inequalities, calling for the end of them, and for justice.

The Western concept of justice originated in ancient Greece and is strongly linked to the formation of citizenship and direct democracy in ancient Athens (Soja 2010: 75). With the creation of the Nation-State, the idea of justice has been conceptualized as provided by the State, but not as part of the concept of citizenship. However, justice cannot only be linked to the kind of justice administered by the State. It assumes a broader meaning of *just* or *fair*, linked to "the qualities of a just society: freedom, liberty, equality, democracy, [and] civil rights" (Soja 2010: 20). For Soja (2010), justice is a concept that should go beyond class, race, and gender. Justice and injustice, as concepts, pervade our world on multiple levels and are deeply nested in the current socioeconomic system, but they can be challenged and changed through social and political action (Soja 2010). As Harvey recognises, economic inequality and injustice are both a production of capitalist urban development:

> Capital represents itself in the form of a physical landscape created in its own image, created as use values to enhance the progressive accumulation of capital. The geographical landscape which results is the crowning glory of past capitalist development. (1985: 25)

Subsequently, Soja (2010) also recognised the importance of looking at the spatial dimension of justice and developed "spatial justice" as a core concept. Even without negating the importance of the historical and sociological approaches of justice, focusing on the spatial helps highlight hidden aspects or discover new perspectives for action. In a recent discussion on spatial justice, Iveson (2011: 255) affirms that "the attention to space can help highlight the spatial relations in which place-based issues and actors are enmeshed".

Spatial justice, as a concept used in analysing current urban crises, can firstly help cast "new light on the processes through which socio-spatial injustice is reproduced, perpetuated and sometimes aggravated in our times" (Souza 2011: 73). Thus, focusing on the negation of spatial justice can be a powerful tool, both helping to understand how injustice is created and highlighting where to act.

Secondly, a focus on the affirmation of spatial justice can help reveal "the spatial practices by means of which protagonists of socio-spatial change (above all emancipative social movements) are challenging injustice and trying to build alternatives" (ibid). As with the right to the city, spatial justice becomes an agenda for urban social movements to follow in order to reshape the city. A connection can be made between the two concepts, as I will show in the next section.

A Convergence of Concepts

The concepts of right to the city and spatial justice can both be used as analytical tools to highlight current urban crises and as proactive slogans upon which to build social struggles. Looking at the intersection between the creation of space, the negation of rights, and social injustice is crucial to understanding the urban crisis and developing strategies for social change.

In this section I argue that there is a further connection that needs to be made between the right to the city and spatial justice. As Uitermark (2012) considers, a just city presupposes equity, distribution of resources and democratic control toward the full implementation of the right to the city. The right to the city and spatial justice thus work hand-in-hand towards the construction of a just city. This link is very clear, for example, when Zárate (2015) titles an essay *The Cities We Want: Right to the City and Social Justice for All*. In the same vein, Marcuse (2012: 35) stresses that the right to the city is not a mere set of individual rights but connected to the idea of justice: "The right to the city is a moral claim, founded on fundamental principles of justice". The concept of rights and justice refer to a similar moral stand. Moreover, "a good [and just] city should not be simply a city with distributional equity, but one that supports the full development of each individual and of all individuals" (Marcuse 2009: 2).

In their positive affirmation, both spatial justice and the right to the city are demanding fulfilment for humans in the urban environment. In their negation they are also deeply connected: spatial injustice is the negation of the right to the city (and vice versa). Moreover, they are determined or negated under the same political frame: "Urban rights and justice are therefore mediated by the spatial organization of political powers" (Harvey and Potter 2009: 42). It is thus clear that the two concepts of right to the city and spatial justice are strictly interdependent and intertwined (Mitchell 2003)—one needs the other for its full positive realization. Both concepts go beyond class, race, and gender, and should be able to mobilize a large part of the population (Harvey 2003; Soja 2010). Furthermore, they both refer to the need to create a true citizenship. However, the concept of citizenship is a "multifaceted idea" (Souza 1999: 171) theorized by various authors and traditions, depending on specific national and juridical contexts. Often, innovations have been implemented under pressure from urban social movements, as stressed by Holston: "The right to the city arguments of the urban social movements embodied the struggle of residents for this recognition of being citizens who bear the right to rights" (2008: 241). Citizenship is conceived as a distinction between those who may access rights in their daily life in the city and those who cannot. There is a continuous struggle for expanding the concept of citizenship and recognizing the rights of everyone, especially the oppressed.

Lefebvre explicitly said that a true right to the city "implies nothing less than a revolutionary conception of citizenship" (in Merrifield 2017: 23). From this perspective, urban social movements have actively built an insurgent citizenship (Holston 1998; 2008), a citizenship that attempts to subvert state agendas and enact real forms of citizenships based on "civil, political, and social rights available to people" (Holston 1998: 50), beyond formal forms of citizenships granted (and restricted) by the State. Insurgent citizenship is critical here and its objective is the disruption of granted norms and a transformation of the city (Holston 1998).

However, despite the normalised use of the concept of citizenship in society, contemporary urban social movements remain sceptical about using this concept as it indicates "distance, anonymity, and uncommon ground" (Holston 2009: 250). Citizenship is commonly used by institutional frameworks that do not easily allow for revolutionary usage. Furthermore, citizenship, in all its expression, is based on who is a citizen and who is not—as determined by the Nation-State (Sassen 2002). In this way urban social movements continuously struggle with public officials, but also with the public, to enlarge the base of citizenship.

Moreover, the concept of the right to the city has also been co-opted and distorted (Souza 2010; Kuymulu 2013). One example is the drafting of the Brazilian constitution, which actively engaged civil society, but led to a depletion and co-optation of urban social movements (Souza 2001).

Reconceptualising Citizenship, Justice, and Freedom

The concept of citizenship, despite its potential role in addressing urban crises, is thus deeply contested—social ecology offers a way forward. Bookchin's approach can be illustrated on two levels. On the first, he defends a system based on rights (defined alternately as civil rights or human rights) and duties.[3] They represent a crucial stage of social development, with the move from the uncertainty of tribal times to the introduction of a justice system based on laws (Bookchin 2005a). Rights represent the important achievements of popular struggles and should be preserved and defended (Bookchin 1986; 1999; Bookchin and Biehl 1991).

The second level is more fully developed and articulated, and addresses the core of the social ecology project, whose aim is to go beyond "contemporary citizenship within a depersonalized formal system of "rights" and "duties"" (Bookchin 1988: 238).[4] Bookchin tries to recover the "true" meaning of citizenship, referring to the Athenian formulation:

> The Athenian notion of *arete*, the daily practice of *paideia*, and the institutional structure of the *polis* were synthesized into an ideal of citizenship that the individual tried to realize as a form of self-expression, not an obligatory burden of self-denial. Citizenship became an ethos, a creative art, indeed, a civic cult rather than a demanding body of duties and a palliative body of rights. (Bookchin 1995b: 75)

Citizenship thus needs to be affirmed as a praxis of citizens' expression towards self-realization. Moreover, Bookchin recognises the need to move towards a universal human commonality (Bookchin 2005a), thereby surpassing the parochial and non-universal connotation of citizenship as formulated in ancient Athens (Bookchin 1995b).

The concept of community, then, is crucial. An authentic community is "not merely a structural constellation of human beings but rather the practice of communizing" (Bookchin 2005a: 349). The expression of an active citizenship is then linked to the final expression of freedom, where citizenship can be conceived as a direct action that expresses itself in the practice of direct democracy, in the possibility to make decisions for one's own community (Bookchin 2005a).

Freedom thus also becomes a crucial concept in discussions of citizenship and, most importantly, of justice. As a concept, freedom is preferable to justice, being able to more fully address the problem of inequality:

> Unlike justice, which works with the pretension that all are equal in theory, despite their many differences in fact, freedom makes no pretense that all are equals but tries to compensate for the inequalities that occur with age, physical infirmity, and different abilities. (Bookchin 1995a: 260)

Classically, the concept of justice was based on the fundamental idea of equality of human beings. The reality, however, is different:

> To assume that everyone is "equal" is patently preposterous if they are regarded as "equal" in strength, intellect, training, experience, talent, disposition, and opportunities. Such "equality" scoffs at reality and denies the commonality and solidarity of the community by subverting its responsibilities to compensate for differences between individuals. (Bookchin 2005a: 219)

These differences mean that human beings vary with respect to their potentials and needs. Freedom, for Bookchin, recognises this point and posits the basis for a rational society on the idea that "as long as the means exist, they must be shared as much as possible according to needs—and needs are unequal insofar as they are gauged according to individual abilities and responsibilities" (Bookchin 2005a: 219). In social ecology, the concept of freedom is thus embedded in the idea of equality of unequals, an "unreflective form of social behaviour and distribution that compensates inequalities and does not yield to the fictive claim…that everyone is equal" (Bookchin 2005a: 219).

This is opposed to the use of justice, which "turns the equality of unequals into the inequality of equals" (Bookchin 2005a: 224). Bookchin agrees with the Marxist formulation of "from each according to his/her ability, to each according to his/her needs" In opposition to a "bourgeois right", which claims "equality of all," freedom abandons the very notion of "right" as such (Bookchin 2005a: 219). Freedom is thus a crucial pillar for an alternative society.

Reconceptualising the Right to the City and Spatial Justice

Just as we reconceptualised citizenship and justice, highlighting the importance of freedom is thus necessary to reconceptualise the right to the city and spatial justice through social ecology. The libertarian or anarchist tradition seems to remain impermeable to or suspicious about the idea of rights (Turner and Miller 2005); it is uncommon for radical thinkers to use this term.[5] Contemporary rights are guaranteed and determined by states and international bodies, and, despite many significant improvements, their track record, from the standpoint of the libertarian or anarchist tradition, is poor and demands a radical change.

Questions regarding how rights are institutionalized, who guarantees them, and by what means can lead to a slippery debate. Fotopoulos (1997: 231–232), an author close to social ecology, affirms that there are two different traditions of rights. The first meaning is rooted in the "liberal conception of freedom, which is defined negatively as the absence of constraints on human activity; these rights are also defined in a negative way as 'freedom from', their explicit objective being to limit state power". The second meaning, connected to the socialist tradition, opposes the liberal one, and affirms instead "social equality, mainly in the form of an equitable participation in the production and distribution of the social product, achieved through state intervention. These rights are therefore "collective" in the sense that they belong more to communities or whole societies rather than to individuals". For Fotopoulos, however, both conceptions have limitations. Firstly, they are grounded on the reductionist idea that the political and economic spheres are always separated, missing a holistic approach to human rights. Secondly, and most importantly, both forms of rights make sense only in a statist form of government, and presuppose the existence of "political and economic power...concentrated in the hands of elites", while, "in a non-statist type of democracy, which by definition involves the equal sharing of power, these rights become meaningless". Bookchin goes in the same direction and, although having explored the concept of rights, he values and elaborates more on the social dimension of concepts like cooperation and mutualism, a position that is shared among social ecology authors, who have avoided basing their work on the concept of rights.[6]

A similar approach is taken with respect to the concept of justice, as seen in the previous section. Social ecology aspires to a broader change than the one proposed, for example, within the idea of a just city "in which public investments and regulation would produce equitable outcomes rather than support those already well off" (Fainstein 2010: 3). Social ecology aspires to go beyond a mere fix of the current problems, aiming at affirming the freedom for all to self-determination.

Moreover, for social ecology it is important to go beyond the distinction between right and justice. Even if we consider the right to the city as a different right, the definition remains vague. For example, for Marcuse (2014: 5) the right to the city is "not a Right in the sense of a legal claim enforceable through the judicial system, but a moral right, an appeal to the highest of human values". However, these highest human values remain again opaque or vague. Furthermore a radical social change cannot be limited only to the full and equal enjoyment of the resources and services concentrated in cities, as instead prescribed by the right to the city.

According to dialectical naturalism, the crucial point is to consider whether rights or justice, or other concepts, are able to foster mutualism, differentiation, and development, as proposed by Heller (1999), for the creation of an ecological society. In this way social ecology is able to broaden the discussion around those terms and put them at the service of social change. For example, in an attempt to go beyond particularism and expand the notion of the right to the city, Souza (2014) proposes the right to the *planet*, bridging it to the experience of social ecology (and of Cornelius Castoriadis). Moreover, the notion of a right to the planet, which is based on the affirmation of freedom, can help establish who is a citizen or not, and move us towards affirming the concept of world-wide citizenship, echoed by the verse "our homeland is the whole world, our law is liberty" (from an anarchist song of the 19th century).

Lefebvre spoke about a planetary urbanization (2003), echoing a city without limits (Bookchin 1986). Indeed, Lefebvre (2013) agrees with Bookchin's claim that today's cities are creating an amorphous urban environment that absorbs all the space, negating nature and the social aspects of the original meaning of city. Given this kind of planetary urbanization, it is becoming difficult to speak about a right to the city. From this perspective, Merrifield (2013) argues that Lefebvre's right to the city may not be useful simply because we no longer have cities.

Social ecology's proposal for a new society is, therefore, more articulated than the concept of the right to the city or spatial justice. As suggested by Souza (2012a: 24), a grassroots revolution for a new world "should be conceived as something even more complex than just the 'right to the city' in Lefebvre's sense". As we struggle, it is necessary to include concepts like political decentralisation, economic de-concentration, and "conviviality" (Illich 1973), ecological soundness, egalitarian access to resources and opportunities of self-development, and ethno-diversity. And here, it is probably accurate to say that Murray Bookchin can help us better than

Henri Lefebvre". Social ecology, with its dialectical naturalism and analysis of freedom and domination, offers powerful tools to carve out new modes for society (Venturini forthcoming).

In any case, rights to the city and spatial justice remain important concepts to be used, especially by urban social movements, as mobilizing concepts that are able to speak to a broad, transclass and transnational audience. Moreover, both concepts focus their attention on the spatiality and geography of the city and its crises. What I propose is a *spatial turn* for social ecology—it should pay greater attention to spatial dynamics and processes. For example, the individuation of the negation or lack of rights to the city and of spatial justice (for example where the right to the city is negated or where there is spatial injustice) would make it possible to highlight the urban crisis, and prepare the ground for struggle and the construction of an ecological society.

Further, both concepts are transformative; they presuppose a sea change in the social, economic and political sphere, clearly connecting with the power and transformative agenda of urban social movements.

However, I agree with Uitermark Nicholls and Loopmans (2012: 2548) that "while there certainly are movements claiming a right to the city, it is clear that the concept remains much more popular in academic than in movement circles". To break this elite perspective and offer a new perspective to urban social movements, the right to the city and spatial justice assumes real value only when paired with the concept of domination. For example:

> Social justice—including in this spatial justice...is, of course, fundamentally a matter of power, not simply of ethics. If injustice is supposed to be related to illegitimate, unequal access to resources and means of exercising some rights, it is related to heteronomous power: that is, to oppression and domination. (Souza 2011: 73)

The concept of "fighting against all forms of domination" towards freedom developed in social ecology can be taken as a unifying concept that includes and amplifies the agenda of both right to the city and spatial justice.

In particular, the use of the concept of "domination" allows a more holistic vision of the social issues. Social ecology does not single out specific struggles, but moves holistically against domination, with a broader understanding of crises. Social ecology, highlighting the linkages between all forms of domination, not only calls for the coordination of different struggles that urban social movements pursue, in order to reinforce them, but also highlights the need to focus on a change that is broader and more fundamental.

Conclusion

To conclude, the right to the city and spatial justice are concepts that share three principle areas of common ground. First, they go beyond class, race, and gender. Second, each is used in order to mobilize large parts of the population. Finally, they both refer to citizenship. However citizenship is not a concept that is commonly used by urban social movements because they are suspicious of a term already co-opted by the State.

Today we live in a world where we must deal with the State while finding a new revolutionary path, in an approach that Souza (2006: 327) called "together *with* the State, *despite* the State, *against* the State". The concept of the right to the city is a necessary mobilizing concept, but alone it is not sufficient. Indeed, D'Souza (2018: 210) reminds us that:

> We have inherited rights-based institutions. Do we need to, for that reason, demand rights, struggle for them and place our futures in its power of promise, knowing the promises are empty for most people most of the time? What did the socialists and the freedom fighters in anti-colonial movements do? They demanded the real thing—food not right to food, national independence not right to independence, peace not right to peace, debt-repudiation not forgiveness.

If urban social movements want to recuperate key terms like citizenship, rights, and participation for building a truly revolutionary citizenship, they could link them to freedom and to the project of direct democracy—not only as a practice, but as a discourse. Linking these key concepts with something not yet incorporated into the current dominant system could help develop a coherent and resilient project, and gain popular support for ecological and democratic cities.

References

Attoh, K. A. 2011. What Kind of Right Is the Right to the City? *Progress in Human Geography*. 35(5), pp.669-685.

Bookchin, M. 1986. *The Limits of the City*. Montreal: Black Rose Book.

Bookchin, M. 1988. *Toward an Ecological Society*. Montreal: Black Rose Books.

Bookchin, M. 1995a. *Re-enchanting Humanity: A Defense of the Human Spirit Against Anti-Humanism, Misanthropy, Mysticism and Primitivism*. London: Cassell.

Bookchin, M. 1995b. *From Urbanization to Cities: Toward a New Politics of Citizenship*. New York: Cassell.

Bookchin, M. 1999. *Anarchism, Marxism, and the Future of the Left: Interviews and Essays, 1993–1998*. Oakland: AK Press.

Bookchin, M. 2005a. *The Ecology of Freedom*. Oakland: AK Press.

Bookchin, M. and Biehl, J. 1991. A Critique of the Draft Program of the Left Green Network. *Anarchy Archive*. [Online]. [Accessed 20 August 2014]. Available from: http://dwardmac.pitzer.edu/Anarchist_Archives/bookchin/gp/perspectives23.html

D'Souza, R. 2018. *What's Wrong With Rights? Social Movements, Law and Liberal Imaginations*. London: Pluto Press.

Evanoff, R. 2007. *Social Ecology: Basic Principles, Future Prospects*. [Online]. [Accessed 25 January 2018]. Available from: http://new-compass.net/articles/basic-principles-future-prospects

Fainstein, S. 2010. *The Just City*. New York: Cornell University press.

Fotopoulos, T. 1997. *Towards an Inclusive Democracy: The Crisis of the Growth Economy*. London: Bloomsbury.

Gibbons, A. 2010. Bridging Theory and Practice. *City*. 14(6), pp.619-621.

Griffin, Toni, Ariella Cohen and David Maddox, 2015. *The Just City Essays*. [Online]. J. Max Bond Center, Next City and the Nature of Cities. [Accessed 25 January 2019]. Available from: https://static1.squarespace.com/static/56266613e4b0a5df57a46c9d/t/5629464de4b05257bed3c507/1445545549774/TheJustCityEssays.pdf

Hamel, P., Lustiger-Thaler, H. and Mayer, M. eds. 2000. *Urban Movements in a Globalising World*. London: Routledge

Harvey, D. 1985. *The Urbanization of Capital: Studies in the History and Theory of Capitalist Urbanization*. Baltimore: John Hopkins University Press.

Harvey, D. 2003. The Right to the City. *International Journal of Urban and Regional Research* 27(4), pp.939-941.

Harvey, D. 2008. The Right to the City. *New Left Review*. (53), pp.23-40.

Harvey, D. and Potter, C. 2009. The Right to the Just City. In: Marcuse, P. et al. eds. *Searching for the Just City: Debates in Urban Theory and Practice*. New York: Routledge, pp.40-51.

Heller, C. 1999. The Ecology of Everyday Life: Rethinking the Desire for Nature. Montreal: Black Rose Books.

Holston, J. 1998. Spaces of Insurgent Citizenship. In: Sandercock, L. ed. *Making the Invisible Visible: A Multicultural Planning History*. Berkeley: University of California Press, pp.37-56.

Holston, J. 2008. *Insurgent Citizenship: Disjunctions of Democracy and Modernity in Brazil*. Princeton: Princeton University Press.

Holston, J. 2009. Insurgent Citizenship in an Era of Global Urban Peripheries. *City & Society*. 21(2), pp.245-267.

Illich, L.D. 1973. *Tools for Conviviality*. London: Calder & Boyars.

Iveson, K. 2011. Social or spatial justice? Marcuse and Soja on the Right to the City. *City*. 15(2), pp.250-259.

Kropotikin, P. 2011. *The Conquest of Bread*. New York: Dover Publication.

Kuymulu, M. B. 2013. The Vortex of Rights: 'Right to the City' at a Crossroads. *International Journal of Urban and Regional Research*, 37(3), pp.923-940.

Lefebvre, E. 2003. *The Urban Revolution*. Minneapolis: University of Minnesota Press.

Lefebvre, H. 1968. *Le Droit à la Ville*. Paris: Anthopos.

Lefebvre, H. 1996. *Writings on Cities*. Oxford: Blackwell.

Lefebvre, H. 2003. *The Urban Revolution*. Minneapolis: University of Minnesota Press.

Marcuse, P. 2009. Spatial Justice: Derivative but Causal of Social Injustice. *Justice Spatiale/Spatiale Justice*. [Online]. [Accessed 25 January 2015]. Available from: http://www.jssj.org/wp-content/uploads/2012/12/JSSJ1-4en2.pdf

Marcuse, P. 2012. Whose Right(s) to what City? In: Brenner, N. et al. eds.*Cities for People, not for Profit: Critical Urban Theory and the Right to the City*. London: Routledge, pp.24-41.

Marcuse, P. 2014. Reading the Right to the City. *City*. 18(1), pp.4-9.

Marcuse, P. Connolly, J., Novy, J., Olivo, I., Potter, C. and Steil, J. eds. 2009. *Searching for the Just City: Debates in Urban Theory and Practice*. New York: Routledge.

Mayer, M. 2012. The "Right to the City" in Urban Social Movements. In: Brenner, N. et al. eds. *Cities for People, not for Profit: Critical Urban Theory and the Right to the City*. London: Routledge, pp.63-85.

Mayer, M. 2013. First World Urban Activism. *City*. 17(1), pp.5-19.

Merrifield, A. 2013.*The politics of the encounter: Urban theory and protest under planetary urbanization*. Athens, Georgia: University of Georgia Press.

Merrifield, A. 2017. Fifty Years On: The Right to the City. In: Verso editors,*The Right to the City: A Verso Report.*[iBooks]. London: Verso, pp.18-32.

Mitchell, D. 2003. *The Right to the City: Social Justice and the Fight for Public Space*. New York: The Guilford Press.

Roussopoulos, D. 2013.The Politics of Neo-Anarchism. In: Graham, R. ed. *Anarchism: a documentary history of libertarian ideas* (Vol. 3). Montreal: Black Rose Books, pp.31-42.

Roussopoulos, D. 2015. *The Politics of Social Ecology*. Porsgrunn: New Compass.

Roussopoulos, D. 2017a. From the Rise of Cities to the Right to the City— By Way of an introductionl In: Roussopoulos, D. ed. *The Rise of Cities*. Montreal: Black Rose Books, pp.7-33.

Roussopoulos, D. ed. 2017b. *The Rise of Cities*. Montreal: Black Rose Books.

Sassen, S., 2002. The repositioning of citizenship: Emergent subjects and spaces for politics. *Berkeley journal of sociology*. 46, pp.4-26.

Soja, E. 2010. *Seeking Spatial Justice*. Minneapolis: University of Minnesota Press.

Souza, M. L. de 1999. O Desafio Metropolitano. Rio de Janeiro: Bertrand Brasil.

Souza, M. L. de 2001. *Mudar a Cidade: Uma Introdução Crítica ao Planejamento e à Gestão Urbanos*. Rio de Janeiro: Bertrand Brasil.

Souza, M. L. de 2006. Together with the State, Despite the State, Against the State: Social Movements as 'Critical Urban Planning' Agents. *City*, 10(3), pp.327-342.

Souza, M. L. de 2010. Which Right to which City? In: Defence of Political-Strategic Clarity. *Interface*. 2(1), pp.315-333.

Souza, M. L. de 2011. The Words and the Things. *City*. 15(1), pp.73-77.

Souza, M. L. de 2012a. The City in Libertarian Thought. *City*. 16(1-2), pp.4-33.

Souza, M. L. de 2012b. Challenging Heteronomous Power in a Globalized World: Insurgent Spatial Practices, 'Militant Particularism', and Multiscalarity. In: Stefan Krätke; Kathrin Wildner; Stephan Lanz. eds. *Transnationalism and Urbanism*. London: Routledge, pp.172-196.

Souza, M. L. de 2014. Towards a Libertarian Turn? Notes on the Past and Future of Radical Urban Research and Praxis. *City*. 18(2), 104-118.

Turner, S. and Miller, D. 2005. Anarchist Theory and Human Rights. In: *British International Studies Association Conference St. Andrews, Scotland 2005*. [Online]. [Accessed 10 December 2015]. Available from: www.anarchist-studies-network.org.uk/documents/anarchist_theory.doc

Uitermark, J. 2012. An Actually Existing Just City? In: Brenner, N. et al. eds. *Cities for People, not for Profit: Critical Urban Theory and the Right to the City*. London: Routledge, pp.197-214.

Uitermark, J., Nicholls, W. and Loopmans, M. 2012. Cities and social movements: theorizing beyond the right to the city. *Environment and Planning A*, 44, pp.2546-2554.

United Nations Human Settlements Programme. 2010. *Report of the Fifth Session of the World Urban Forum: The Right to the City: Bridging the Urban Divide*. Nairobi: World Urban Forum Secretariat.

Venturini, F. forthcoming. The Value Of Social Ecological Theory in the Struggles to Come. In: Springer, S. et al. eds. *Anarchist Political Ecology: Epistemologies and Ontologies of Resistance*.

Zárate, L. 2015. Right to the City for All: A Manifesto for Social Justice in an Urban Century. In: Griffin, T.L. et al. eds. *The Just City Essays*. [Online]. J. Max Bond Center, Next City and the Nature of Cities, pp.25-28.

Notes

1. I would like to thank Janet Biehl for advising me on relevant Bookchin's quotes.
2. For reason of space, this work does not explore the debates on the origin of rights, individual legal rights and natural rights.

3. For Bookchin, rights are a human construction and need to be based on objective assumptions. When based on freedom or self–consciousness, they would better be called "norms" or "ethical standards". These are things that people would ultimately want to achieve (Bookchin, in Evanoff 2007).

4. Although Bookchin seems to side with a natural conception of rights, he sidelined the debate on the origin of rights.

5. An interesting exception is the work of Kropotkin that speaks extensively about the right to live, to have food and to resist. His slogan is emblematic: "What we proclaim is the Right to Well-Being: Well-Being for All!" (Kropotkin 2011: 14).

6. The only exception is the work of Roussopoulos (2013; 2015; 2017a), who explores the use of the right to the city and its implementation, using the creation of charters as his main example. This implementation is for him a way to incrementally address the possibility of citizenship being affirmed. However, this approach cannot clearly define the connection between the affirmation of such rights and the social ecology project. Moreover, it is not able to respond to the aforementioned critiques of the use of charters by Mayer and Souza.

PART 3:
THE KURDISH ANSWER:
DEMOCRATIC CONFEDERLISM

The Evolution of the Kurdish Paradigm

Havin Guneser with Eleanor Finley

What sets us apart as humans—especially those who struggle for freedom and reject injustice, inequality, oppression, and exploitation—is our imagination. We can refuse to accept that which is simply handed over to us as truth. Let us begin here in our exploration of the journey of the Kurdish people in their quest for freedom over the last 45 years. Where are Kurds coming from? How can we holistically understand what has happened to the PKK and the strategic thinker Abdullah Öcalan and why? Let me briefly lead you all through this journey.

So where are we coming from? This is what I want to get into: to be able to holistically understand what happened and why it happened. There's a lot of contention around that issue.

The Early Years (1970–1989)

Obviously, struggles for freedom are not unique to Kurdistan or to the region. They happen across the world. Many people like to think that Öcalan's thinking changed suddenly in 1999 after his abduction in Kenya. In fact, at that time, many people believed that he betrayed the Kurdish people's cause. But when we look at 45 years of the struggle of the PKK, we can see that the organization has continuously moved forward and developed itself. The Kurdish freedom movement has seen many movements and struggles emerge and then wither away (for example, real socialism, national liberation movements, feminism, and anarchism). The PKK's ability to evolve lies with its analysis of these movements, deducing lessons that it then applies to itself.

When the PKK was gathering in order to take up the Kurdish issue during the 1970s, there was very limited information available about *leftism*. Around the time of the military coup in Turkey, the first of which was in 1960, there were translations of leftists into Turkish available only from Russian and French. There existed a bit of Marxism, feminism, Leninism, Stalinism, and Maoism, but no Gramsci, Bookchin, or other contemporary thinkers back in those years. It was not until the 1990s that the work of alternative movements began to be translated from English; even those that *were* translated were subsequently censored. For example, *The Origin of the Family* by Engels went against the traditions of society, so it was censored.

Even the history of the Middle East itself was suppressed. Throughout the region, the nation-states that had formed were interested in completing processes of cultural homogenisation. The information least available of all was Kurdish history. By the 1970s, they had nearly succeeded in getting Kurdish people to forget that Kurdistan was divided into four parts. The majority of Kurds knew only the history of the part in which they lived. In this way, it came to be inscribed in the minds of Kurds themselves that Kurdistan was barren, nowhere worth living in, backward, etc. They were participating in auto-assimilation. Thus, the founding members of the PKK (and especially Öcalan) gave a great deal of importance to education, reading, and the ability to draw conclusions from different movements and great deal of studying was done during this period.

The founding members of the PKK were not all Kurdish and not all male. They came not only from one social class. Already within the initial group, we see the presence of students, workers, women, and people of different ethnicities. This point is very important to making sense of how and why the group developed the way that it did. If we were to say that Öcalan and the PKK knew what they were doing from day one and that they had already arrived at their own paradigm in the 1970s, that would be incorrect. However, it would be correct to define Öcalan and the early founding members as people in the process of questioning everything. They questioned what was being presented to them—even from the Left.

The initial group began with a simple premise: Kurdistan is a colony. The issue is not simply about Turkey, but also about Iran, Iraq, and Syria, and as well about the hegemonic system in which they lived. That's why they started saying that Kurdistan was an inter-state colony, an international colony. During this questioning, they established a political party that was Marxist–Leninist. To do so at the time of the Cold War time was like creating a Molotov cocktail. One was banned from saying even the words "Kurd" or "Kurdistan" and instead people would use the letter "K". So not only were they a political party that demanded freedom for Kurds and their homeland, but on top of that, they were Marxist–Leninist. Of course, people used to say "There's no proletariat in Kurdistan, so you can't be socialists! You have to first become a proletariat and then become a socialist." There were all sorts of funny and odd situations like that happening in the Middle East at that time.

The relationship between the PKK and the Turkish left was complex. On the one hand, Kurds needed to form a separate movement because the issue of Kurdish colonization would not be taken up by the Turkish left. The PKK were also emboldened by national movements around the world, such as the Vietnamese liberation movement and the ideas of Franz Fanon.

On the other hand, the PKK was inspired and influenced by the Turkish Left and leftists who were killed by the Turkish state. Öcalan and the founders saw that in order to unite, first you had to separate and build yourself on your own roots. Today, we're seeing that there is indeed a re-emergence of unity and coming together. Öcalan was also very cautious not to become the disciple of some kind of centre, which was common in those days—either Moscow, Albania, or China. Öcalan refused all that. He said that what was needed was to be able to understand Marxism and Leninism and to implement the ideas according to the conditions of Kurdistan.

Öcalan was very critical of so-called "real socialism" at the time. Can you imagine the Molotov cocktail here as well? Firstly, you're Kurdish. Secondly, you're Marxist–Leninist in the 1970s. But then you're *also* critical of the Left within the Middle East and in Turkey as well as the mainstream Left, including USSR or China. This was a very difficult situation in which to stay alive. Apart from the Kurdish people themselves, there really has been no support for the Kurdish movement itself. If the USSR was what it was claiming to be, why did it ignore the Kurdish people if they are also Marxist–Leninists? If the Iranian Left, the Iraqi Left, and the Turkish Left are also Marxist–Leninists, why were they doing the same? Although it appeared like a negative situation (and in many respects was), the fact that they were ignored or excluded from virtually all other political tendencies gave them the courage to question all of these tendencies. Until very recently, if you asked anyone but Kurds about the PKK, you got a very negative answer. The left wing would say they're nationalist. The religious wing would say they're atheist. The Turkish state would say they're Armenian, which is a terrible word to say in Turkey, it's like a blasphemy. You get all these contradictory descriptions about one and the same organisation and movement. It means that the Kurdish movement has questioned everything that was there.

Soul-Searching within the PKK (1990–2010)

During the early 1990s, the world witnessed the collapse of the USSR. Although Öcalan was already critical of the Soviet Union, he saw this happening and started to analyse. He didn't give up on socialism or communism, but instead he wrote a book called *To Insist on Socialism is to Insist upon Being a Human-Being*.

Thus, during this period, there was a great deal of questioning about activities within the PKK. In 1996, his analysis concluded that we need to kill the dominant male. I remember very distinctly that from the years 1997 to 1998, Öcalan spoke about real socialist practices within the PKK. That is why this is such a dynamic and non-dogmatic movement. The questioning was not only towards the outside, but also towards the inside. The PKK did a lot of doing and thinking, thinking and doing at the same time. And that's something very important for Öcalan, and he continues to say it to date. He's very much of a dialectical thinker in that way, insisting that you should think as you do and do as you think so that you may find different ways of doing and different ways of thinking.

Öcalan set up a school garden, which he likened to Socrates' garden. There, revolutionaries would discuss the developments of the organisation, the questions that face the movement, and the questions that face revolutionary people and humanity in general. He drew many conclusions from those discussions. He did not allow himself to be affected negatively by a question or criticism. Instead, he would go and re-question and try to understand why things happened the way they did. For example, he said that you cannot doubt the intentions of the people who make revolution. Instead, you must go back and interrogate the tools and the meanings that were given to do things. He made similar remarks regarding feminism. Feminism has been great at making invisible the loss of women's freedom, but where did this go wrong? How did it become elite and come to lack grounding within the people?

There were pragmatic points as well. From the very beginning, Öcalan was looking at the question of the State. But neither the Left nor the Right addressed this problem, apart from anarchism, but even this tendency didn't offer an alternative solution. Perhaps in this we can see why he was later inspired by Bookchin. The freedom movement imagined an independent and free socialist Kurdistan within a Middle Eastern confederation—there was always the hope of this re-unification at some point. However, in 1993, Öcalan said for the very first time that there could be talks with Turkey, that there could be a solution within the official borders of Turkey. Of course, outside observers thought this decision was entirely tactical. Although it was arguably more of a practical than paradigmatic step, it was also the first time that Öcalan definitively broke away from the idea of a separate state. At a practical level, he approached the issue so that it could be resolved within the borders of the Turkish state.

I should emphasise the developments concerning women's freedom during this period. The dimension of freedom for women had been formed as a branch of the party, just like any other party or national liberation movement. In the early 1990s, however, there was a huge influx of young women into the PKK, which represented a hope for freedom not only in terms of ethnic repression on the Kurds, but also regarding social relations. Because the PKK was Marxist–Leninist, it rejected feudal relationships and ways of treating women. In fact, before the PKK fought the Turkish state, it fought the feudal lords. Early on, it was the feudal lords who showed resistance to this movement. As agents of the State, they prevented the PKK from growing, so it could not enter into the rest of society.

Ocalan's Abduction and Captivity (1999–)

In 1999 Öcalan was in Kenya and, as a result of a NATO operation led by USA, UK, and Israel, he was handed over to Turkey. All of these discussions lay in the background alongside the ever-present need for Öcalan to find a solution to what was happening to the Kurds. Those who know Kurdish history know that supressing rebellions is actually about capturing the leader, killing the leader, and then massacring the people. The Kurds are acutely aware of this history. There were approximately 20 rebellions in the recent past of the Kurds—they have experienced this day in and day out. Thus, when Öcalan was abducted, all Kurds were on the streets protesting what they knew was coming if he was killed in the hands of the Turkish state.

There's a very strong link between how the Kurds see Öcalan and what he represents for the Kurdish people historically and presently. He is of course a tested leader who has guided the Kurds in and out of grave situations. Moreover, he has helped Kurds become proud of who they are and helped show them that they have dignity. The Turkish state wrote volumes about how Kurds are in fact "mountain Turks": it is an ideology of the State. They claimed that as Kurds walked in the snowy mountain trails, they made the sound of "kat-kurt-kat-kurt," and that's where the word *Kurd* comes from. Can you imagine? This was considered rational thinking by university professors in Turkey! Can you imagine?

Thus, the abduction of Öcalan in 1999 was a major rupture because of what it represented in the history of the Kurdish freedom movement and the history of the Kurds in general.

Öcalan's abduction was also historically significant because of the way he handled this chaotic moment. Many movements within the Middle East—especially in Turkey—exclaimed that the PKK's leader had just betrayed them and called upon them to take their weapons and join them. Instead, what Öcalan asked for was for countless people to go onto the streets around the world in protest. Some even burned themselves alive. This direct action by Kurdish people stopped many horrible possibilities, including any plans there may have been to harm Öcalan during his abduction from Kenya to Turkey. There were many who expected him to go on a hunger strike, but instead he asked for calm.

Öcalan and the movement could foresee the intervention of the world system into the Middle East. In fact, he dates the beginning of this intervention to October 9th, 1998, the day he was pushed out of Syria. In his books, Öcalan recalls that in 1998 Israel sent an envoy to him. They wanted him to accept Israel's patronage regarding the Kurdish question and its resolution. Öcalan could neither accept it morally nor politically. As a result, his odyssey began, which Kurds call the "international plot".

Öcalan made use of this rupture quiet positively. In prison, he had more time to read. He requested thousands of books and one of the authors, of course, is Murray Bookchin. One could say that the Kurdish freedom movement revitalized Bookchin's ideas; the Kurdish freedom movement is the most influential struggle in the world that has been inspired by him. What Bookchin wrote helped Öcalan immensely to find his own questions from a philosophical background.

Just as it was a Molotov cocktail in the 1970s to be Kurdish and Marxist–Leninist, in the 2000s—just when people expected something else of him—Öcalan declared, "No, we don't want a state". Can you imagine the world's reaction? Some people said it must be out of personal fear. The Kurds thought, "It's tactical, it must be definitely tactical". At the time, it was thought that peoples without a state are like people without a father: a bastard. Without a state, you're bullied, massacred. Therefore, you aspire to have a state because that this is where liberation lies. As Öcalan went into questioning, he realized that was one of the traps that most of the Left fell into.

In 1999, with local elections in Turkey, Kurds began to be active in the municipalities for the very first time. They became mayors and council members of the municipalities. Öcalan had told all of the mayors about Bookchin's *Urbanisation Without Cities* and instructed them to have this book on their table, to study and read it. He also studied *The Ecology of Freedom* in depth. The title of Öcalan's third major volume, *Sociology of Freedom*, reflects that. The book that most reflects inspiration from Bookchin is currently in process of being translated. It is a huge book and it's the foundation of *Manifesto for a Democratic Civilisation*, two volumes of which you see here. This book is where he deals with issues of hierarchy, domination and state theory.

Öcalan wanted to understand the source of the problem of the State in the depths of history. As he got in deeper and deeper, he reached some conclusions. He looked at how slavery was built and the basis of the State on three pillars. As Bookchin emphasized, it doesn't happen through the use of pure violence. Rather, it's coupled with other things. For example, Öcalan says that when violence wasn't enough, ideological and religious narrative had to come into play. So if you don't accept what's going on through sheer force, there's the ideological narrative as well. If you're not accepting that, then your livelihood and economy are taken away from you, so you're made economically dependent as well. We see all of this reflected in mythology. This is why Öcalan describes his method as interpretive. He looks at mythologies and tries to see what they are telling us in terms of the struggle.

The difference between Öcalan and Bookchin is that Öcalan stretches back to the Neolithic period and he associates the issue of class and nation with the loss of freedom of women and her system.[1] Öcalan doesn't attribute the loss of woman's freedom to her biology; he sees it as the loss of the moral and political society that she founded and guided. He says that in order for society to be subdued and dominated, women had to be subdued and dominated. The beginning of state society is the institutionalisation of patriarchy. It's not to say that there wasn't any hierarchy or domination, but that statist class civilisation as we know it begins with the institutionalisation of hierarchy, and not just hierarchy alone. This is very important.

Öcalan is thus asking what happened to what he calls "moral and political society" throughout history. His point of departure is the Kurdish question. Throughout 48 years, throughout asking all of these questions, and throughout the seemingly impossible resolution to the Kurdish question due to national, regional, and international issues, he came to the point of trying to understand in depth what is actually happening to us as humans. That is why, in the 2000s, when everybody expected him to come up with something utterly different, he came out with democratic confederalism: a non-state solution for not only the Kurdish question, but for the social questions we are experiencing throughout the world. Bookchin was very important for Öcalan, especially the several books he obtained, and he continually asked for others that had been translated into Turkish.

The Present: Where Do the Answers Lie?

Öcalan looks at it like this. There are three components to how we are enslaved: (1) violence; (2) ideology; and (3) economic. Where do the answers lie? Firstly, it's important to remember that we're not the first in this freedom struggle; we are part of and linked to a chain. But this chain is dispersed. It needs to be brought together. Öcalan attempts to do this, which he outlines in an essay *Sociology of Freedom*, by linking together the people, the communities, the women who have struggled for freedom. If there is a history of states, domination, hierarchy, the city/class/state civilisation, he argues, then there is *another* civilisation, which he calls the *democratic civilisation* of peoples, women, workers, craftspeople, clans, tribes, etc. who resist these centralisations. Therefore, he clarifies, "I'm not doing anything new, I'm just trying to make visible what is already there".

Öcalan's unit of history is moral and political society, which I believe Bookchin calls organic society. However, Öcalan bases this moral and political society on the loss of women's freedom, so women are key agents. Therefore, he realizes that freedom and revolutionary struggles of the past fell into some traps regarding violence of the army and the military (including the PKK) and he asks, "How do we redefine this?" There's extraordinary violence being applied against the people, even at this very moment. It's not just economic, there's sheer physical violence at the same time. There needs to be what he calls self-defence, to protect yourself—not to attack, but to protect yourself. He feels that there needs to be a force to open space for this.

The second piece is ideology. This is why there is *Jineology* [a science of women], so that women can decide on what their history is and not just rely on the history that is given to us. And this is necessary for the history of the people as well.

How do you become independent of state structures? As we can see, states today are grabbing people off the land and putting them in the middle of the road, especially in the Middle East. But this is also happening across the world. We are witnessing a reconquering of these geographies, of their land and riches. Through them, they are making the European and Anglo-Saxon world a little bit scared so that they'll go and embrace the State as a "protection" against what's coming. They're using populations against one another. And they are using economics. So how do we develop an independent economics and living from the State in response? This is the fundamental point. Öcalan says that you can't conquer the State and then make it useless and have a classless society. No, forget about that. What is crucial is to organise the people so that they can organise their spaces independent of the State, which is nothing but a monopoly and the peak of all monopolies that have arisen throughout time: military, ideological, cultural, industrial, monetary, etc.

He's separating governance from the State and he's creating tools like democratic confederalism that can find a compromise with the State. It goes over boundaries; it goes to individuals as well. We cannot expect to change the system if we don't change ourselves. However, our change cannot be on the basis of the individual; we need to have an organised society. We're seeing capitalism destroy society, not only nature—Öcalan calls it *societycide*, the killing of society. He believes this is the biggest problem at present. What revolutionaries should do is keep these forces off of society so that moral and political society has the space to reawaken and to function once again.

This is the soul of the matter: whatever format you have, it means nothing if the soul isn't in the right spot. But the soul must be accompanied by tools that can further it.

The Nation-State defines itself on a mindset of nationalism. How do we define ourselves, what is our mindset? The same as Bookchin—freedom. This is something dynamic. The nation is static. That's why Öcalan defines the democratic nation on two characteristics: freedom and solidarity. It is a mutualistic and dynamic identity.

Note

1. While Bookchin carefully examines Neolithic society in the *Ecology of Freedom* and traces the development of hierarchical society in Sumer in

contrast to the rest of Mesopotamian society, he does not link specifically the loss of freedom with the loss of freedom of women. See also Chapter 2, *The Emergence of Hierarchy* and Chapter 3, *The Legacy of Domination*. Similarly, the first chapter of *Urbanization Without Cities* focuses on early Mesopotamian cities and he remarks on Kurdistan by name.

The Democratization of Cities in North Kurdistan

Ercan Ayboga

The History of Cities in North Kurdistan

After the foundation of the Republic of Turkey, the cities in North (Turkish-occupied) Kurdistan became progressively poorer relative to those in the Turkish state. This led to comparatively weak municipalities ruled by so-called system parties, which were hierarchical, corrupt, and extremely alienated from the population. They also formed part of the repression mechanism. There were no big investments by the colonialist state in North Kurdistan (also known as Bakur), except in the three provinces in the western part of Bakur with a high non-Kurdish population: Meletî (Malatya), Xarput (Elazığ) and Dîlok (Gaziantep). While the biggest city in Bakur, Diyarbakir (Amed) was, in the 1920s, the third most important economic city within the Turkish state after Istanbul and Izmir, 70–80 years later it became one of the poorest. However, in terms of Kurdistan, Turkey, and the Middle East we have to consider that municipalities were historically weaker than those in Europe. While the smaller cities often had no municipal administrations, the mid-sized and large cities were administered directly by an appointed governor. Communities organized themselves in large part outside of municipalities—it was different, but not necessarily better.

In the 1950s a steadily increasing migration wave started from the Kurdish cities and some regions of Anatolia to the larger cities in the West and South of the Turkish state, particularly Istanbul. Thus Turkish cities grew at a faster rate compared with Kurdish cities. Nevertheless, many people also moved to the cities of North Kurdistan. Due to limited financial capacity, most new housing buildings were built by the migrating people, leading to poor neighbourhoods and slums. In the 1970s strong leftist Turkish and Kurdish movements became stronger and won local elections in some cities in Turkey and Bakur. Together with social movements some of these cities could be even governed with elements of direct democracy. However, the cities ruled by leftist socialists/communists led to better social services, more democratic rights and more cultural opportunities for the people. While not used as a term, *the right to the city* could be realized better this way than through the party systems. In these years the Kurdish Freedom Movement (KFM), with the PKK in its centre, evolved among other political Kurdish and revolutionary movements and gained, within a short time, serious support by the proletarian and student youth. PKK candidates could also win elections—for example, in Elîh (Batman).

But the military coup in 1980 eliminated all achieved rights in these cities and the whole state of Turkey established a fascist regime, laying the basis for neoliberalism, which spread, although more slowly than in other countries. In Turkish cities life quality fell. For example, almost all social and cultural centres, cinemas and theatres were shut down, and the first steps of privatization were initiated—bus lines were the first areas dominated by privatization. While in the 1970s villages were more at the heart of the society, in the 1980s migration away from rural areas increased.

In 1984 the Kurdistan Workers Party (PKK) started an armed rebellion against the colonialist Turkish state. In the beginning of the 1990s it developed as a mass movement in several Kurdish provinces. In 1991 and 1992, when repression was still not absolutely dominating everything, a short but strong civil dynamic evolved in a number of cities in Bakur. The KFM also gained support in cities. In parallel, in some Turkish cities leftist organizations became a bit stronger, but could not achieve the level prior to the military coup of 1980. But in the second half of the 1980s the social democrats won local elections in most big cities, but with absolutely no democratic impulse, ending up in corruption and mismanagement. From 1993 onwards the revolutionary dynamic in Bakur's cities was oppressed completely, ushering in difficult times. In rural areas the Turkish Army destroyed up to 4,000 Kurdish villages and forcibly displaced more than 2 million people. While some fled to Europe, the majority moved to Turkish cities. Still, a significant number moved to the cities of Bakur. Several cities doubled the number of residents—Amed, Elîh, Nisêbîn (Nusaybin) and Cizre. Those cities were totally unprepared and could not cope with the sudden mass migration, resulting in serious problems with water supply, sewage water, housing, waste and health. The central government did not help with anything. An increasing proletarianization of the cities was the result with a high poverty, street children, prostitution and perceivable crime. In cities, civil society was either politically and democratically disorganized, or had no capacity. Yet, they were under political pressure to show solidarity with refugees, who arrived with almost nothing. It took several years to overcome the worst impacts. However in these years, although the State implemented broad state terrorism, the KFM could not be defeated; rather an equilibrium was maintained between 1994 and 1999.

An international plot led to the kidnapping of Abdullah Öcalan, leader of the PKK and central to the KFM, to Turkey in February 1999 in which the Greek state was also involved. This led to the cessation of armed struggle in the ensuing months. The KFM commenced fresh discussions about a new strategy on a theoretical and practical basis. The political struggle in the cities moved into the centre of the whole struggle. Within this approach the municipalities played an important role. Just at the time of the international plot local elections were held in Turkey.

Cities Under the Governance of the Kurdish Freedom Movement

The Kurdish Freedom Movement (KFM) has achieved increasing successes in local elections since 1999. In a surprise win in 1999, the legal party of the KFM—HADEP (People's Democracy Party)—won several big cities like Amed, Wan, Elîh and Agirî (Ağrı). The KFM was challenged with governing several big cities and needed to prove it had better social-democratic concepts than other parties for the local level. The end of the war in Bakur led to less oppression by the Turkish state and some space to act politically at a legal level. While the KFM ruled, some infrastructure and basic services experienced significant improvements, but concerning democracy and people's political participation, development was slower and characterized by structural difficulties. Considering centuries of authoritarianism, oppression, assimilation, corruption and a lack of open democratic relations, this was not surprising. A positive aspect in these years was that civil society and social movements became stronger in Bakur, becoming important actors in the cities. They joined the discussions to develop more social and ecological cities, and made multiple proposals and requests to the municipalities for which they voted too. So the right to the city began to be discussed the first time in a broad way in Bakur.

The KFM discussed generally in these years the new political concept until in 2005 democratic confederalism was declared by Öcalan. It was the first main step of systematizing the new approach, which developed over the years. Between 2005 and 2008 the PKK Guerrilla and Turkish Army clashed briefly because the Turkish AKP government did not take essential steps for the solution of the Kurdish question—it just ignored it and reduced the question to individual rights. In 2006 a big uprising occurred in Amed and several other cities, leading to the collapse of the State for some days. Proletarian youth were at the forefront of this revolt. The State was shocked and commenced measures to quell the uprisings.

In 2007, when the framework was discussed for two years, the Democratic Society Congress (KCD; also named DTK) was founded and many KFM members started to reorganize society based on the "paradigm of a democratic, ecological and gender liberated society" as democratic confederalism proclaimed. The KCD is an umbrella of all organizations close to the KFM, with a leftist democratic stand, and is considered a platform with a new approach for doing politics. At the same time the KCD is an alternative to parliamentarian democracy, which is in a structural crisis in both Turkey and the rest of the world. It propagates radical democracy and has many structures expressed in its councils and assemblies at different levels. There are today 14 sectors, also called political spheres, covering a wide range of focus areas (e.g. politics, women, youth, economy, health, ecology, justice, beliefs, education and diplomacy). In other words the KCD is the "council of councils". The model it is developing in practice is called "democratic autonomy".

With democratic confederalism the theoretical base of "free municipalism" has been laid in principal. In this sense the first steps have been taken to set up people's assemblies at the neighbourhood level, as well as women and youth councils wherever the KFM had substantial support in Bakur, and even in those cities in Turkey where there are significant Kurdish populations. At higher levels the delegates of these people's assemblies meet social movements, NGO's, parties, municipalities, unions and other organizations and sectors in city/district and provincial councils. At the top is the general assembly of the KCD with 501 members. The inclusion of all willing organizations and players at these higher levels in society is a crucial element of the new political project.

In 2010 the "First Conference on Ecology and Local Authorities" was realized. Its framework stated that municipalities organize society based on four pillars: organized society and participative approach; ecological life; gender-liberated approach; and participative social economy. Crucially, its focus was on cities, considering that the majority of the population of Bakur was living in cities—migration never ceased due to economic reasons. At the conference, the search for radical democracy and self-organization far away from the (nation) State and representative democracy was discussed in depth with strong emotions. Strengthening the women's movement was considered elementary for successful progress, as the gender question is believed to be the main contradiction in society. Without the strong involvement of women and a raised consciousness regarding gender relations, emancipative processes can lack substance.

After the intensive war period of 2011 and 2012, democratic autonomy and its related self-organizing structures like the people's assemblies became stronger. In 2013 and 2014 the women's movement spread to all parts of society, leading economics and ecology activists to create real social movements and implement the first projects and campaigns. This was the result of raising critical consciousness in the society of Bakur. Crucially, the first urban struggles came up against some large housing projects, the cutting of green areas and forests, the construction of shopping malls, the transformation of state areas in city centres into commercial areas, and intervention by the State into city planning. The struggles were a reply to increased pressure by the AKP government for gentrification, commercialization and control of cities with a so-called "security" motivation. The AKP wanted to increase profits in all areas and cities of the country where what the DBP (Party of Democratic Regions, the KFM party within the People's Democratic Party—HDP) considered were an obstacle. The HDP/DBP municipalities and several social movements resisted against gentrification and the displacement of residents of poor neighbourhoods. Some struggles succeeded; some did not.

But some social movements protested against the HDP/DBP municipalities, where they had (perhaps deliberately) failed to grasp the implications of development or the logic of capitalism and simply followed the market-based approach of the State. A serious number of projects like housing estates and parks, as well as some elements of city planning were oriented towards neoliberal capitalist policies. It took years for social movements and civil society organizations to have a strong impact against these neoliberal projects of the HDP/DBP municipalities. This was made possible through public critique, political actions, face-to-face meetings, as well as the KCD umbrella structure. As a whole the KCD took the critique of municipalities seriously and started a broad discussion with all member organizations. In the years 2012–2013 the municipalities redirected their policies towards a more ecological and socially-oriented direction.

The KCD has to be understood as a structure where it sometimes requires a long time to make decisions as discussions are requested by many organizations and members. When a decision is taken, it is binding on all member organizations, although there is no basis for enforcement within the Turkish legal system. The people's council at city level of the KCD system stands over the official city council. If the city council has a majority from the KCD, then they must take decisions in line with the decisions of the KCD. Furthermore, the municipalities have to work closely with the people's assemblies at the neighbourhood level.

The neighbourhood people's assemblies are key to developing democratic and participative cities. People's assemblies have to be considered the main driver, especially considering the existing representative political structures, which are not able to develop political solutions to local needs.

This mechanism allows civil organizations and groups in the city to influence decisions about the city and is crucial for limiting corruption and reducing alienation of the population. If there is a critical, social, ecological and gender-free awareness in society, decisions will improve and the right to the city will be better realized. In the early years the municipalities and city councils ruled by the people and parties of the KFM often failed to follow the principles and decisions of the KCD, but in the last 4–5 years it has changed for the better. Nevertheless the contradictions within the system remain.

When the terrorist Islamic State (IS) besieged Kobanî in Rojava in fall 2014, millions of people in Bakur and also Turkey revolted in dozens of cities. The Turkish state lost control of many cities and could not hold its position without terrorizing the population; many people were systematically shot. In three days over 40 civilians were murdered. This strong uprising, led by broad masses and joined by many leftist people and other movements in

Bakur and Turkey, was a bigger shock for the Turkish state than the uprising of 2006. It showed how weak the base of the Turkish state in Bakur actually was in reality.

Between 2013 and 2015 people's assemblies emerged in most urban neighbourhoods of Bakur, partially overcoming the weaknesses of the first years (2007–2011). The internal democratic processes, women's participation and a communal ecological awareness became significantly stronger. The people's assemblies acted more confidently in their cities and society. This was an important contribution to democratic culture and decision-making. In 2015 the foundation of hundreds of communes spread to the politically well-organized cities of Bakur (e.g. Cizre, Gever, and Nisêbîn). This development followed the practice in Rojava, the Syrian part of Kurdistan liberated in 2012 in the midst of the intensifying war, where a social revolution progressed quickly towards implementing radical democracy. The reason is obvious: people's assemblies at the neighbourhood level were not enough for a strong self-organized society and large-scale participation. In the neighbourhoods many people remained outside of the political structures.

In many cities the declarations of self-governance in summer 2015 were a result of this strengthening of the people's assemblies and the setting up of communes—i.e. the deepening and enlarging of radical democracy. But they were subsequently made instrumental by the Turkish state in its new war against the Kurds.

Challenges

When the KCD was founded, neoliberalism within the Turkish state was becoming very strong. The economy policies of the KFM in the first years were too weak to counter the State or capitalism. Neoliberalism created a strong pressure on KFM municipalities where decision-makers were often politically and ideologically too weak to understand or challenge capitalist mechanisms. Neoliberalism also affected many political activists from the KFM. Yet in spite of these forces, the KFM pushed forward and achieved some results, including setting up dozens of cooperatives in 2014.

However, the constituent actors have a problem in that they are unable to balance theory and practice. One of the main problems in practice is the hierarchy within the KFM member organizations, particularly the municipalities. While on the one hand a participative democracy and a horizontal and decentralized social life is aimed for and developed, on the other hand hierarchical and centrist relations between constituent actors continue to exist in a hidden way. Within the new organizational structures hierarchies continue to exist and even, under certain circumstances, grow from time to time.

The interventions of the Turkish nation-state against the constituent actors has led to instability. In 2009 massive arrests started against activists and continued until 2012 as the so-called "KCK operations", which interrupted the development of participative structures, bringing numerous organizations to existential problems. After the new war commenced in 2015 arrests and repressions far exceeded those of prior years, and some organizations could no longer function. Since then, municipalities have been usurped by the Turkish government and the war has affected many cities in a number of ways.

Urban Warfare and the New Wave of Gentrification

When the Turkish government unilaterally recommenced war in July 2015 against the PKK and Kurds, it was a matter of a few weeks until the war reached the cities of Bakur. State forces met the strong resistance of the organized population with such heavy and brutal military means that hundreds of civilians were murdered. However, the massive physical destruction of cities occurred after the cessation of armed conflict. The State blockaded the contested cities, systematically erasing parts of the cities of Cizre and Gever, most of Şirnex and Nisebîn, and half of the old city of Amed, called Sur. The houses of more than 200,000 people were destroyed, leaving refugees to disperse to other cities of Bakur.

The war has been used by the Turkish state as an opportunity to destroy cities or neighbourhoods where the population was very oppositional and politically well organized. It continues to punish the population and implement longstanding gentrification policies. Since 2017 the State has been building new houses in the ruined neighbourhoods according to a new plan for wide roads. Through a permanent change to the demography it wants to destroy forever the social and cultural structures in these cities so that the displaced people will be unable to organize themselves again in a political way. What the Turkish government calls "urban transformation" can just as easily be implemented in neighbourhoods where no armed clashes took place—no neighbourhood is safe!

The war in the mountains of Bakur between the Turkish Army and the PKK guerrilla continues at an intensive level. Political pressure on the whole population in Bakur is increasing, particularly through the state of emergency declared in July 2016. More than 10,000 public employees have lost their jobs, and 10,000 politically active Kurds have been arrested, almost all HDP-ruled municipalities have been seized by the State through the appointment of state commissioners. Hundreds of associations in Bakur have been closed and the oppression on the Kurdish media is so strong that all free media has been shut down.

The State has banned de facto the Kurdish language in cities —signs are no longer bilingual, municipal-operated Kurdish kindergartens and theatres have been shut down, and Kurdish books have been destroyed. In the streets fly tens of thousands of Turkish flags. All youth, cultural, social, and women's centres have been shut down or seized, with new personnel and materials replaced with totally contrary content. More than two dozen co-operatives linked to the municipalities have been shut down. Most social, ecological and women-focused developments implemented since 1999 by the KFM have been destroyed or reversed. What is being experienced in Bakur is open dictatorship—fascism is not far away.

The larger aim of the State is to create contradictions among the Kurds and marginalize the KFM in Bakur. But it has not worked. Although people do not demonstrate much and seldom join protest actions, they are yet to support the State. Any suggestion they do is merely Turkish propaganda. People still feel close to the KFM, recalling its long struggle for freedom and democratic organization since 2000. Kurds who support the AKP are still a minority.

Despite the repressions, the vast majority of the Bakur people remain in their homeland. The number of refugees in Europe or elsewhere from Bakur is still small—only people faced with arrest leave Bakur. This is a key difference compared with the 1990s. The majority of the population feels that the AKP government cannot maintain this level of oppression in the long term, and the day of its breakdown is close. It seems that an appropriate moment to revolt against the State awaits the cities and villages of Bakur.

PART 4:
TRANSFORMING SOCIAL THEORY

Do We Need a New Theory of the State?
Metin Guven

The struggle for the right to the city is growing in different contexts all over the world. For example, tens of thousands of people rebelled to protect Gezi Park in Istanbul in 2013, yet their actual driving motivation was resisting the authoritarian government that is trying to control every aspect of citizens' lives and to suppress every movement that raises concerns. Therefore, it is becoming increasingly important to understand how that context is changing in a dynamic world that is transitioning into a new world order. Old powers are losing their ground and new powers are rising. The neoliberal policies of globalization are adversely affecting the living conditions of people. Because of these changes, authoritarian governments and right-wing populism are becoming more common.

I will try to explore what kind of transformation period we are going through first, then I will try to explain the historical differences of domination among the main civilizations and why I think we would understand the outcome of the current transformation better if we develop a new theory of the State that includes the various state evolutions, especially in Asia.

The Current Transition of World Leadership
Fourteen years ago the Iraq war was on the agenda, neocons of the US were planning to take over Iraq in order to establish a friendly government and access cheap oil to stop the decline of the US economy. Within a few years it became a debacle; Iraqi resistance increased the cost of the war to trillions of dollars. It also caused the collapse of the US hegemony project. In 2006 neocons left all positions in the US government. The US entered into so much debt that it hasn't been in a position to start another war since. Yet the actual decline of the US started in 1970s, with the loss of the Vietnam War being an important turning point. Some relief was provided by neoliberalism and monetary policies during the late 1980s, as well as new economic and financial expansion in the 1990s. However, these policies could not prevent the 2001 recession. The US succeeded in attracting capital flow, but manufacturing in the US was too costly and profit rates were too low. Most investment went to new technologies, but the expected

rate of consumption was not realized. The recession of 2008–2009 was even worse, and the next recession could be the worst of all given that income and wealth imbalances are at a historical high.

If we look at the decline of the US in a historical perspective this seems inevitable. Giovanni Arrighi (2007, p.235) explains four systemic cycles of capital accumulation:

> Recurrent system-wide financial expansions appeared to return, new rounds of inter-capitalist competition, interstate rivalries, accumulation by dispossession, and production of space on an ever-increasing scale revolutionized the geography and mode of operation of world capitalism, as well as its relationship with imperialistic practices. Thus, if we focus on the "containers of power" that have housed the "headquarters" of the leading capitalist agencies of successive cycles of accumulation, we immediately see a progression from a city-state and cosmopolitan business diaspora (the Genoese); to a proto-national state (the United Provinces) and its joint-stock chartered companies; to a multinational state (the United Kingdom) and its globe-encircling tributary empire; to a continent-sized national state (the US) and its world-encompassing system of transnational corporations, military bases, and institutions of world governance.

One hundred years ago the world was in another transition period, with the UK's global leadership of capitalism on the decline. Investing in the UK was not profitable; capital was flowing to the US for a higher profit. The US economy was already the largest in the world. The UK economy had been financialized just as the US economy today has been financialized. A 30-year period, including two world wars, brought the end of UK leadership. For the US, a similar period started with Iraq War. There likely will not be another war since the US doesn't seem to be able to reduce its foreign debt and prepare for another war. Also, other opportunities to start a war between rivals seems very difficult. However, the period of the US global leadership either has already ended or it will end in the near future depending on how that leadership is defined. The US elite are in disarray regarding decisions on how to spend limited resources – whether to erect a wall on the Mexican border or to develop military capacity to match rivals China and Russia (Sonne and Harris, 2018).

There are many possibilities for the next period. One possibility is a new world system with strong global actors including US, EU, China and India. But among these powers China might have much more power than others. The Chinese economy became the largest economy based on purchasing power parity in 2014. It is expected to be the largest in nominal prices during next decade and China is expected to be number one in wealth during the 2030s when India's economy is expected to catch up to the size of the US economy (pwc.com, 2017).

If we witness another big recession due to the current financial bubble it may also mean the end of liberal capitalism. According to Forbes, currently four of the top ten global corporations are Chinese state banks (Forbes.com, 2018). During the most recent recession China and India were affected the least. Even though they promote capitalist development in manufacturing and service sectors, they regulate and control their finance sector by state banks. For more than a thousand years Chinese bureaucracies have maintained a tradition of controlling capitalist development and preventing it if they think it could be a threat to the Chinese economy or state power. On the other hand, elites of Western countries have started to realize that they don't benefit from globalization anymore. The Trump administration has already started implementing a reversal of globalization by restricting imports and other state interventions. The US might be forced to implement measures such as universal basic income to reduce social tensions as well.

The Heritage of Domination

In short there is a high probability that states will play a more crucial role to maintain current domination forms; states may become the main driving force to change the balance of different domination forms in favour of themselves. I think the concept of the heritage of domination is useful in understanding relationships between different domination forms. During the nineteenth century, revolutionary thinkers tried to explain social relationships based on class domination, as class struggle was mainly determining these relationships at that time. Then all other types of social domination and the idea of domination over nature became critical to understanding social contradictions in the twentieth century.

Social ecology provides a strong framework with which to explain how the legacy of domination and the legacy of freedom played their roles throughout history and brought humanity into the current social and ecological crisis. However, since capitalism and Western powers were so dominant in determining social change during the twentieth century, the focus was mostly on capitalism, even though social ecology advocates the end of all hierarchies and all types of domination to create a free society. We may need to change that focus to the State in the near future if state domination prevails over capitalism.

Murray Bookchin (1982, p. 95) elaborates state domination:

> The State is not merely a constellation of bureaucratic and coercive institutions. It is also a state of mind, an instilled mentality for ordering reality. Accordingly, the State has a long history—not only institutionally but also psychologically. Apart from dramatic invasions in which

conquering peoples either completely subdue or virtually annihilate the conquered, the State evolves in gradations, often coming to rest during its overall historical development in such highly incomplete or hybridized forms that its boundaries are almost impossible to fix in strictly political terms. ...Its capacity to rule by brute force has always been limited. The myth of a purely coercive, omnipresent State is a fiction that has served the state machinery all too well by creating a sense of awe and powerlessness in the oppressed that ends in social quietism. Without a high degree of cooperation from even the most victimized classes of society such as chattel slaves and serfs, its authority would eventually dissipate. Awe and apathy in the face of State power are the products of social conditioning that renders this very power possible.

The evolution of the State, Bookchin explained, will not stop and the State seems to increasingly manipulate the economy while developing tools to enhance the cooperation between the State and lower classes of population.

Historically, social theories have concentrated on European states, which were formed during cycles of capitalist accumulation with strong allegiance to merchants and bankers. These states became capitalist nation-states at the end of those state-making processes. However, states all over the world have been formed in a variety of ways during decolonization in the twentieth century. Also cultural differences have made crucial differences in the evolution of the State in different countries. If we compare the oldest civilizations, states first emerged in Mesopotamia and Egypt more than five thousand years ago. These two civilizations had hierarchical social structures, leaving remnants of big temples and palaces. However there is no evidence that similar buildings were constructed during Indus Valley civilization despite the fact that they built larger cities with better designs and more advanced water and sewage systems. Archaeologists haven't yet found any evidence of kings or military organizations or indications of a hierarchical social organization in the Indus Valley. Some Indian scholars suggest that it could have been a democratic society, even though their writings haven't been deciphered (Mayank and Nisha, 2011). It seems that the State emerged in India not as a result of internal social dynamics, but was imposed by outsiders, namely Aryan invaders. Also, there is no correlation between the level of civilization and the hierarchical structure of a society. Eventually, the native people of India accepted the imposed institutions, but Jainism and Buddhism—which were against the Aryan's religion and the class system it brought—could have been influenced by their earlier civilization, and may have been part of their culture, yet surfaced in a different form.

The evolution of the State in China was very different, too. It seems that states emerged during the second millennium BCE—with a gap of more than one thousand years between the oldest states, which had different characteristics. The first kings presented themselves as a God, or representative of God, to legitimize their rule. However, in China the legitimacy of the king or emperor was based on a mandate of heaven (or cosmos). They did not need to be a noble to gain that mandate, but if they ignored the welfare of the masses, or if a natural disaster caused widespread misery, the people might assume that he had lost the mandate of heaven. In such cases rebellion was seen as legitimate. This pressure on emperors to be just led to periods when land was distributed to peasants equally (it was very common during the period of the Warring States). Also, local rebellions were monitored and taken seriously by rulers. The Chinese State has evolved with its own authoritarianism and rationality over more than two thousand years.

The Axial Age and Later Developments

The Axial Age is defined as the period between 800 and 200 BCE in which the main religions and philosophies were shaped throughout Eurasia. Before this period great empires collapsed and small kingdoms and states began fighting each other. As opposed to the times when empires lasted for long periods, there was uncertainty and insecurity during the Axial Age. As a result, many scholars started to think about the meaning of life and how to deal with uncertainties. Then very different new ways of thinking appeared (Graeber, 2011). We can compare these developments in three regions where the oldest civilizations emerged.

In the region of the Middle East/Europe both the first monotheistic religion and rational thinking appeared in Axial age. Greek democracy emerged based on ethics developed by rational reasoning, while Judaism was being shaped in the Middle East. Greek civilization attained peak achievements in many areas. However, even though the Macedonian and Roman empires later helped spread Greek culture throughout most of Europe and the Middle East, the core ideas of Greek civilization—democracy and ethics—disappeared. Instead, the Roman Empire adopted Christianity as its official religion well after the Axial Age. Philosophy was suppressed in favour of monotheistic thought. Romans ransacked Greek cities taking writings and sculptures to Rome, sometimes killing or enslaving Greek philosophers and artists. They used the engineering knowledge of Greeks and copied their architecture and aesthetics. On the other hand, emperor Jovian in 363 CE burned the Royal Library of Antioch as well as the temple since there were pagan writings there. At the end there was no continuity in Greek ideals. Those ideals, such as democracy and ethical society resurfaced as part of the heritage of freedom about two thousand years after direct democracy was destroyed in Greece. Europe was under religious dogmatism until the seventeenth century while philosophy and science were being developed in other parts of Eurasia.

In India both Hinduism and Buddhism appeared during the Axial Age. Basic concepts of Hinduism were defined in the Upanishads written in this age. However, this philosophy has been adopted in a variety of different ways. Eventually polytheistic forms of Hinduism became dominant in India. Even though Buddhism shares some of the concepts with the Upanishads, there is no worshiping of any God in Buddhism. It teaches that "man can gain deliverance from suffering by his own efforts" (Accesstoinsight.org, 1995). During the late Axial Age, the Maurya Dynasty ruled almost all of the Indian subcontinent. Ashoka was the grandson of the founder of the Maurya Dynasty and he became a Buddhist after a bloody war to conquest Kalinga about 263 BCE. That war converted him to a stable and peaceful emperor as a result of the sorrow and regret he felt. He became a patron of Buddhism until he died in 232 BCE. He left a legacy of peaceful ruling in harmony and diversity based on ethics he wrote in his edicts. These edicts included banning animal sacrifice and elimination of meat eating on many holidays. But this legacy did not provide a way of self-defence for people in India, nor could it prevent development of the caste system. The history of India has been mostly the history of foreign invasions by nomadic nations or imperialists, which were catastrophically worse than the former.

The Axial Age in China was the period of small kingdoms or states. Those states were consolidated into seven main states by 476 BCE. Then the Warring States period started. This was also a legalist period in which a realistic consolidation of the wealth and power of autocrats and the State was emphasized while ignoring morality and the goal of an ideal rule. On the other hand, Confucius developed a philosophy based on secular morality. His rationality was mostly applied to the conduct of state rule by an elite as opposed to the Greek rationality of rule by the people. Confucian ideas presumed that human nature is potentially good. Rituals and self-cultivation provide a means to attain that potential. He emphasized leading by virtue rather than enforcing by law. Confucianism became the philosophy of most dynasties during Chinese history starting with the Han Dynasty (206 BCE–220 CE) at the end of the Axial Age. Starting in 136 BCE the Han Dynasty sponsored Confucianism and encouraged nominees for office to receive a Confucian-based education. During the Han Dynasty the total number of bureaucrats employed by central and local governments was estimated to be more than 130,000 in 5 BCE (Keay, 2009).

Confucian studies were heavily influenced by Daoism and Buddhism after the Han Dynasty. Then during the Sui (581–618) and Tang dynasties (618–907), Buddhism became widespread and supported by the emperors. However, it was crushed between 843 and 848 BCE when Buddhist temples had accumulated most of the available gold, silver and copper as statuary while the government was not able to find enough precious metals to mint coins. At the end, superstitious and mystical elements of Taoism and Buddhism were eliminated from Confucian studies and the new orthodoxy emerged in the 11th century as Neo-Confucianism. Also in the Tang dynasty, the examination system superseded the apprentice/nomination alternative, and was formally institutionalised by the Song emperors to recruit officers in the years 960–1279 (Watson, 2006). The number of candidates taking officer exams in the thirteenth century reached 400,000.

China in the Twenty-First Century

The Chinese state has evolved in continuity over three millennia. Its huge bureaucracy has historical experience controlling the spread of religion and capital accumulation, and mobilizing people for a variety of goals such as education, agricultural projects, and war. We shouldn't expect that such a state would become a capitalist state. On the contrary, such a state with its own traditions of protecting its interests may shape capitalism into a new form by using its own rationalism.

Murray Bookchin (1982, p. 127) warned us about state power: "Like the market, the State knows no limits; it can easily become a self-generating and self-expanding force for its own sake, the institutional form in which domination for the sake of domination acquires palpability."

China had a "century of humiliation" between the mid-nineteenth and mid-twentieth centuries, starting with the Opium Wars and the invasion by European states, and then by Japan. Now China is regaining confidence under Chinese Communist Party (CCP) rule, as John Osburg (2013:, p.822) explained:

> In many ways, the financial crisis of 2008 gave the Chinese leadership even more confidence in the superiority of their form of state-managed authoritarian capitalism to the laissez-faire capitalism of the United States. In the most basic terms, the CCP hopes to maintain the embeddedness of the market in state structures that it controls in order to ensure that the market is harnessed to serve political goals, such as fostering indigenous innovation, maintaining social stability, and preserving CCP rule (not to mention the unstated goal of enriching elite families). As China has become less reliant on foreign investment in recent years, it has been able to more assertively promote and protect its own companies and interests, much to the annoyance of the Global North. ...Despite the fact that many SOE (state-owned enterprises) are publicly traded in overseas stock markets, the Chinese state is still the majority shareholder in these companies, which are overseen by the State-owned Assets Supervision and Administration Commission of the State Council (SASAC). Their CEOs are appointed by the CCP's Organization Department, the same bureau that appoints all other CCP officials. They control all industries deemed of strategic and national importance: steel, petrochemicals, transportation, utilities, and virtually all banking and financial institutions.

Apparently the Chinese state seeks "domination for the sake of domination" and also revanche for the century of humiliation.

The Strength of the Chinese State Model

The early twenty-first century witnessed a historical transition—the failure of the world hegemony project by the US and the rising power of "emerging markets." This transition can be interpreted in many other ways as well: the revival of Asian states from the destruction of colonization in the nineteenth century; the re-emergence of China after a century of humiliation and taking over its previous role as the largest producer and innovator of the world; the rising old superpower of Russia after the collapse of "real-socialism" during the 1990s; or all of them at the same time. But one aspect of this transition is clear: homogenization of the world by globalization is over. Quite to the contrary, cultural differences are becoming more effective in shaping the new world order. China doesn't compromise when it comes to state domination of the economy and India didn't compromise on protecting small farmers during the Bali and Doha rounds of WTO discussions, even the country permits large agricultural projects.

Also, for example, Bookchin (1982, p. 139) commented that: "The legacy of domination thus culminates in the growing together of the State and society—and with it, a dissolution of the family, community, mutual aid, and social commitment." But, generally, this doesn't apply to Asian societies with their gregarious culture. Confucian authority of parents in the family is still common in China and the CCP is using Confucian ideas to strengthen its authority. The fact that 88.4 per cent of marriages in India are arranged by parents shows how family ties are still strong there.

The capitalist nation-states of Europe evolved from weak kingdoms in the periphery when the production centres of the world were in Asia. Europe didn't have much to sell to Asia in exchange for tea, spices, silk, porcelain and other luxuries at that time. These states had few choices to accumulate power other than developing military technologies and expanding their overseas colonies, which they plundered. In the end, an irrational capitalism dominated Europe since there was no strong State with an ethical tradition. On the other hand, the State has evolved in China for over four thousand years. Confucian traditions have provided this state an authoritarian rationalism with a secular ethic. Today China not only provides a model to other states in the developing world, but also finances most of the projects in those countries. Eventually that model may affect capitalism in developed countries as well. It is hard to predict how it would manifest itself, but we can see some trends as President Trump advocates protectionist policies for the US. However, in the long run an authoritarian rationalism may become more dominant.

A New State Theory for the Struggles to Come

Neoliberal capitalism destroys safety nets in society, increases inequality and makes people more atomized by increasing competition for jobs. On the other hand it makes the balance between society and nature more fragile as it relentlessly destroys nature. However, all these irrational developments may eventually cause the collapse of modern society—the existence of humanity is seriously threatened. An authoritarian rational state may ease these policies and make capitalism a less urgent existential threat to humanity, presenting itself as a solution to such a threat.

The heritage of domination needs to provide some hope to make people's lives better. Currently neoliberal capitalism claims that new technologies, such as driverless cars or artificial intelligence, will make life easier. But they will only increase the profit of corporations while people will experience the same difficulties. On the other side of the world hundreds of millions of people were lifted out of extreme poverty as a result of the CCP's policies, and new reforms are on agenda in order provide more people with safety nets. During the nineteenth National Congress of the CCP, President Xi Jinping said, "What we now face is the contradiction between unbalanced and inadequate development and the people's ever-growing needs for a better life" (Chinadaily.com.cn, 2017). This definition of the new era shows that the CCP will follow more rational policies while strengthening its authoritarian power.

In the end, a struggle for freedom against such a rational State poses a much more difficult challenge than a struggle against an irrational capitalism. Current state theories that include only developments in the region of the Middle East/Europe will be of limited use for this challenge. These theories assume that states in other civilization centres would evolve in the same way. But the current reality doesn't show any evidence in that direction. Therefore, I think a new state theory that elaborates the differences in the evolution of states and the possibilities for the role of the State in the near future is crucial as we prepare ourselves for new struggles against the kinds of hierarchies and domination we will face in the future.

This theory should help the Left to understand and foresee how authoritarian states have evolved and are likely to evolve and influence other states in the future. Such a theory would be crucial for the Left to prepare itself for struggles in the upcoming political environment. Moreover, it would provide a perspective such that class reductionism does not blind the Left when it is becoming ever more critical to fight against domination by the State, so that we might all live in a society free from all forms of oppression.

References

Accesstoinsight.org 1995. *Buddhism in a Nutshell, Access to Insight.* [Online]. [Accessed 25 January 2017]. Available from: http://www.accesstoinsight.org/lib/authors/narada/nutshell.html

Arrighi, G. 2007. *Adam Smith in Beijing.* London, New York: Verso.

Bookchin, M. 1982. *Ecology of Freedom.* Palo Alto, CA: Cheshire.

Chinadaily.com.cn 2017. "Principal Contradiction Facing Chinese Society Has Evolved in New Era: Xi" [Online]. [Accessed 25 January 2017]. Available from: http://www.chinadaily.com.cn/china/19thcpcnationalcongress/2017-10/18/content_33401026.htm

Forbes.com 2018. The World's Largest Public Companies. *Forbes* [Online]. [Accessed 25 March 2019]. Available from: https://www.forbes.com/global2000/list/#tab:overall

Graeber, D. 2011. *Debt: The First 5,000 Years.* New York: Mellville Publishing House.

Keay, J. 2009. *China: A History.* London: Harper Press.

Mayank N. V. and Nisha Y. 2011. Reconstructing the History of Harappan Civilization. *Social Evolution & History,* 10(2), pp.27-49.

Osburg, J. 2013. Global Capitalisms in Asia: Beyond State and Market in China, in *The Journal of Asian Studies,* 72(4), pp.813-829.

Pwc.com 2017. *The World in 2050, PwC Global.* [Online]. [Accessed 25 March 2019]Available from: https://www.pwc.com/gx/en/issues/economy/the-world-in-2050.html

Sonne, P. and Harris, S. 2018. U.S. military edge has eroded to 'a dangerous degree,' study for Congress finds. *Washington Post.* 14 Nov. [Accessed 25 March 2019]. [Online]. Available from: https://www.washingtonpost.com/world/national-security/us-military-edge-has-eroded-to-a-dangerous-degree-study-for-congress-finds/2018/11/13/ea83fd96-e7bc-11e8-bd89-eecf3b178206_story.html?utm_term=.9196dd6746e6

Watson, P. 2006. *Ideas.* New: Harper Perennial.

Direct Democracy, Social Ecology, and Public Time

Alexandros Schismenos

One could argue that since the dawn of modernity, humanity has been in a situation of constant crisis. Today we find ourselves amidst a nexus of crises: an economic crisis, a political crisis, and an ecological and anthropological crisis where both the human and natural environments are threatened. The privatization of public time and space, under the false identification of public with state, transforms social geography and the public architecture of life. We are also witnessing a rapid transformation of national politics under the grid of transnational networks of power, combined with a revival of nationalistic rhetoric as a means for manipulating populations.

In order to clarify the current crisis—a *crisis of significations*—it may be useful to delimit, schematically, some areas of its manifestation. I use the term "significations" in the Castoriadean sense, namely, the "pre-eminent element in and through which the social-historical unfolds" (Castoriadis, 1997, p. 201), which includes the dominant norms, purposes and attitudes that characterize a specific society. The purpose of this article is to correlate central aspects of the crisis of established significations in order to highlight the opportunities for social emancipation that emerge through collective forms of direct democracy inspired by social ecology that create a free public time. I use the term "public time" as defined by Cornelius Castoriadis, as the "dimension where the collectivity can inspect its own past as the result of its own actions, and where an indeterminate future opens up as domain for its own activities" (Castoriadis, 1997, p. 281).

My main point is that the creation of a free public time implies the creation of a democratic collective inspired by the project of social ecology. The first and second parts of this article focus on the modern social phenomena correlated to the general crisis and the emergence of the Internet Age (Castells, 2012). The third and fourth parts focus on new significations that seem to inspire modern social movements and the challenges that modern democratic ecological collectivities face. I use the term "social ecology" as defined by Murray Bookchin: "Social ecology is based on the conviction that nearly all of our present ecological problems originate in deep-seated social problems" (Bookchin, 2006, p. 19). And I use the term "democracy" exclusively in the original, true meaning, of direct democracy where society is self-governed by the equal participation of every individual to political decisions and functions, as opposed to a modern representative democracy or republic, where political decisions rest in the hands of an oligarchy. In this sense, a truly democratic political collectivity is a truly ecological collectivity and vice versa.

Aspects of the Global Crisis of Significations

The globalization of power and market mechanisms has spread the net of bureaucratic capitalism across the globe and stretched it to its limits, both internally and externally. Internally, because capitalism waives the requirement to provide a coherent meaning for the populations it dominates. It deregulates processes that are necessary for social cohesion, and ensures a psychical internalization of norms for the purposes of the system among the majority.

Externally, because the capitalist political and economic system, which was never actually controlled or regulated, is unable to fulfil both its general purpose, namely the unlimited dominance of rationalistic control and capital growth, and the specific purposes of elites and trusts that constitute the power network of globalized bureaucratic capitalism. A fraction of this network was revealed in the Panama papers imbroglio (Obermayer and Obermaier, 2016).

The system has approached its natural limit as available resources, both environmental and human, appear close to exhaustion. Besides capitalism's unlimited ambition, there is a destruction limit onto the brink of which we walk blindfolded—the brink of natural disaster, environmental disaster, social disaster, and even nuclear disaster. The whole range of nightmares and dystopias stand like potential realities before us.

The core values of Western societies have been reduced to the capitalist irrationality of economic growth. Formerly prosperous civilizations have been subdued by imperialism, their cultures destroyed by the advance of colonization and capitalization. Both the inner collapse of communal and social values within Western societies and the external destruction of other communities and cultures have resulted in a modern society that is incapable of creating social significations that constitute a positive common meaning towards a positive common future. Ultimately, this process has undermined the foundations of social belonging and identification, producing a world where the only value afforded any kind of worth is monetary. Money in itself is only a measure of value and, in this sense, is actually valueless.

The most recent and visible aspect of this multifaceted crisis of significations is the economic crisis associated with the burst of the subprime mortgage bubble in 2008. However, this process actually began in the 1970s during the OPEC oil crisis, which saw the surrender of North American labour unions and the launch of Reagan and Thatcher's neoliberal doctrine. The main feature of this doctrine was the triumph of closed interest groups that promoted a version of capitalism even more predatory than the New Deal or the European social-democratic versions of post-war capitalism—those at least had provided some degree of social security measures. State authorities swiftly and voluntarily abolished financial regulation tools that formally kept multinational private capital in check. Society also adopted the "Shock Doctrine", which Friedman characterized as modern capitalism's core tactic for the subjugation of societies and the dismantlement of labour (in Klein, 2007, p. 6).

The construction of huge megacities smothered the urban public space under a network of commercial zones. The basis of societal cohesion, the spirit of community, withered away. When community between people vanishes, the communal bond between nature and society is also shattered. The privatization of urban public space began under what can be described as a false conflation of the public and the State. As Murray Bookchin understood, it was a consequence of the failure of collective initiatives that had "stagnated as moribund relics of an era washed away by the social reaction of the 1990s, or regrettably, [had] become purely privatized" (Bookchin, 1995).

The implementation of these policies fundamentally altered the social geography and the public architecture of the city. Major cities became dense population hubs with energy demands in excess of the levels formerly required by entire countries. Inner-city landscapes became divided into three discrete zones with exploitative relations—housing blocks for the majority, mansions for the dominant elites, and ghetto jungles for marginalized minorities. A vast network of markets divides and at the same time connects these isolated zones under the circulation of products. As cities expand, the foundations of community and the conditions for democracy narrow, transforming cities into hives of private cells where circulation replaces community.

The transformation of cities into zoned areas of product circulation stems from the expansive capitalist imagination of the Industrial Revolution. The phenomenon of modern urbanization is distinct from the development of cities as independent political entities—for example, just as urbanization had occurred in late Medieval Italy. Modern urbanization transforms urban communities into production and distribution hubs with little consideration for public human life and public social space.

Alongside the destruction of public social space and community, there has been large-scale destruction of the natural environment. The destruction of nature that began with the dawn of industrial capitalism has led to the current ecological crisis whose effects are evident in an undeniably emphatic way. There is no need to argue here for what everyone knows and witnesses in the perturbation of natural processes, extreme meteorological phenomena, and mass extinction of species. Scientists recently attributed the term Anthropocene (Carrington, 2016) to the period since the Industrial Revolution, elevating modern human activity to the level of geological forces.

These two types of crisis, economic and ecological, constitute a broader crisis of significations that includes the social, cultural and anthropological (Castoriadis, 1982). In the sense that the misguided signification of unlimited growth has made a desert of the human environment itself, and in the sense that it seeks to dominate the totality of society, it has accelerated desertification on both the natural and the cultural dimension. The system has failed to legitimize its core impetus for growth, creating a hollow meaning that is reducible to bottom-line profitability.

In my opinion, the full implementation of the growth doctrine seems to be hindered by three main factors:

1) the exhaustion of natural resources;
2) the collective resistance of communities and the psychic resistance of individuals who create new, global networks of sociality at a time when traditional institutions are being dismantled; and
3) the fundamental contradiction within capitalism itself, which objectifies people while its function is based precisely on the exploitation of human ingenuity.

To the extent that the economic motivation of unlimited growth and profitability remains the dominant imaginary signification, the tension between systemic pursuits and the rapid self-destruction brought about by their achievement has resulted in a field of constant reproduction of the crisis.

Currently, the abandonment by the State, not only of financial regulations, but also of social services, deprives it of any social rooting. As a result, while a nationalistic propaganda still pervades all modes of discourse from entertainment to politics, the real strength of the Nation-State is declining. A globalised economy transfers power to international institutions, which help elites bypass national constraints. At the same time the use of a nationalistic rhetoric keeps populations under control within those constraints.

This blurs the precise borders between countries, as the distinction between interior and exterior liquidates, while war fronts multiply. Modern warfare and the rise of "anti-terror" campaigns creates new borders within societies, within cities, and across countries. At the same time, there are signs of a deep corrosion of republican representative politics, revealing the ever-present divide of interests and sentiments between society and the State. The Trumpian degradation of US politics signifies something by signifying nothingness, the representative void.

The decline of nation-state power is indicated not only by the enforcement of austerity by organizations like the IMF, the World Bank, and the European Central Bank on countries like Argentina and Greece,[1] but also by the emergence of secessionist movements that have emerged in response to international politics (e.g. Cataluña). The local has become inextricably linked with the global. Societies are both local and global in the sense that everything that happens locally is projected globally, and what is displayed globally is diffused locally. There is no detached place since information has the ability to exceed geographical boundaries and spatial limitations, while satellites map every corner of the planet. When ecological or social disasters are viewed and felt around the world, a consciousness of global interdependency seems to be formed in terms of either common despair or common solidarity.

Murray Bookchin warned us that "unless we realize that the present market society, structured around the brutally competitive imperative of "grow or die", is a thoroughly impersonal, self-operating mechanism, we will falsely tend to blame other phenomena—such as technology or population growth—for growing environmental dislocations" (Bookchin, 2006, p. 20). Consequently, the project of ecology cannot be separated from the project of social transformation; social ecology thus implies a need to emphasise social equality and democracy.

In conclusion, it is obvious that the different aspects of the global crisis of our time are interlinked by the main social imaginary impetus of capitalist globalization, which is expansive growth and total exploitation of human and natural resources. The crisis is self-generated by the expansion of the capitalist system inwards and outwards. As this expansion reaches the limits of the human and natural environments, the political character of the problem cannot be concealed, nor can its ecological ramifications. The values of human liberation and natural balance remain interlinked with the principles of direct democracy and social ecology, which provide the conceptual framework of a different way of societal life.

The Problems of the Internet Age

We live in the first period in history when the urban population exceeds the rural. At the same time the city, as a political and social entity and unity, is being dismantled. It is being rebuilt into a set of segregated functions, with respect to public space and public time. Likewise, personal time is sliced into distinct occupations defined by production or consumption. Public time is also sliced into "zones of leisure" and "zones of labour", both of which are exploited for profit. Commodities of leisure are presented as common values while the vast majority of humanity is excluded from leisure and commodities. The division of wealth, exploitation of both workers and the unemployed, and the gap between privileged elites and excluded populations are now at the widest and deepest points in history.

Within the current socioeconomic landscape the emergence of the internet has brought a new field of projection and reconstruction of public and personal identities, enabling almost infinite possibilities. The digital person—fragmentary, but at the same time a multiplicity of representations of the natural person—brings forth a new problematic of the individual's relation to themselves and to society. It offers a worldwide surface for the reflection, projection, and re-creation of personal preferences and views, in a completely disembodied and virtual manner.

On one hand, the internet seems to provide a medium for even deeper personal fragmentation and isolation. Online, the user is at the same time invulnerable and vulnerable. Invulnerable as a digital self materially detached from its physical existence, vulnerable as a physical/psychical subjectivity with a social identity embedded in the broader social environment. The digital self is a patchwork of images, preferences, comments, trends, and contacts—a conscious reconstruction of the individual projected onto a virtual global public platform. Social cohesion of the personal image, which was formerly dependent on the natural presence of the individual, dissolves within the digital multiplicity of pseudo-personas. Personal identity loses its original foundation, the social significance of the individual's consistency as a singular, actual personality.

On the other hand, the internet, as a medium for direct and simultaneous global communication, has demonstrated many liberating capabilities: disseminating knowledge, socializing research, communicating societies, overcoming censorship, and overcoming ethnic and cultural exclusions. Although it has become an instrument of widespread control, it is also a tool for widespread solidarity and the emergence of new social movements (Castells, 2012). For the first time there is a global public time within a virtual space.

This global temporality that has formed in and through the internet is at the same time synchronic and diachronic. Nevertheless, it is not in accordance to social time, which is essentially local. Direct accessibility flattens the critical significance of information within its continuous flow, where information sets can be articulated into pseudo-narratives, and where the quantity of information ultimately constitutes the quality of meaning, however absurd. The fundamental properties of the Internet—speed and condensation—express precisely this principle of expansion through contraction.

Without a common criterion of value or truth, which is offered in the non-digital world—at least partially—by the social-historical reality and the real limitations imposed by society as the "objective" world (in the sense that it transcends subjectivity) or by "nature", the only criterion of value that remains is *popularity*.

At the same time, every marginal idea, whether radical and liberating or reactionary and obscurantist, now shares an ability of propagation previously limited to the dominant discourse. Every individual or group now shares, at least in theory, the same potential public audience—the whole of digital humanity. Without a mechanism for proof of validity, validity is gained and lost through the flow of information itself. New online funding tools, such as crowdfunding, are widely visible to the public and offer money for projects that would otherwise be hopeless or even non-existent. This visible public surface seems unlimited in range, but is actually limited in scope as the majority of the Internet lies within unsearchable areas called the "Deep Web", which includes the "Dark Web", where black market economies flourish.

In sum, the internet has created new challenges for direct democracy, but one should always keep in mind that a precondition for democracy is a community that exists in relation to its natural environment—antithetical to the Internet. The emergence of new significations of global solidarity, liberated knowledge and free community has been augmented by the Internet, but in fact needs to take place in actual social reality.

The Emergence of New Significations

The twenty-first century has, thus far, been marked by financial crises, the implementation of neoliberal policies on a supranational level, the ascension of international financial organizations to a central decision-making level, the violent dissolution of local communities, and the fragmentation of public time. However, this corrosion has been met with successive revolts, the awakening of a universal solidarity and resistance, the creation of imaginary communities, and the spreading of the concept of the commons. The anti-globalism movement, the Occupy Movement, the movement of the Kurdish people in Rojava, and the Zapatistas movement as the first groups to use the internet as a means of global solidarity, are all examples of the dynamic struggle for autonomy and democracy. Although the outcome of these movements and social conflicts remains uncertain, the rise of the internet has meant they are now performed for a global audience with variable levels of involvement. Meanwhile, what is at stake is the future itself in the most comprehensive sense—the existence of a future.

Against every manifestation of a given crisis, new possibilities open, new significations emerge, and the values of solidarity and community are revived on a broader scale. They emerge within a radical political context, into forms of self-governed communities that aspire to direct democracy.

What is apparent in recent years is a multifaceted resistance of societies. A resistance formulated not in terms of electoral representation, but in terms of direct democracy, within communal forms of life. The refutation of sovereign institutions becomes even more obvious, by the positive activity of social movements, by the creation of primary institutions of direct democracy, social solidarity and local self-government, to some extent, like the aforementioned Zapatista communities, the Kurdish horizontal assemblies and, temporarily, the occupied factories in Argentina and Greece (VIO.ME in Thessaloniki). The VIO.ME factory was occupied by its workers in 2011, who decided not only to self-manage their working space, but to transform it into a space of democratic cooperation and political decision. A columnist of *The Guardian* described VIO.ME thus:

> For a start, no one is boss. There is no hierarchy, and everyone is on the same wage. Factories traditionally work according to a production-line model, where each person does one- or two-minute tasks all day, every day: you fit the screen, I fix the protector, she boxes up the iPhone. Here, everyone gathers at 7am for a mud-black Greek coffee and a chat about what needs to be done. Only then are the day's tasks divvied up. And, yes, they each take turns to clean the toilets. (Chakraborttya, 2017)

We should also note that the VIO.ME workers organized open assemblies with the local community, solidarity actions to immigrants and ecological movements. Most importantly they have criticized not only the structure of labour, but also the product itself. VIO.ME have decided against chemical products and now produce eco-friendly soap and cleaning products.

Against such examples of social movements organizing themselves using methods of direct democracy, the crisis of political representation and identity has largely manifested itself as a revival of nationalistic rhetoric. Still, global networks of solidarity challenge the validity of official borders, forming nodes of free social space and free collectivities that challenge the jurisdiction of the State.

Fukuyama's doctrine of the "end of history" (1992) is a symptom of the crisis of the association of public time with subjective temporality—a crisis of our relation to the past and the future, a loss of the future and a levelling of the past. Yet, social struggles and social movements can create new forms of free public time and an opening to a common future. A new ecological consciousness has arisen—democratic, anti-authoritarian, and connected to the environment. Pro-environmental protests and political struggles, such as the US anti-pipeline movement in Dakota and the anti-gold movement in Chalkidiki, Greece, provide the seeds for a new *sensus communis*, a new sense of common good and humanity.

We are also witnessing the emergence of new social movements, unrelated to traditional trade unions or parties, which do not seek to implement ready-made plans but to create a new open free public space and time. Besides the aforementioned movements, such urban grassroots networks are present not only in Western countries, but in many other parts of the world, including South America, Africa, East Asia, and Central/Eastern Europe.

These are movements without leaders—movements that seem fragmented, but which allow for the creation of free networks and mutual complementary structures on many fields and places within the broader social-historical narrative, precisely because they have a common project and create a common meaning. That is, self-governing direct democracy without authoritative power, without party representatives, and without state officials.

And this indicates a different answer to both the crisis of political representation, and to the identity crisis of the individual who finds it difficult to identify with national state mechanisms. This is not because propaganda is insufficient, or because there is access to a wider world, but because these mechanisms themselves have been exposed to signify nothing except empty automations deprived of their original meaning and their old vision.

Democratic ecological movements redefine private and public relations in the sense that they create a free public space that belongs neither to private capital nor to the State. And this implies a free public time of social interaction and political decision, like the *Nuit debout* movement—symbolically expressed by the creation of a prolonged month of March, and a significant example of the correlation between public time and political action.

The Political Significance of Public Time

Following major protests on 31 March 2016, against proposed labour legislation and the subsequent loss of workers' rights, the Nuit debout movement flooded the squares of French cities. The manifold manifestations of this movement can be seen as a symbolic act with deep political connotations. The people who participated in the movement defied the official calendar by counting the days of March beyond 31, renaming 1 April as *32 March*, 2 April as *33 March*, and so on. This new "Martian" revolutionary calendar echoed the proclamation of Year 1, and the replacement of the official calendar, by the revolutionaries of 1792. The renunciation of the official calendar, however theatrical, is a French revolutionary tradition. It is a public gesture that exposes the deep dependence of authorities upon an established social temporality, both daily and historical.

By symbolically deregulating the official calendar, the movement defined itself as a historical event and widened its temporal horizon with the proclamation of a different social temporality. This symbolic expression liberated public space and created a common public time. Of course, this was never going to be enough to radically bend the established domination or derail the dynamics of regularity, but it reveals a certain autonomy and self-consciousness of the movement as a creator of its own free public time.

If one looks to the past, one can find many examples that underline the close dependence of political time on public space. Each society is structured in three realms: (1) the private sphere; (2) the private/public (i.e. the sphere of communication and culture); and (3) the purely public sphere—the field of political decision-making. In societies where political power lies within a state hierarchy, public functions, both cultural and political, are subordinate to state power and private space–time becomes contracted and isolated.

The division of the day into equal hours is not natural (since the length of a natural day varies), but was an achievement of the monastic movement based on the needs of common prayer (division of the day into equal 3-hour periods). It was also the first disciplinary normality imposed on social temporality and the first attempt to measure time, regardless of the social activities of rural life (Landes, 1983). The bell tower became the regulator of public time, while public space was restricted to ecclesiastical courtyards.

When political power was transferred to the cities in the late Middle Ages, at the time of the invention of the mechanical clock (around the thirteenth century), the new symbol of public time first appeared on the towers of the rulers, as power leaned towards the secular sphere. The mechanical clock bridged the feudal and proto-capitalist worlds.

Industrial organization required more accurate measures, while time units were diminished to picoseconds (10^{-12} seconds). The dominance of economic activities over other social functions, the dominance of the capitalist imaginary, and the primacy of production transformed social life in terms of functionality. Conflict between the State and society meant conflict over public time and public space.

The mechanical watch, when it became a portable pocket or wrist watch did not mean an inconceivable personalization of social time, but the colonization of personal time by regulatory mechanisms that already organized productive public time.

The recent neoliberal attack on nature and society marks the concession of state-managed public space to private capital, granting its full privatization. It also signifies the transformation of private time in terms of productivity, since the equation of time with money, a fundamental principle of capitalist production, is rooted in the equation of the user with the product. The globalization of information and product circulation organizes the regulation of private time on a global level, under a variable but unified timetable of financial procedures.

On the other hand, the global diffusion of information produces cracks in the dominant social temporality and regularity, offering opportunities for the creation of social networks beyond the dominant constraints. Under these conditions political time becomes "dense", and seems to expand and contract depending on the social occupation and recreation of free public space.

But the social background of modern human existence—the urban landscape of megacities—is a problem in itself. The modern city is not an ancient democratic polis, but rather, as Aristotle would claim, *Babylon.* Modern collectivities create, within the urban network, new and free egalitarian social spaces, like Nosotros in Athens or Micropolis in Thessaloniki. They are self-managed and open to anybody, hosting a wide range of social and self-educational activities. They utilise a form of direct democracy at the levels of individual participation and collective decision-making. Nosotros was founded in Athens in 2005, in the centre of

Exarcheia, by an anti-authoritarian initiative, while Micropolis was founded in Thessaloniki in 2008 amidst the December riots. Both are based on principles of direct democracy, equality, and actual creative participation.

Since their inception, a constellation of free social places have emerged in other neighbourhoods and in smaller Greek towns such as Ioannina, Larisa, and Komotini. They form a network of political, social and cultural activities without any exclusions or separations. Seeds of new democratic forms of life, perhaps, but against the dominant paradigm they face tremendous pressure and depend upon remaining open to the broader society. They alter the social landscape of the city through their activities. These are not self-referential, but refer to society, interacting with and acting on the city. They embody the project of a democratic ecological society, albeit in a limited but inspiring manner, both by their activities and their presence, which depend on individuals interacting with mutual respect for one another.

Democratic ecological collectivities, which explicitly combine the project of social ecology with the project of direct democracy, must move beyond the collegial and create institutions of education and communication marked by cohesive political activity across a wider social-historical field. We may, perhaps, schematically designate four moments of political time to autonomous collectivities. They all involve and presuppose a public conflict with established authorities.

The first moment, when the collectivity first opens up to society, involves the initial creation of a broader social environment. The creation of free social spaces seems to be the limit of this moment. If this limit is not exceeded through connection with broader society, free social spaces can become self-referential and, sooner or later, collapse internally.

If this limit is exceeded, then we proceed to the next moment, which can only occur within society—that is, beyond the collective since the activity of the collectivity exceeds the collectivity itself. It involves the co-creation of networks of solidarity, communication and action on local, regional and global scales. It involves the creation of free open public spaces. It means creating a limited public space–time for communication and a limited public space–time for political decisions.

Opening a free public space presupposes a break with state and capitalist mechanisms. It is an initial step. The second step is explicit self-determination to enact institution-building through direct democracy and public deliberation, in order to realize autonomy in terms of social functions and a complete rupture with the State. I use the word "autonomy" not in reference to the Italian "*autonomia*" or to the Kantian concept, but as defined by Castoriadis: "the self-positing of a norm, starting from some content of effective life and in relation to this content" (Castoriadis, 1997, p. 401). In this sense, social autonomy is direct democracy as it is essentially linked to the autonomy of the individual and enabling society to create its own institutions.

We can imagine explicit self-determination if we consider a self-sufficient local network that is not subject to state or capitalist taxation or oversight. It constitutes a fundamental division between free communities and the State. However, it is not yet an autonomous society until a complete public space is established along with a public time for free communication, yet with limited public space–time for political decision-making.

In order for social autonomy to be realized, society must have the power to explicitly re-create its central institutions, namely politics, justice, and education, in a democratic and egalitarian manner. The people, as free individuals, must be able to establish laws by means of open public deliberation and through the establishment of direct democracy. This would presuppose abolishment of the State and subordination of the economy to democratic politics. But it also presupposes the psychical transformation of the individual to an autonomous, reflective and deliberative subjectivity. It presupposes a democratic education that cannot be separated from the experience of direct democracy in practice, via a praxis of autonomy. It also means establishing a complete public space and time for free communication, and a complete public space and time for political decision and action.

Back in 1969, Ecology Action East—a collective that included Murray Bookchin—published a statement that asserted, "We hope for a revolution which will produce politically independent communities whose boundaries and populations will be defined by a new ecological consciousness." It is now evident that this ecological consciousness is also a political consciousness that demands a self-reflecting direct democracy against hierarchy and economic growth— one that combines ecological and social struggles within the project of building a democratic ecological society. Under the global threat of disaster, this is the challenge facing communities and societies today; for the future remains, as always, open for societies themselves to determine.

References

Bookchin, M. 2006. *Social Ecology and Communalism*. Oakland: AK Press.
Bookchin, M. 1995. *Comments on the International Social Ecology Network Gathering and the "Deep Social Ecology" of John Clark*. [Online] [Accessed 25 March 2019]. Available from:
http://dwardmac.pitzer.edu/anarchist_archives/bookchin/clark.html
Carrington, D. 2016. The Anthropocene epoch: Scientists declare dawn of human-influenced age. *The Guardian*. 29 August.
Castells, M. 2012. *Networks of Rage and Hope: Social Movements in the Internet Age*. Cambridge: Polity Press.
Castoriadis, C. 1982. The Crisis of Western Societies. *Telos*, 53, 17-28.

Castoriadis, C. 1997. *The Castoriadis Reader.* London: Blackwell .

Chakrabortty, A. 2017. How could we cope if capitalism failed? Ask 26 Greek factory workers. In: *The Guardian.* 18 July 2017. [Online] [Accessed 25 March 2019]. Available from: https://www.theguardian.com/commentisfree/2017/jul/18/cope-capitalism-failed-factory-workers-greek-workplace-control

Ecology Action East 1969. *The Power to Destroy, the Power to Create.* [Online]. [Accessed 25 March 2019]. Available from: https://rioprarua.noblogs.org/files/2015/05/1969-Power-to-Destroy.pdf

Fukuyama, F. 1992. *The End of History and the Last Man.* New York: Free Press.

Klein, N. 2007. *The Shock Doctrine: The Rise of Disaster Capitalism.* New York: Picador.

Landes, D.S. 1983. *Revolution in Time.* Massachusetts: Harvard University Press.

Obermayer, B. and Obemaier, Fr. 2016. *The Panama Papers.* New York: Oneworld Publications.

Notes:

1 In Greece, austerity measures were imposed by a Troika comprised of the IMF, the ECT and the Eurogroup, the unelected assembly of EU Ministers of Finance.

The Present is Pregnant with a New Future
Olli Tammilehto

A key focus in social ecology has been the bringing about of profound societal change. This has been thought to mean a period of groundwork after
which there would be a rapid revolutionary transition. Social movements,
especially in cities, are seen as agents of change to a decisively more democratic and ecological society. This article contributes to an understanding of
the dynamics of major societal shifts and the role of movements. It develops a theory of a pre-existing world—a "shadow society"—which enables
societal transition, and makes a "societal phase shift" possible.

The first section of this article sketches out western thinking about
gradual versus abrupt change in nature and society. The following section
describes historical and recent instances of abrupt social change. The third
section introduces the concepts of "shadow society" and "shadow personality" and delineates how they help to understand the dynamics of societal
phase shift. The fourth section outlines how abrupt changes have been
theorized in biology and asks if this theory can be applied to society and
how it relates to the theory based on shadow society. The last section examines the implication of the societal phase shift perspective for social
movements and their strategies.

Gradual versus Abrupt Change in Western Thought
The paradigm of gradual change has been very influential in western
thought. In this view, real change only happens little by little (Brinkmann,
1974; Scoville, 2017). To force abrupt change is dangerous. Since Aristotle's
time the principle "nature does not make jumps" (in Latin, "*natura non facit
saltus*") has been widely accepted in natural philosophy (Franklin, 1986).

Also in social and political philosophy, and in social sciences, gradualism
and its variation, reformism, have been popular. Social evolution has usually
been interpreted as occurring bit by bit, in contrast to the notion of revolutionary change. Revolutions are considered to be normal in technology, but
not in society. Technological revolutions are thought to come about because
of the inner logic of scientific research and market competition. They are
something to which society and people must just adapt. However, according
to the cultural lag hypothesis, social structures follow technical change only
gradually (see e.g. Wilterdink and Form, 2009). On the other hand, if social
revolutions occur, they are doomed to fail. Since the French Revolution, the
phrase "the revolution devours its children"[1] has been repeated frequently.

After the revolts of 1968 and after the postmodern turn, it has been
common to think that even aspirations to a revolutionary change are
inherently dangerous. They contain a totalizing view on society which—if

the movement in question is successful—is bound to lead to a totalitarian state (see e.g. Best and Kellner, 1997).

Yet, as a matter of fact, even nature does make jumps. This is most obvious in phase shifts. For example, ice turns into water at 0°C without any intermediate stage. Ice does not become softer and only then liquid. There is a clear-cut jump in the constitution of H_2O.[2]

Leaps also take place at the macro scale. For example, a clear shallow lake can abruptly become turbid or muddy, even though the flow of nutrients to the lake has been constant for a long time (see e.g. Scheffer et al., 2001). Also, the global bio-geophysical system has experienced many rapid shifts during its aeons. A geological period may end and a new one begin very rapidly—even in just one year (see e.g. Masson-Delmotte et al., 2013). Human-induced climate change may also leap to a new state in the near future (e.g. due to the disappearance of the summer ice sheet in the Arctic). Such jumps can be expected to produce catastrophic consequences (see e.g. Collins et al., 2013). Thus, gradual change is only one possible pattern exhibited by nature.

Abrupt Social Changes in the Past and Present

Rapid and extensive social changes are also common as a consequence of wars, collapses of stock exchanges, etc. Yet, societies usually remain structurally the same after such changes. Therefore, you cannot speak about a societal phase shift or a change in the basic functioning of society. However, in some cases, local or wider society may abruptly alter course through a fundamental change.

When an earthquake, destructive flood or other natural disaster destroys the physical infrastructure of a locality, it also knocks down social hierarchies and market relations. However, according to many empirical studies, social chaos or general panic does not usually ensue. Only elites panic because they lose their power (Solnit, 2009; Quarantelli, 2001; Clarke and Chess, 2008). The rest of the population immediately organizes itself horizontally; they form grassroots rescue teams and arrange food, shelter, and other support for survivors (Solnit, 2009; Fritz, 1996; Stallings and Quarantelli, 1985). Thus, new egalitarian social structures arise in a moment.

Fundamental structural changes also happen during social revolutions or insurrections. In the Finnish language "revolution" is *vallankumous*, which literally means abolishing power (in the sense of domination). This gets close to what often has really happened in the first stages of historical revolutions. Various hierarchies and many kinds of domination (power over) dissolves. In their place, councils, factory committees, assembles and other entities pursuing direct democracy are created. These organizations certainly have a lot of power or capability to get things done co-operatively, but power over or domination is severely restricted. Unfortunately, this stage usually only lasts a short time, and old domination structures are restored or new ones created (Bookchin, 1996; Bookchin, 1998; Foran, 2002).

Many examples of such grassroots organization during revolutions include the following:

- sectional assemblies of the French Revolution in 1790–1793 (Bookchin, 1996; Tønnesson, 1988);

- factory committees, city and district councils, village assemblies and soldiers' councils flourishing in Russia from February until October 1917, maintained until the Bolsheviks consolidated their power (Voline, 1990; Brinton, 1975; Bookchin, 2004);

- the 2,100 councils established in 12 days during the Hungarian revolution of 1956 before the Soviet invasion destroyed these councils (Gutiérrez, 2004; Arendt, 1958; Kosuth, 2007);

- shoras (workers' councils) during Iranian revolution of 1978 (Landy, 1981);

- neighbourhood and workplace assemblies during and after the economic crisis that hit Argentina in 2001 (Sitrin, 2012; Fifth Estate, 2002); and

- the network of communes and councils which were put together in 2011, the development of which currently continues in Rojava, northern Syria (Knapp et al., 2016; Strangers in a Tangled Wilderness, 2015).

Thus, as in nature, gradual change is only one of the ways that society modifies itself. In certain situations abrupt structural changes can occur in societies.

Shadow Society and Abrupt Change

How is it possible for society to change abruptly? One explanation is that society is never a fully integrated whole. In any society there are always conflicts, fractures and undercurrents. These are so widespread that you can speak about the *shadow society* that exists side-by-side the official society.[3]

An essential part of the shadow society is the *shadow economy*. It comprises the production and distribution of goods and service that are not recognized in the official economy, and thus not usually taken into account when calculating Gross National Product (see e.g. Bennholdt-Thomsen and Mies, 1999; Gibson-Graham, 2006). This economic field is referred to by many terms with partially overlapping meanings: unofficial, informal, social, autonomous, post-capitalist, expolary, community, solidarity, subsistence, traditional, unregistered, indigenous, underground, family, black, grey, lumpenbourgeois, or third sector (Shanin, 1999). Examples include: unpaid service production in households; unofficial exchanges of goods and services among friends, acquaintances and neighbours; and unpaid peer support in solving various technical problems. The shadow economy is huge, especially in poor countries, but even in western Europe it is about as big as the official economy when measured in working hours (Stiglitz et al., 2009 p. 127).

The shadow economy has been conceptualized in terms of flows— production, distribution and consumption—as is common in economic discourse. However, it can also be perceived in terms of reserves or accu- mulated resources. From this perspective it is easy to see that both the official and shadow economies are based on resources that are neither paid for nor included in economic calculations. Part of this *common wealth* is hu- man-made, such as our cultural heritage. Most of these reserves are, however, created by nature over millennia and aeons. When a resource is taken care of by a local, regional or global community, we can speak of a *commons*. Commons play an essential role in the shadow economy and many popular movements have risen to defend them against encroachment by the capitalist economy (see e.g. Bollier and Helfrich, 2012; Berkes, 1989).

These movements belong to a large body of social movements that at- tempt to create and change the rules under which they live.[4] They are important political actors. Yet political discourse usually ignores these actors and keeps silent about them. Accordingly, there exists a kind of *shadow polity* alongside the shadow economy. A part of this shadow polity includes their internal decision-making processes. In many cases, these processes try to prefigure democratic decision-making in a hoped-for future society (Day, 2005; Graeber, 2013). In situations where open movements or social action groups are too hard or impossible to organize, the shadow polity takes the form of an invisible resistance, which can include loitering, disobedience and sabotage. These kind of activities have been widespread in peasant so- cieties and in state-socialist—a.k.a. state-capitalistic—countries (Scott, 1985; Filtzer, 1996; Kopstein, 1996).

The shadow society carries on the traditions of countless movements, and former less hierarchic and more democratic societies that attempted to turn the course of history. Bookchin calls this important history "the legacy of freedom", knowledge of which can lessen control of the future[5] by the powers-that-be (1982). The use of the concept of "democratic civilisation" by the imprisoned Kurdish leader, Abdullah Öcalan, has similar meaning (see Öcalan, 2016).

Human beings are social creatures and, as such, social conditions are re- flected at the individual level. Like society, hardly any human mind or personality is a fully integrated whole. In different social circumstances we think and react differently and make different value judgements. This idea has been common during recent decades in post-structural thought: in dif- ferent discourses the same person takes different subject positions (see e.g.

Foucault, 1982; Henriques et al., 1984). Also, it has been widespread in Buddhist philosophy (see e.g. Kvaløy, 1992). Yet, the idea of the normality of a mildly divided self has appeared occasionally also in mainstream western philosophy ever since Aristotle. It appears whenever the phenomena of self-deception and weakness of will or *akrasia* (Aristotle, 1925 bk. VII; Rorty, 1988) are discussed.

Accordingly, we can speak about a *shadow personality* that manifests itself when people act in a shadow society. We can include with it many traits that are repressed in present social circumstances. They exist only as desires and dreams, often only on a subconscious level.[6] This sphere of the unfulfilled and subliminal constitutes a hidden potentiality in any human being.

We can now put forward an explanation for rapid and profound societal change: In natural or human-caused disasters and revolutions all the functions of the prevailing society weaken or stop working altogether. This side of society moves to the background. At the same time the repressed, under-used or underestimated functions of shadow society become essential. The other side of society gets stronger and moves to the fore. The roles of these social spheres are swapped. The same happens on an individual level: the shadow personality comes to the fore and the former normal personality must go by the wayside.

Yet if the new situation stabilizes it is conceivable that in the new shadow society qualitative changes will occur. It no longer only represents the former dominant society but, in part of it, develops seeds and seedlings of new social forms ready to come to the fore in the next societal phase shift. The process of social change may have a dialectical character, as many thinkers have proposed (see e.g. Marx, 1996; Bookchin, 1990; Bhaskar, 1993).

In a sense, the theory of shadow society is a generalization or extension of the theory of dual power in social ecology (Bookchin, 2000; Biehl, 1998, pp. 123–124). Dual power theory deals with the best case scenario, where social movements have been able to organize a strong counter-power based on a confederation of municipalities before any societal phase shift. This has not proved the case in most historical revolutions—most organization occurs during and after the shift. The theory of a shadow society tries to explain why the shift was, and will be, possible in these bad cases.

Regime Shift Theory in Biology and its Relevance to Society

We could simply leave our pursuit of understanding abrupt social change at this. However, it would be good to develop a more nuanced picture of societal phase shift, especially of the social dynamics during periods of approaching rapid change. Therefore, it might be useful to look at how rapid structural changes are understood in biology, and attempt to apply those ideas to society.

In ecology, *regime shift theory* has been popular during recent decades. It developed from complexity theory, which originated in mathematics as a description of non-linear systems. Complexity research tries to understand how complex systems exhibit simple, system-wide behaviour.

A regime is a certain behaviour pattern or an oscillation range of an ecosystem. Regime shift theory tries to understand, on the one hand, how a certain regime is maintained or why normally the variability of the system is within certain bounds and, on the other hand, how a rapid shift to another regime is possible (Scheffer and Carpenter, 2003; Stockholm Resilience Centre, 2015)

The key is the existence of negative and positive feedback mechanisms or loops. These exist where the "output" of the system has an effect on its "input". Negative feedbacks maintain a system in its present regime. For example, when an influx of nutrients increases the amount of turbidity causing algae in a lake, the number of daphnia (small plankton animals) that eat them also increases and the clear-watered regime is maintained.

Positive feedbacks, instead, try to move the system to a different regime. For example, a small increase in turbidity kills some big water plants that protect daphnia. Fish then catch daphnia more easily, allowing algae to grow. The following turbidity increase kills more plants, which means that more daphnia get caught—causing more turbidity, and so on (Scheffer and van Nes, 2007; Jeppsen, 1998).

In normal circumstances, negative feedback loops dominate and the regime is preserved. Yet, in situations where the system reaches a tipping point, negative feedbacks may weaken and/or positive feedbacks may become so strong that the system rapidly moves to another regime.

Could this model be applied to society? What were the feedbacks that maintain the present order or try to change it? We could categorise as negative feedbacks all processes that gain strength when social order is endangered. For example, when a social change movement grows, there are attempts to undermine its influence by two opposite processes. On the one hand, a part of the movement is marginalized by labelling it violent and extremist, something from which ordinary people should keep at a distance. On the other hand, another part of the movement is integrated into the powers-that-be. It then seems that the movement proper is no longer needed because it has gained representation in the power structures (Mathiesen, 1982; Neocosmos, 2018).

Positive feedbacks, on the other hand, could be conceptualised as processes that potentially get stronger when the present order is challenged. For example, a social movement may encourage new people to join a movement or form new ones. A stronger and more versatile movement scene may encourage still more people to join, and so on. The same applies to many other things that happen in the shadow society. For instance, experiences in the shadow economy may provoke thoughts about alternatives, delegitimizing the prevailing order, and stimulating other activities in the shadow society, and so on.

One could further adapt the language and evidence of regime shift and complexity theory, but the scope of this essay is limited. Complexity theory forms part of systems theory, to which Bookchin and many other thinkers maintained an aversion because of its mechanistic approach (Bookchin, 1990 p. 149). Such an aversion is justified in regard to much of system discourse. However, complexity research goes beyond mechanistic models and tries to understand entities with memory, history, evolution and "revolutions" (Ernst, 2009; Ramalingam, 2013 p. 142). In fact, it has much common with dialectical thinking (Ernst, 2009).

Nevertheless, complexity theory uses many of the same concepts as the rest of the systems approach, such as feedback loops. This is a significant problem if it results in forgetting the uniqueness of life and human society. One solution is to take some relevant ideas from regime shift theory but reformulate them. For example "positive feedback loop" could be called "self-reinforcing social process" and "negative feedback" could be called "self-attenuating social process".

Societal Phase Shift and Social Movements

So, what is the relevance of all of this? If this theory of shadow society helps to adequately explain abrupt social changes, what are the consequences?

First of all, this view can provide hope in our seemingly hopeless situation. Climate change, biodiversity loss, and other dangerous trends will lead to a global catastrophe if they are not stopped soon (see e.g. Steffen et al., 2015). It is easy to see that the reasons for inaction are the structures of our society. Yet, social change is usually thought to be very slow. This contradiction creates hopelessness. Therefore, seeing that, in principle at least, society can change very rapidly brings hope.

However, within this chain of thoughts lurks a danger. It can create a complacent attitude. Our analysis shows that revolution happens anyway. We don't have to do anything—just wait and relax. This would be a wrong conclusion: the counter currents or positive feedback loops upon which societal phase shifts or revolutions are based are precisely our activities. If we are not active, counter currents will be too weak and there won't be any revolution or, if it starts, it will fail quickly.

Although this analysis does not weaken the importance of movements and alternative projects, it provides another perspective for them. Making a systemic change in society is not building a new society one block at a time. Movements and projects cannot do it because no one knows which of their achievements will remain, and under present circumstances it is probable that many of them will falter. Instead, a reason why these activities are important is that they defend the existing shadow society and prefigure what society should and could be after a phase shift. Another reason is that they advance and work out processes—which can be called positive feedbacks—that, when a suitable situation arises, shift society to another phase. In other words, they can contribute to a revolution.

So far, in societal phase shifts, the "grassroots regime" has lasted only a short period of time. There are many reasons for the restoration of the hierarchical order. Outside pressure or even war has enforced their return. But often inside forces play an important role. For example, in the Russian revolution Lenin, Trotsky and the Bolshevik party were instrumental in suffocating the grassroots democratic institutions that sprang up all over the country in 1917 (Bookchin, 2004; Brinton, 1975).

For many it is difficult to believe that the grassroots democratic regime is the real thing upon which a future society could be built. They think that this is just a party after which the party takes over and surpasses the "inefficient" grassroots structures. Indeed, real democracy is very different from the present governance with its hierarchical structures.

However, for most people it is not so strange because, in its embryonic form, it has been widely exercised in the shadow society. Keeping in mind the utter destruction and misery caused by the existing order and the bleak or non-existent future it is promising us, one may wonder if we are under a spell of some sort when we regard the predominant form of society as normal. Perhaps the feeling that this is normal and there are no alternatives is an effect of the distorted mirror that the prevailing society and its cultural machinery keeps in front of us. Shadow society and its blossoming in crisis situations may show us a more adequate image of what we are, and what future society could be.

References

Arendt, H. 1958. Totalitarian Imperialism: Reflections on the Hungarian Revolution. *J Polit.* 20(1), pp.5-43.

Aristotle 1925. *The Nicomachean Ethics of Aristotle.* Oxford: Oxford University Press.

Baumeister, B. and Negator, Z. 2005. *Situationistische Revolutionstheorie, Eine Aneignung, Vol. I: Enchiridion.* Stuttgart: Schmetterling Verlag.

Bennholdt-Thomsen, V. and Mies, M. 1999. *The Subsistence Perspective, Beyond the Globalized Economy.* London: Zed Books.

Berkes, F. ed. 1989. *Common Property Resources, Ecology and Community-Based Sustainable Development.* London: Belhaven.

Best, S. and Kellner, D. 1997. *The Postmodern Turn.* New York: Guilford Press.

Bhaskar, R. 1993. *Dialectic, The Pulse of Freedom.* London: Verso.

Biehl, J. 1998. *The Politics of Social Ecology, Libertarian municipalism*. Montreal: Black Rose Books.

Bollier, D. and Helfrich, S. eds. 2012. *The Wealth of the Commons: A World Beyond Market and State*. Amherst, Massachusetts: Levellers Press.

Bookchin, M. 1982. *The Ecology of Freedom, The Emergence and Dissolution of Hierarchy*. Palo Alto: Cheshire.

Bookchin, M. 1990. *The Philosophy of Social Ecology, Essays on Dialectical Naturalism*. Montréal: Black Rose Books.

Bookchin, M. 1996. *The Third Revolution: Popular Movements in the Revolutionary Era, Volume 1*. London: Cassell.

Bookchin, M. 1998. *The Third Revolution: Popular Movements in the Revolutionary Era, Volume 2*. London: Cassell.

Bookchin, M. 2004. *The Third Revolution: Popular Movements in the Revolutionary Era, Volume 3*. London: Continuum.

Bookchin, M. 2000. Thoughts on Libertarian Municipalism. *Left Green Perspectives*. [Online]. 41. [Accessed 13 March 2018]. Available from: http://social-ecology.org/wp/1999/08/thoughts-on-libertarian-municipalism/

Brinkmann, H. 1974. Gradualism. In: Ritter, J. ed. *Historisches Wörterbuch der Philosophie, Band 3*. Basel: Schwabe & Co.

Brinton, M. 1975. *The Bolsheviks & Workers' Control 1917 to 1921, The State and Counter-Revolution*. Detroit: Black & Red.

Clarke, L. and Chess, C. 2008. Elites and Panic: More to Fear than Fear Itself. *Social Forces*. [Online]. 87(2), pp.993-1014. [Accessed 25 March 2019]. Available from: http://sf.oxfordjournals.org/content/87/2/993.abstract

Collins, M., Knutti, R., Arblaster, J., Dufresne, J. L., Fichefet, T., Friedlingstein, P., Gao, X., Gutowski, W.J., Johns, T., Krinner, G., Shongwe, M., Tebaldi, C., Weaver, A.J. and Wehner, M. 2013. Long-term Climate Change: Projections, Commitments and Irreversibility. In: Stocker, T. F. Qin, D. Plattner, G.-K. et al. eds. *Climate Change 2013: The Physical Science Basis. Contribution of Working Group I to the Fifth Assessment Report of the Intergovernmental Panel on Climate Change* [Online]. [Accessed 25 March 2019]. Cambridge University Press, pp.1029-1136. Available from: www.climatechange2013.org

Complex Systems Group 2015. *Amorphous materials*. [Online]. [Accessed 10 October 2017]. Available from: http://web.physics.ucsb.edu/~complex/research/amorphous.html

Day, R.J.F. 2005. *Gramsci is Dead, Anarchist Currents in the Newest Social Movements*. London: Pluto Press.

De Angelis, M. 2007. *The Beginning of History, Value Struggles and Global Capital*. London: Pluto Press.

Ernst, G. 2009. *Komplexität, 'Chaostheorie' und die Linke*. Stuttgart: Schmetterling Verlag.

Fifth Estate 2002. Que se vayan todos! — Out with them all!: Argentina's Popular Rebellion. *Fifth Estate.* [Online]. 359. [Accessed 10 October 2017]. Available from: http://theanarchistlibrary.org/library/various-authors-que-se-vayan-todos-out-with-them-all-argentina-s-popular-rebellion

Filtzer, D. 1996. Labor Discipline, the Use of Work Time, and the Decline of the Soviet System, 1928–1991. *International Labor and Working-Class History.* [Online]. 50, pp.9-28. [Accessed 10 October 2017]. Available from: http://libcom.org/history/labor-discipline-decline-soviet-system-don-filtzer

Foran, J. ed. 2002. *The Future of Revolutions, Rethinking Radical Change in the Age of Globalization.* London: Zed.

Foucault, M. 1982. The Subject and Power. In: Dreyfus H.L. and Rabinow, P. eds. *Michel Foucault: Beyond Structuralism and Hermeneutics.* Chigaco: The University of Chigaco Press, pp.208-228.

Franklin, J. 1986. Aristotle on Species Variation. *Philosophy.* [Online]. 61(236), pp.245-252. [Accessed 22 September 2018]. Available from: https://www.cambridge.org/core/journals/philosophy/article/aristotle-on-species-variation/B456B714693BF058D6EA3029C02FD0AD

Fritz, C.E. 1996. *Disasters and Mental Health: Therapeutic principles drawn from disaster studies.* [Online]. [Accessed 22 September 2017]. Available from: http://udspace.udel.edu/bitstream/handle/19716/1325/HCpercent2010.pdf

Gibson-Graham, J.K. 2006. *A Postcapitalist Politics.* Minneapolis: University of Minnesota Press.

Graeber, D. 2013. *The Democracy Project, A History, a Crisis, a Movement.* London: Penguin Books.

Gutiérrez, J.J.G. 2004. Hungarian Revolution and Workers Councils. In: *St. James Encyclopedia of Labor History Worldwide, Vol. 1.* Detroit: St. James Press, pp.440-443.

Henriques, J., Hollway, W., Urwin, C., Venn, C. and Walkerdine, V. 1984. *Changing the Subject, Psychology, social regulation and subjectivity.* London: Methuen.

Heywood, A. 2013. *Politics.* Basingstoke, Hampshire: Palgrave Macmillan.

Jeppsen, E. 1998. *The Ecology of Shallow Lakes, Trophic Interaction in the Pelagial.* [Online]. Silkeborg: National Environmental Research Institute. [Accessed 22 September 2017]. Available from: http://www2.dmu.dk/1_viden/2_Publikationer/3_fagrapporter/rapporter/FR247.pdf

Knapp, M., Flach, A. and Ayboga, E. eds. 2016. *Revolution in Rojava, Democratic Autonomy and Women's Liberation in Syrian Kurdistan.* London: Pluto Press.

Kopstein, J. 1996. Chipping Away at the State: Workers' Resistance and the Demise of East Germany. *World Polit.* [Online]. 48(3), pp.391-423.

[Accessed 22 September 2018]. Available from:
http://libcom.org/history/workers-resistance-demise-east-germany-jeffrey-kopstein.

Kosuth, D. 2007. Revolution in a "workers' state". *Int Social Rev.* [Online]. (51). Available from: http://isreview.org/issues/51/hungary1956.shtml

Kvaløy, S. 1992. Complexity and time—Breaking the pyramid's reign In *Wisdom and the Open Air, The Norwegian Roots of Deep Ecology.* Minnesota: University of Minnesota Press.

Landy, S. 1981. Iran: Revolution, War and Counterrevolution. *Socialist Voice.* [Online]. (14). [Accessed 22 September 2017]. Available from: https://www.marxists.org/history/etol/newspape/socialistvoice/iran11.html.

Marx, K. 1996. *Capital, Volume One, The Process of Production of Capital.* [Online]. Marx/Engels Internet Archive. [Accessed 22 September 2018]. Available from:
https://marxists.catbull.com/archive/marx/works/cw/volume35/index.htm

Masson-Delmotte, V., Schulz, M. and Abe-Ouchi, A. 2013. Information from Paleoclimate Archives. In: Stocker, T. F. Qin, D. Plattner, G.-K. et al. eds. *Climate Change 2013: The Physical Science Basis. Contribution of Working Group I to the Fifth Assessment Report of the Intergovernmental Panel on Climate Change.* [Online]. Cambridge University Press, pp.383-464. [Accessed 22 September 2018]. Available from: www.climatechange2013.org

Mathiesen, T. 1982. *Makt og Motmakt.* Drammen: Pax.

Neocosmos, M. 2018. Thinking freedom: Achieving the impossible collectively, Interview with Michael Neocosmos. In: Buxton, N. and Eade, D. eds. *State of Power, 2018 edition.* [Online]. Amsterdam: Transnational Institute, pp.33-48. [Accessed 22 September 2018]. Available from: https://www.tni.org/files/publication-downloads/tni-stateofpower2018-webversion.pdf

Öcalan, A. 2016. *Democratic Nation*[Online]. Cologne: International Initiative Edition. [Online]. [Accessed 22 September 2018]. Available from: http://www.ocalan-books.com/downloads/en-brochure-democratic-nation_2017.pdf

Orwell, G. 1955. *Nineteen eighty-four: a novel*Repr. London: Secker & Warburg.

du Pan, J.M. 1793. *Considerations sur la nature de la revolution de France.* [Online]. London: Emm. Flon. [Accessed 5 October 2017]. Available from: https://ia601204.us.archive.org/13/items/bub_gb_yIA8AAAAcAAJ/bub_gb_yIA8AAAAcAAJ.pdf

Quarantelli, E.L. 2001. Panic, Sociology of. *International Encyclopedia of the Social & Behavioral Sciences.* [Online]. Pergamon, Oxford, pp.11020-11023. [Accessed 22 September 2018]. Available from: http://www.sciencedirect.com/science/article/pii/B0080430767018672

Ramalingam, B. 2013. *Aid on the Edge of Chaos: Rethinking international cooperation in a complex world.* Oxford: Oxford University Press.

Rorty, A.O. 1988. Self-deception, akrasia and irrationality. In: J. Elster, ed. *The Multiple Self.* Cambridge: Cambridge University Press.

Scheffer, M., Carpenter, S., Foley, J.A., Folke, C. and Walker, B. 2001. Catastrophic shifts in ecosystems. *Nature.* [Online]. 413(6856), pp.591-596. [Accessed 22 September 2018]. Available from: http://dx.doi.org/10.1038/35098000

Scheffer, M. and Carpenter, S.R. 2003. Catastrophic regime shifts in ecosystems: linking theory to observation. *Trends in Ecology & Evolution.* [Online]. 18(12), pp.648-656. [Accessed 22 September 2018]. Available from: http://www.sciencedirect.com/science/article/pii/S0169534703002787

Scheffer, M. and van Nes, E.H. 2007. Shallow lakes theory revisited: various alternative regimes driven by climate, nutrients, depth and lake size. In: *Shallow Lakes in a Changing World, Developments in Hydrobiology, Vol. 196.* [Online]. Developments in Hydrobiology. Springer Netherlands, pp.455-466. [Accessed 22 September 2018]. Available from: http://dx.doi.org/10.1007/978-1-4020-6399-2_41

Scott, J.C. 1985. *Weapons of the Weak, Everyday Forms of Peasant Resistance.* New Haven: Yale University Press.

Scoville, H. 2017. Gradualism vs. Punctuated Equilibrium. *ThoughtCo.* [Online]. [Accessed 6 March 2018]. Available from: https://www.thoughtco.com/gradualism-vs-punctuated-equilibrium-1224811

Shanin, T. 1999. Ekspoljarnye struktury i neformaljnaja ekonomika sovremennoj Rossija. In: *Neformaljnaja ekonomika, Rossija i mir.* Moscow: Logos, pp.11-32.

Sitrin, M.A. 2012. *Everyday Revolutions, Horizontalism and Autonomy in Argentina.* London: Zed.

Situationist International 1963. Ideologies, Classes, and the Domination of Nature. *Internationale Situationiste.* [Online]. (8). [Accessed 22 September 2018]. Available from: http://libcom.org/library/internationale-situationiste-8-article-6

Solnit, R. 2009. *A Paradise Built in Hell: The Extraordinary Communities That Arise in Disaster.* New York: Viking.

Stallings, R.A. and Quarantelli, E.L. 1985. Emergent Citizen Groups and Emergency Management. *Public Adm Rev.* [Online].45(Special), pp.93-100. [Accessed 22 September 2018]. Available from:

http://search.ebscohost.com/login.aspx?direct=true&db=ehh&AN=1199 7563&site=ehost-live&scope=site

Steffen, W., Richardson, K., Rockström, J., Cornell, S.E., Fetzer, I., Bennett, E.M., Biggs, R., Carpenter, S.R., de Vries, W., de Wit, C.A., Folke, C., Gerten, D., Heinke, J., Mace, G.M., Persson, L.M., Ramanathan, V., Reyers, B. and Sörlin, S. 2015. Planetary boundaries: Guiding human development on a changing planet. *Science*. [Online]. [Accessed 22 September 2018]. Available from: http://www.sciencemag.org/content/early/2015/01/14/science.1259855.abstract

Stiglitz, J.E., Sen, A. and Fitoussi, J. P. 2009. *Report by the Commission on the Measurement of Economic Performance and Social Progress*. [Online]. Paris: Commission on the Measurement of Economic Performance and Social Progress. [Accessed 22 September 2018]. Available from: http://www.stiglitz-sen-fitoussi.fr/documents/rapport_anglais.pdf

Stockholm Resilience Centre 2015. *Regime shifts*. [Online]. [Accessed 22 September 2018]. Available from: http://www.stockholmresilience.org/download/18.3e9bddec1373daf16fa438/1381790210379/Insights_regimeshifts_120111-2.pdf

Strangers in a Tangled Wilderness 2015. *A Small Key Can Open a Large Door: The Rojavan Revolution*. San Bernardino, California: Strangers in a Tangled Wilderness.

Tammilehto, O. 2010. Major Intentional Social Change as a Political Perspective. In: Martin, G. Houston, D., McLaren, P. and Suoranta, J. eds. *The Havoc of Capitalism: Publics, Pedagogies and Environmental Crisis*. Rotterdam; Boston: Sense Publishers, pp.195-206.

Tammilehto, O. 2012. On the Prospect of Preventing Global Climate Catastrophe due to Rapid Social Change. *Capitalism Nature Socialism*. [Online]. 23(1), pp.79-92. [Accessed 22 September 2018]. Available from: http://dx.doi.org/10.1080/10455752.2011.648842.

Tønnesson, K. 1988. La démocratie directe sous la Révolution française—la cas des districts et sections de Paris. In: *The French Revolution and the Creation of Modern Political Culture, Vol. 2, The Political Culture of the French Revolution*. Oxford: Pergamon, pp.295-308.

Voline 1990. *The Unknown Revolution*. [Online]. Montréal: Black Rose Books. [Accessed 22 September 2018]. Available from: http://www.ditext.com/voline/unknown.html.

Wilterdink, N. and Form, W. 2009. Social change. In: *Britannica Academic*. [Online]. Encyclopædia Britannica, Chicago. [Accessed 3 October 2017]. Available from: http://academic.eb.com/

Notes

1. Originally in French (du Pan, 1793 p. 80): "A l'exemple de Saturne, la révolution dévore ses enfants".
2. An abrupt change takes place if the solid is crystallized. Some solids—e.g. glass—are not crystallized and they turn into liquid gradually. These solids are called amorphous (see e.g. Complex Systems Group, 2015).
3. I have developed this thesis earlier in Tammilehto (2010; 2012). A similar theory is presented in De Angelis (2007).
4. Heywood, in his widely used textbook, defines "politics" as "the activity through which people make, preserve and amend the general rules under which they live" (Heywood, 2013 p. 2).
5. As George Orwell writes in his novel *Nineteen eighty-four*: "'Who controls the past,' ran the Party slogan, 'controls the future: who controls the present controls the past.'" (Orwell, 1955).
6. The situationists hinted at revolutionary desires that are repressed but exist in the subconscious (Baumeister and Negator, 2005, pp. 38–40; Situationist International, 1963).

PART 5:
WALKING WITH THE RIGHT TO THE CITY

Squatting as Claiming the Right to the City
Diana Bogado, Noel Manzano and Marta Solanas

Introduction
The phenomena of *squatting* and *occupying* currently constitute global methods of resisting the "neoliberal" dynamic of the global metropolis. We use the term *occupy* to refer to housing occupations that seek to guarantee shelter for populations without resources, and the term *squat* to allude to occupation processes that try to generate spaces for public meetings and political discussions. In Brazil and Spain, both kind of spaces push towards claiming social rights. Some essential similarities and differences between them will be described in this article.

The neoliberal city is built on a new form of "entrepreneurial" urban management, whose consequences are, among others, the accentuation of territorial segregation (Harvey, 2005, 2011). In the current global context, the action of civil society culminates in movements demanding the accomplishment not only of basic needs, but also the quality of urban life: the *right to the city* (Lefebvre, 1968). This right is under constant threat by the gradual imposition of financial interests in global cities (Sassen, 2001). However, insurgent social networks make possible to endorse local struggles on a global scale. Both local and global trends, occupying and squatting have been described together as a single phenomenon, a product of comparable economic and institutional processes, in both the global North and South (Aguilera and Smart, 2016). This essay presents the hypothesis that the similarities between occupying and squatting in Spanish and Brazilian metropolises are the counterpart to the homogeneous processes of transforming housing and the city into speculative objects (Rolnik, 2016; Harvey, 2005; 2011), with specific, but equivalent, popular reactions.

In recent years, significant success has been achieved by the public space *squatting* and *occupy* movements in both countries, in their struggles for the right to decent housing and to the city, but along different dimensions. In Spain, the so-called *15M movement*, starting in May 2011, contributed to the birth of the PAH,[1] the main housing movement in Spain. In Brazil, the demonstrations of June 2013, known as the *June Days*, began in Rio de Janeiro and spread throughout the country and other Latin American countries, inspiring a whole generation to engage in socio-political struggles. These movements represented key moments in each location, and a new cycle of social revindications, with significant political consequences and global impacts, and appeared related to the global wave of popular resistance movements that began in Tunisia (2010) and Egypt (2011) known as the *Arab Spring*, with further manifestations in Europe and Latin America. These movements also represented a variation of traditional occupational forms by occupying public spaces instead of buildings (Erensü, Karaman, 2017). Furthermore, they claimed shared roots—the struggle for fundamental urban rights.

Related to these, a process of legitimizing housing occupation occurred in a context of accelerated dispossession processes (Harvey, 2005), both in Spain and in Brazil. In this text, we will compare their similarities and differences, studying the explicitly political occupy and squatting movements.

Our purpose will be to contextualize the global transformations in housing and city rights, both in Brazil and Spain, relating them to "the era of finance" (Rolnik, 2016), and the occupying/squatting patterns that emerged as reaction to it.[2] In the context of financial capitalism, housing policies, housing complexes, public spaces and their idiosyncrasies become affected by the political process of financializing life. Public space becomes speculative and housing becomes a luxury item, transformed by speculation and gentrification, both in Brazil and in Spain, as a consequence of the commodification of cities for the global market (Rolnik, 2016). Such a management model leads to violations of civil rights, particularly with respect to the right to decent housing.[3] Precarious populations were expelled to the extreme metropolitan periphery, threatening the right to the city both in Rio de Janeiro and in Spain.

These urban changes lead us to address the following issues: How have cities threatened the popular classes in both countries by transforming the city to allow the attraction of international speculative capital? How have local populations reacted in order to maintain their rights to the city?

Methodological Frame

This article is based on the personal and activist experiences of its three authors, as well as on materials collected during their respective academic trajectories. The methodology includes direct and participant observation (Becker, 1993; Whyte, 1943), or *observant participation* (Wacquant, 2000) in the occupy and squatting movements. At the same time, militancy and research were carried out in occupations for the right to housing and to the city (Lefebvre, 2001) in Rio de Janeiro, Seville and Madrid. In addition, at various moments, over the last few years, free conversations and structured interviews were conducted in different "squats" as part of the master's and doctoral theses of the authors.

Diana Bogado's (2011) master's thesis was entitled *The Okupa movement: Resistance and autonomy in occupy buildings in central urban areas*. This text, written between Seville and Rio de Janeiro, comprises a theoretical analysis of occupying and squatting, using the existing literature and developing hypotheses linked to the experiences of the author-activist in squats and occupations in Brazil and Spain. She then wrote a Ph.D. thesis about the right to the city. The author participated in the 15M movement, in Spain, and in the demonstrations of June 2013 in Brazil, among other manifestations, and participated intensely in the fight against eviction and removal of the "favelas" in Rio de Janeiro from 2013 to 2016. The author built a museum of popular resistance with the community of the Vila Autódromo favela in Rio de Janeiro: The *Museu das Remoções* (Eviction Museum).

Noel Manzano's (2015) master's thesis in sociology was entitled *People without houses, houses without people: Urban financialisation and housing appropriation in the new Madrilenian periphery*. His research was carried out between Paris, Madrid, and Rio de Janeiro, and contains a strong empirical component based on a participative immersion in the social housing movements of Madrid, and 68 semi-structured interviews with urbanists, activists and members of informal occupations.

Marta Solanas' doctoral thesis, *Uruguayan housing cooperatives as a system of social production of habitat and neighborhood self-management*, examined the horizontal and self-organized forms of popular housing in Latin America, with fieldwork in Montevideo. This experience was put into practice in spaces such as the "Corrala Utopia" in Seville—a building occupied by squatters at the beginning of the Spanish economic crisis (2012–2014).

This article is born, therefore, from the crossroads of theoretical research, fieldwork, and transnational experiences on the right to the city of the three authors. The activism practice within social movements permitted the authors to observe the squats' dynamics, as well as enabling access for interviews. In an action-research process, practical actions constitute the initial provision of inputs, as well as a base with which to verify conclusions (Tripp, 2005). Dealing with the debate of subjectivity and objectivity, and also about the illusion of scientific neutrality, the path adopted is an exercise of objectification—not of objectivity—(Bourdieu, 1977), which does not treat reality as objective and admits that it can be treated as in search of objectification. In this way, the scientific principle upon which the methodology is grounded is not objectivity, but reflexivity. Our academic production is based on the theory of "ecology of knowledge" (Boaventura de Sousa Santos, 2010), which proposes the fusion of popular and scientific knowledge.

For this reflection we considered the everyday micro-processes that developed in the heart of the case studies, adopting them as key elements for understanding and explaining complex global macro-processes. We have considered squatting, and its logics, as spaces of struggle for the right to the city and conflict against neoliberal interests. This assessment was based on the regressive-progressive method, as designed by Lefebvre (1949, 1953, 1960, 1968), which allows for sketching the historicity of social processes, from a look at daily life and the spatialization of social dynamics (Lefebvre, 1991).

Our hypothesis is that the processes of exclusion— the consequence of market management of cities—generates new dynamics of struggle in social movements, and explains the plurality of forms of occupation and emerging squatting practices. In other words, new forms of entrepreneurial management and their impacts require the creative re-articulation of social movements, which subsequently leads to the emergence of different claims to the right to the city.

Financial Urban Management and the Right to the City in Brazil and Spain

The current era differs from other moments of the capitalist system lifecycle by some. unique characteristics related to economic and financial dynamics. During the last decades, urban life has been increasingly mediated by the consumption of urban life, turning relationships and spaces into spectacles (Debord, 1969) and pressing them into competition. Competitiveness is not only restricted to the sphere of individual relations; it also becomes the predominant hegemonic logic that justifies itself (Santos, 2011). Within this logic fit the cities—they compete among themselves to become more attractive.

Urban planning, theoretically responsible for providing basic infrastructure, is managed as a tool for transforming spaces into international showcases. The emergence of the entrepreneurial protagonist within the urban management landscape is determined by its direct relationship with international financial capital, highlighting the speed of business processes and the presence of authoritarianism by a *state of emergency* in the execution of measures that serve corporate interests (Agamben, 2005; Aguilera and Naredo, 2009).

In Brazil, the traditional context of the chronic housing deficit was aggravated by initiatives trying to position the Brazilian metropolis as a priority focus for speculative real estate investments: the organization of macro-events, mainly the 2014 World Football Cup and the 2016 Olympic Games. Commuting global capital into local real estate projects, the increase in real estate prices produced, as a consequence, an urban policy of "evictions",[4] which was undertaken in several informal urbanizations (favela), such as the famous "Vila Autodromo" of Rio de Janeiro (Bogado, 2017). Producing both an alarming increase in rates of eviction and expulsions of low-income families (Azevedo and Faulhaber, 2015), the gentrification of already built areas, such as the port area of Rio de Janeiro,[5] and the speculative construction of new buildings, which remain currently empty. This process was accompanied by a violent eviction policy to occupations and favelas.

In Spain, entry to the Eurozone in 2001 facilitated the raising of international capital and, as a result, the generation of a colossal real estate bubble. The national urban planning frame was transformed, deregulating the whole country by the national Land Law of 1997, which declared suitable to build on any land not specifically protected. In Madrid, the modification of the General Plan of Urban Planning, foresaw since 1995 the construction of new speculative neighborhoods and infrastructure, frequently (as in the Brazilian case) justified by unsuccessful applications to host the Olympic Games. Allowing local and regional housing companies, EMVS[6] and IVIMA,[7] to speculate on residential land prices.

The explosion of the real estate bubble, linked to the global subprime crisis in 2008, led to the privatization of a large part of social housing, and to a great number of evictions, producing a "housing emergency" (PAH, 2013) that remains today.

Faced with the rational use of housing, the massive non-payment of debts provoked a "promotion of high levels of indebtedness that reduced the whole populations to a condition of credit slavery" (Harvey 2005, p.173–174), thanks to the coercive mechanism of "mortgage evictions". At the "macro" level, various financial speculative mechanisms privileged the maintenance of empty houses in the whole country to increase market prices of real estate, forbidding their social use (Manzano, 2015). This contradiction was visible in the most part of Spanish cities by the presence of abandoned urbanizations and empty blocks (Observatorio Metropolitano, 2013) being illegally, but rightfully, used both by social housing movements and individuals as a shelter solution.

In Spain, the sudden arrival of global capital to the real estate market, and the further dramatic capital outflow produced a huge economic crisis, stopping social housing programs and accelerating asset accumulation through a dispossession process (Harvey, 2005). The absence of a public housing park for rent (Naredo, 2013) forced the use of empty buildings as a precarious alternative to social housing.

In Rio de Janeiro, the construction of the neoliberal city is characterized not only by the commercialization of urban territory, but by the absence of public power in the construction of adequate housing units, as well as the lack of distribution to those who really need them. Although in Brazil there are programs focused on social housing, they are not efficient due to a range of factors: the dramatic housing shortage; the existence of a large stock of empty buildings for speculation; abandonment of central areas by the State; tourism; gentrification; the absence of social housing in or close to the central areas (with employment opportunities); and real estate interests in areas earmarked for social housing. Entrepreneurial public management is responsible for intensifying the production of urban segregation, a situation that, when combined with the inefficiency of social housing programs, has led to a gradual increase in the occupation of idle buildings and informal constructions in the great metropolis (Bogado, 2011).

Squats and Occupations

Squatting and occupying, both in Spain and Brazil, are booming practices. Although originating from very different socioeconomic realities, the problems from rampant real estate speculation and the lack of public housing forces people to use empty buildings as a precarious alternative to social housing. The basic difference is that a *squat* is an empty building used as common space to claim social rights. We refer to *occupied buildings* as a practice with the direct purpose of using a building as a dwelling, and afterwards developing other claims.

These different forms of *occupation, squat* and *occupy,* are alternatives to access the use of space, and claim the right to housing and the right to the city. The phenomenon of occupation of empty buildings is the direct response to the reproduction of "exceptions" and lack of access caused by real estate speculation and urban sprawl in large metropolises. We consider occupying the public space as one more face of the *squat* and *occupy* movements. To illustrate it, we point out that the "reclaim the street" in London and the "Ocupa Minc", held in Rio de Janeiro in 2016, are demands that, besides the right to housing, presented guidelines on urban social rights and the rights to cities. All forms of occupation contradict the tenets of the neoliberal and commodified city (Harvey, 2005).

The emergence of social organizations that use occupation or squat as a means to claim the use value of buildings is a process with parallel instances and historical evolutions between the two countries. From the emergence of the first "Centros Sociales Okupados" (Squatted Social Centers), in Spain in the late 70s (García, Martinez, 2014), through the "Movimento Nacional de Luta pela Moradia" [National Movement for Housing Struggle] (MNLM), initiated in the main Brazilian capitals in the early 1980s (Martins, 2011), this method of reaction against the speculative logic of the real estate market has been increasing until today.

The *squats movement* is different from housing movements, and essentially questions the behavior established by the language of the capitalist economy and proposes another language, an alternative language to consumer behavior, presenting other perceptions and community organizations for everyday life. The *squats* proposals resemble many other proposals brought by other movements, such as the movement of occupation of real estate in central areas and, especially, the principle of autonomous society. We observe the affinity of the *squats* movement with the principle of autonomy in its most fundamental aspect: the conference of autonomy to the subjects through the passage of knowledge that confers the possibility of discernment and criticism, fundamental factors for a self-managed social organization, as proposed by different kinds of squatters. The *squatter* philosophy is not an exclusive claim to the process of gentrification and maintenance of the local population of a neighborhood, but a claim against the kind of segregation produced by neoliberal economic logic, which puts the capital and exchange value variable above the value of use and all other variables of the social life equation.

The interest of the *squats movement* is not to become the dominant language, it is to encourage people to decide on their own reality. The movement organizes its action as an open system—one that seeks to modify the performance of the subjects in society towards social transformation. In Spain, the links between occupation and squatting is a traditional dichotomy, identified by the terms "okupa" and "ocupa" (Bogado, 2011). The first occupy buildings mainly as a tool to establish social centers, which are open to the neighborhood, in central and peripheral areas to vindicate the common use of the buildings and the city. The second refers to housing squats used mainly as a shelter to impoverished populations (Manzano, 2015), frequently opened or supported by popular housing social movements. In Brazil, although squatted social centers also exist, most of the squatting initiatives are housing occupations, comparable with the Spanish "ocupa" houses, using empty buildings, as a pragmatic housing solution and claim for the right to the city.

Facing the already described speculative logic, social movements have acquired, in the last years, a double role. Firstly, they constitute platforms for the expression of discontent and pressure to change the regulatory framework. The fight for the *Urban Reform*, the control of capitalist urban logics in the Brazilian case, and the demands for modifying the Law Against Evictions in Spain, have been conveyed by social movements and are part of the current political debate in both countries, fighting the local consequences of the global-financial economy. Moreover, it presents disobedient resources and practices to circumvent the model dictated by the theory of consumption, or "tyranny of money in its pure state", according to Brazilian geographer Milton Santos (2013).

Secondly, sectors of these same movements in both countries promote, support and organize collective occupations as a temporary solution for families without resources. In the face of militant squatting, which develops squatted social centers frequently open to citizenship, "collective occupations" would be generalized as a direct and pragmatic action whose study is still embryonic.

161

The Struggle for Housing in Spain

In Spain, the chronification of the "crisis" in the popular classes and the desperate situation of many families provoked a popular reaction, both in Madrid and the whole of the State. It took shape under several housing rights initiatives—La Corrala in Seville, the 15M groups of housing and, mainly, Plataforma de Afectados de la Hipoteca [Affected by the Mortgage Platform] (PAH). Originally born in Barcelona, in the same days that gave rise to the movement of 15 May 2011, this movement took place in a decentralized way, spreading rapidly throughout Spain. The platform is based on mutual legal and psychological assistance among its members. The experience of older members, having learned all the legal mechanisms and passive resistance techniques to stop an eviction, allows it to incorporate new members. The PAH also organizes an occupation movement called the "Obra Social" (Social Work).[8] Heir to the protesting tradition of militant squats, the okupa movement (Martinez, 2002), and based on squats dedicated exclusively to housing, the "Social Work" of the PAH promotes the use of buildings owned by the financial sector, and kept empty for speculative reasons. Their appropriation makes it possible to publicize their demands for legislative change and to negotiate "social rentals" from a strong position when they confront the financial owners.

Spanish occupations are generally undertaken by families weakened by the crisis, perhaps facing foreclosures or claims for the non-payment of rent. Spanish legislation makes it difficult to expel squatter families after 48 hours following their entrance into an empty building, with long judicial procedures, often more than one year, producing a "legal limbo". This allows a large number of precarious people to live in housing squats, even though they may periodically need to change houses. In contrast, PAH "Social Work" fights for families to stay permanently in houses and buildings belonging to banks "rescued" by the Spanish state, or the SAREB,[9] the national "bad bank", that purchased—with public money—unprofitable houses and buildings for the financial and real estate sectors.

For this purpose, activists promote two types of squats: individual and collective. Individual squats begin with the entry of a family into an empty dwelling, supported in this case by one or more activists. Once housed, however, it is relatively independent of the PAH assembly, being supported in particular at the legal level. PAH also helps to regulate individual squats opened by individuals, as long as they are housed in bank properties (previously cleared out after evicting a family that was unable to continue paying their mortgage). Collective squats are directly opened by experienced members of the PAH and serve as a home to households in need of emergency shelter. The buildings occupied are often small, and generally the selection of candidates requires previous assembly work to prepare the entrance and create common links, making easier the adaptation of households to their new life in the collective squat. Involving neighbors is a key element to avoid an early denunciation, reducing enormously the risk of eviction. Sympathy towards PAH in the media also minimizes the risk of expulsion.

The Social Housing Movements in Brazil

In Brazil, movements such as the MNLM[10] and the MTST (Movement of Homeless Workers),[11] frequently occupy empty buildings located in central areas. An important amount of organizational work is usually needed to cope with the creation of collective infrastructures within the housing complexes, such as gardens, libraries, soup kitchens, etc., and to deal with external risks such as police action and infiltrations.

In this country, the occupy phenomenon has strengthened, multiplied and gained more visibility from the various initiatives and forms of occupation carried out over recent years. Faced with the institutional bills approved by the current president, Michel Temer (2016–2018), and the retreat of the social rights they imply, the various manifestations and forms of occupation have become fundamental political actions (e.g. the occupied schools movement). The episode "Occupy Minc" stands out as a symbol of pluralization among the occupation forms and is responsible for spreading the phrase "Fora Temer" throughout Brazil.

Movements of occupation of empty buildings in Brazil are opposed to the interests of the real estate market and seek to provide access to housing for all as an universal right. Opposing the idea of housing as a commodity, occupying empty buildings in central areas, in addition to promoting awareness-raising activities. The National Movement for Housing, the MNLM, and the MTST demand observation of Article 6 of the Brazilian Constitution, which establishes housing as a social right. Moreover, they represent the protest for the right to live and enjoy the city. The slogan of the movement, expresses the government's disregard for housing provision: "If living is a right, occupying is a duty", justifying civil disobedience for the exercise of the social function of property. The MNLM organized itself as an entity in the period of the promulgation of the Federal Constitution, although previously its founders already militated in the National Movement for Urban Reform (MNRU). Before the military dictatorship in Brazil (1964–1985), the militants of the struggle for urban and agrarian reform were linked to the Catholic Church (Souza, 2009). The Central de Movimentos Populares (CMP), together with the MNLM, linked to discussion forums and debates promoting popular mobilization to occupy public buildings (Souza, 2009).

The CMP, which is national in scope and operates in several areas, selects abandoned public buildings available for occupation, although they also organize the occupation of private properties indebted to the municipality. These debts sometimes exceed the value of the property, and in some situations belong to the State (Souza, 2009). The lack of public commitment to housing is the trigger for the action of social movements, which arbitrarily enforce the rights described in the Constitution. However, this action is severely repressed by the police. In attempting to evict families and dismantle the movement the authorities cut the electricity and water supplies and threaten members. The occupation movements in Brazil act against the advance of real estate speculation in the central lands, and represent a radical route of action of re-appropriation of the city through civil disobedience. The existence of innumerable organized occupations in the metropolitan urban centers, mainly in the southeast of the country, testifies to the representativeness of the movements in the struggle for realizing the right to housing. Occupy movements exert significant pressure on governments to enforce the right to the city, although, in recent years, state action has focused more on evicting families than on regulating occupied housing. This conduct of the State is directly related to certain mega-events—the World Cup, 2014 and the 2016 Olympics—and with the troubled political scenario with the appointment of the country's president without elections, accompanied by measures that prioritize individual interests to the detriment of public and collective interests.

A Transnational Comparison between Brazilian and Spanish Practices of Occupation and Squatting

An in-depth comparison of struggles for the right to housing in Brazil and Spain is a project still to be carried out. However, we can point to some schematic similarities and differences between Brazilian and Spanish squats. Predominantly organized or related to housing movements, but also informally executed by individuals, in both countries squatting and occupations are a pragmatic answer to the speculative dynamics that have produced empty buildings. In this way, inhabitants claim their rights to the city. Used as a tool of hard negotiations, in both countries squats and occupied buildings are inhabited for several years, with few expulsions.

Some differences, however, can be pointed out. Firstly, the kind of buildings used and their ownership characteristics. Spanish housing occupations used to be of a small size, re-using empty residential buildings owned by the financial sector, mainly in peripheral areas, to provide individual flats. Brazilian housing social movements frequently occupy much bigger buildings, usually reconfiguring the spaces to provide individual apartments, but also installing basic infrastructure and creating common spaces of collective management.

Secondly, the origin of populations presents some differences. While the Spanish housing squats provide single flats to impoverished populations due to the economic crisis, the Brazilian equivalents house historically disadvantaged and precarious populations, with a more shared ideological background than the Spanish ones. Thirdly, these kinds of social initiatives, linked to the PAH movement, seem to enjoy huge popular support in Spain. In Brazil, the informal occupation of housing has historically been subject to stigma (Gonçalves, 2012) and, since around 2013, evictions accompanied by stigmata have accentuated—mainly during sports mega-events, when inappropriate housing practices were consciously linked, by authorities and the private sector, to marginal populations.

The Brazilian and Spanish legal frames are also different. In Spain, there is no institutionalized regulation to allow squats or occupations to obtain a long-term right to occupy empty buildings, being an object of case-by-case negotiations with public authorities and building owners. The Spanish "okupa" movement, whose motto is "un desalojo, otra ocupación" (one eviction, a new squat) is based on a continuous process of eviction–resettlement. The "ocupa" practices, not related to housing movements, are founded in a situation of high precarity and inhabitants are able to stay just a few months in their occupied houses—the time needed to get a new eviction court order. Although lacking empirical evidence, we estimate that a huge population is currently moving through the empty real estate housing stock, in a continuous process of fighting for survival (Manzano, 2015).

In Brazil, different legislation, such as the "City Statute" (Estatuto da Cidade) and the "usucapião" law, allow for the regularization of individual and collective occupations after some years of pacific, goodwill use of abandoned buildings and lands. In the last years, programs such as "MCMV Entidades" have provided public funds to housing movements, allowing the renovation of occupied buildings in collaboration with architects. Despite these legal advancements in relation to the right to housing, there is still much to be improved, as shown by the frequent evictions of organized occupations.

Conclusion: Towards an Internationalization of Urban Social Movements

Considering this comparative analysis, we believe that the popular answers to speculative processes in both countries are convergent. In spite of cultural differences—and the different positions at the core and periphery of the global economic system—global capitalist mechanics have strongly re-invigorated the "housing problem" in different contexts. The accumulation by dispossession process (Harvey, 2005) has, in both Brazil and Spain, induced massive forced evictions, strengthening the feeling of plunder and a generalized financial "revanchism" (Smith, 2012). As a consequence, the rise of urban social movements has been observed, constituting or supporting autonomous housing alternatives. The motto "people without houses, houses without people" is equally valid and used as a claim on both sides of the Atlantic.

The consolidation of communities generated by social movements is not without difficulties. Although the historical trajectories and the social reality of both countries are very different, the comparison of the respective processes of financialization, and the social reactions that have emerged from it, invite us to propose the existence of a convergence process, both in the commodification of popular urban areas and in the responses of social movements.

On the one hand, financial capital uses the urban space as an object of change, through speculative investment, attacking local populations that would not benefit in any way from these global investment transfers. This makes the "housing problem" (Engels, 1872 [1997]) reappear with force, in contexts characterized by enormous urban and real estate growth. The processes of uncontrolled real estate valuation carried out in both countries, such as the beginning of a crisis of extreme consequences, currently suffered in Brazil seven years after the start of the crisis in Spain, in 2008, could be part of the same process of violent global investment–divestment carried out a few years apart.

On the other hand, the social struggle against the process of financialization of housing and urban management, concretized by the occupy and squatting initiatives, share common elements in northern and southern global contexts, exemplified in the cases of Brazil and Spain. The fact that the struggle for the right to the city and to housing has emerged with force in both countries validates the hypothesis of the emergence of autonomous, self-regulated spaces that overflow the regulation frames and real estate logic of capital gains. Thus, these movements are attacking the core of the global, financial accumulation process with the eruption of popular solidarities by appropriating empty buildings.

Occupying and squatting insert alternative ways of urban life (Castells, Caraça et Cardoso, 2012), which allow populations excluded from the right to the city to become strong and reconquer it. In that sense, occupying and squatting practices are directly rooted in the original sense of Lefebvre's *Right to the City*. As Souza (2010) points out, the original sense of the right to the city goes far beyond the fight against the main manifestations of the neoliberal urban economy, reducing the amount of "horror" of its logics to a "tolerable level". The Lefebvrian purpose was not a fight against the superficial consequences of a capitalist market, but to support a deep transgression of the urban and systemic logic, founded in a subaltern re-appropriation of the city. The common appropriation of public spaces and buildings is materialized by a large range of practices, not only in our cases of study, but in very different countries. This constitutes a historical popular and middle class reaction against the dramatic capitalist exploitation of the city.

The current increase of successful squatting and occupy experiences, and the awareness of the population of the need to build a democratic appropriation of empty buildings, is currently under threat by the rise of conservative forces, both in Brazil and in Spain. However, the current reinforcement of repressive legal frames against self-organized housing initiatives, without providing public housing alternatives, is not sustainable for the hegemonic powers because, as history showed us (Leontidou, 1990; Aguilera, 2017) people need houses, and they will organize to obtain them.

References

Agamben, G. 2005. *Homo Sacer. Sovereign Power and Bare Life.* Stanford: University press.

Agamben, G. 2014. *O amigo & O que é um dispositivo.* Chapecó: Editora Argos.

Aguilera, F. and Naredo, J. 2009. *Interés y contexto del tema tratado. Economía, poder y megaproyectos.* Madrid: Cromoimagen S.L., pp.13-18.

Aguilera, T. 2017. *Gouverner les illégalismes urbains. Les politiques publiques face aux squats et aux bidonvilles dans les régions de Paris et de Madrid.* Paris: Dalloz.

Aguilera, T. and Smart, A. 2016. Squatting North, South and Turnabout: A Dialogue Comparing Illegal Housing Research. In *Public Goods vs Economic Interests: Global Perspectives on the History of Squatting.* New York: Routlegde.

Bogado, D. 2017. *El "Museu das Remoções" de la Vila Autódromo. Potencia de resistencia creativa y afectiva como respuesta sociocultural al Río de Janeiro de los megaeventos.* Ph.D. thesis. Universidad de Sevilla.

Bogado, D. 2011. *Movimento Okupa: Resistência e autonomia na ocupação de imóveis nas áreas urbanas centrais.* Master thesis. UFF.

Bourdieu, P. 1977. Sur le Pouvoir Symbolique. *Annales,* 32(3), pp.405-411.

Bourdieu, P. 1996. *Razões Práticas: sobre a teoria da ação.* Campinas: Papirus.

Bourdieu, P. 1974. *A Economia das Trocas Simbólicas.* São Paulo: Perspectiva.

Bueno, L. 2008. *Forma e sentido da resistência na cidade do Rio de Janeiro.* Master thesis. Instituto de Pesquisa e Planejamento Urbano, Universidade Federal de Rio de Janeiro.

Castells, M., Caraça J. and Cardoso G. 2012. *Aftermath. The Cultures of the Economics Crisis.* Oxford: OUP Oxford.

Debord, G. 1969. *A sociedade do espetáculo.* Rio de Janeiro: Contraponto.

Díaz Parra I. and Solanas Domínguez, M. 2015. De aquel cemento estos lodos. Vivienda, desahucios y okupación en la crisis española. *Servicios Sociales y Política Social,* 108, pp.101-120.

Engels, F. 1872 (1997). *The housing question.* London: Progress Publishers.

Erensü, S. and Karaman, O. 2017. The Work of a Few Trees: Gezi, Politics and Space. *International Journal of Urban and Regional Research,* 4(1), pp.19-36.

Faulhaber, L. and Azevedo, L. 2015. SMH 2016: *Remoções no Rio de Janeiro Olímpico.* Rio de Janeiro: Mórula Editorial.

Gonçalves Soares, R. 2008. O debate jurídico em torno da urbanização de favelas no Rio de Janeiro. *Revista Internacional de Direito e Cidadania*, 2, pp.139-148.

Gonçalves Soares, R. 2013. *Favelas do Rio de Janeiro: História e Direito.* Rio de Janeiro: Pallas/PUC–Rio.

Harvey, D. 1985. *The urbanization of capital.* Oxford: Basil Blackwell.

Harvey, D. 2011. *A condição pós-moderna.* São Paulo: Loyola.

Harvey, D. 2005. *A produção capitalista do espaço.* São Paulo: Annablume.

Lefebvre, H. 2009 (1968). *Le Droit à la ville.* Paris: Anthropos.

Leontidou, L. 1990. *The Mediterranean city in transition. Social change and urban development.* Cambridge, MA: Cambridge University Press.

Logan, J.R. and Molotch, H.L. 1987, *Urban fortunes: The political economy of place.* Berkeley: University of California Press.

Machado Martins, M. 2011. *Les "copropriétés populaires" de l'Avenida Brasil: etude d'une nouvelle forme d'habitat informel a Rio de Janeiro dans les annees 2000.* Ph.D. thesis. Université Paris–Est; Prourb—Universidade Federal de Rio de Janeiro.

Mamari, F. 2008. *Se morar é um direito, ocupar é um dever !: As ocupações de sem-teto na metropole do Rio de Janeiro.* Rio de Janeiro, Universidade Federal do Rio de Janeiro.

Manzano, N.A. 2015. *Casas sin gente, gente sin casas: financiarisation urbaine et appropriation d'immeubles dans la nouvelle périphérie madrilène.* Master thesis. Universidad Paris 8.

Maricato, E. 2008. Brasil, cidades: alternativas para a crise urbana. Rio de Janeiro: Editorial Petrópolis.

Martinez, M. and Bernardos A. 2014. *Okupa Madrid (1985–2011). Memoria, reflexión, debate y autogestión colectiva del conocimiento.* Seminario de Historia Política y Social de las Okupaciones en Madrid–Metrópolis, Diagonal.

Movimiento andaluz por el derecho a la vivienda 2013. *Declaración del estado de emergencia habitacional.* [Online]. [Accessed 22 September 2018]. Available from:
https://granadastopdesahucios.files.wordpress.com/2013/04/emergencia-habitacional-stop-desahucios-15m-granada-1.pdf

Observatorio Metropolitano 2013. *Paisajes devastados. Después del ciclo inmobiliario: Impactos regionales y urbanos de las crisis.* Madrid: Traficantes de Sueños.

PAH 2013. *Emergencia habitacional en el estado español.* [Online]. [Accessed 22 September 2018]. Available from: http://afectadosporlahipoteca.com/wp-content/uploads/2013/12/2013-Emergencia-Habitacional_Estado_Espanyoldef.pdf

PAH 2016. *The PAH'S Green Book.* [Online]. [Accessed 22 September 2018]. Available from:

http://afectadosporlahipoteca.com/wp-content/uploads/2016/06/GreenBook-PAH-21juny.pdf

Rolnik, R. 2009. *Report of the Special Rapporteur on adequate housing as a component of the right to an adequate standard of living, and on the right to non-discrimination in this context.* Geneva: United Nations General Assembly.

Rolnik, R. 2010. *Olimpíada e Copa trazem prejuízo social.* [Online]. [Accessed 22 September 2018]. Available from: http://raquelrolnik.wordpress.com

Rolnik, R. 2013. *A região portuária do Rio de Janeiro.* [Online]. [Accessed 22 September 2018]. Available from: http://raquelrolnik.wordpress.com/2011/06/13/porto-maravilha-custos-publicos-e-beneficios-privados/

Rolnik, R. 2016. *A Guerra dos Lugares: A colonização da terra e da moradia na era das finanças.* São Paulo: Boitempo.

Santos, M. 1996. *A urbanização brasileira.* São Paulo: HUCITEC.

Santos, M. 2013. *Por uma outra globalização: Do pensamento único à consciência universal.* Rio de Janeiro: Record.

Sassen, S. 2001. *The global city: New york, London, Tokyo.* Princeton: Princeton University Press.

Smith, N. 2006. A gentrificação generalizada: de uma anomalia local à regeneração urbana como estratégia urbana global. In: Bidou-Zachariasen, C. *De volta à cidade.* São Paulo: Annablume.

Smith, N. 2012. *La nueva frontera urbana. Ciudad revanchista y gentrificación.* Madrid: Traficantes de Sueños.

Solanas, M. 2016. *Las cooperativas de viviendas uruguayas como sistema de producción social del hábitat y la autogestión de barrios.* Thesis. Universidad Pablo de Olavide.

Solanas, M. 2014. La Corrala Utopía abre puertas. In: *Procesos habitados Las arquitecturas en las que vive el otro 90 per cent.* Universidade da Coruña, pp.60-63.

Solanas, M. 2014. Andalucía hace camino: ocupaciones populares y respuesta institucional. De las Corralas a la Ley de Función Social de la Vivienda. In: Mathivet, C. ed. ¡La tierra es nuestra! Por la función social de la tierra y la vivienda. Resistencia y alternativas. Paris: Colección Passerelle, Coredem, pp.170-175.

Solanas, M. and Lora, M. 2014. Vivienda y organización popular. De la crisis institucional a la utopía. *Vivienda Popular,* 25, pp.90-99.

Sousa Santos, B. 2004. O futuro do Fórum Social Mundial: o trabalho da tradução. *Revista del Observatorio Social de América Latina,* 15, pp.77-90.

Sousa Santos, B. 2010. *Para descolonizar Occidente. Más allá del pensamiento abismal.* Buenos Aires: CLACSO, Prometeo Libros.

Souza, M. L. de. 2000. *A problemática sócio-espacial nas metrópoles brasileiras: o desafio metropolitano.* Rio de Janeiro: Bertrand Brasil.

Souza, M. L. de. 2010. *Which right to which city? In defence of political–strategic clarity.* Interface: a journal for and about social movements. 2(1), 315-333.

Souza, T. R. 2008. *Ocupação de edifícios públicos*. Trabalho Final de graduação, Niteroi: UFF—Universidade Federal Fluminense.

Tripp, D. 2005. "Pesquisa-ação: uma introdução metodológica". *Educação e Pesquisa*, 31(3), pp.443-466.

Notes

1. In Spanish, Plataforma de Afectados por la Hipoteca (Platform of Mortgage-Affected).
2. Another kind of urban squat, land used to build popular housing, although related to housing movements in Brazil, has virtually disappeared in Spain, and will not be examined in this text.
3. As described in the UN report prepared by the Special Rapporteur in charge, Raquel Rolnik (2009), who addresses the right to adequate housing. This report analyses the procedures of those responsible for the mega-events in Brazil, the IOC and FIFA.
4. In Portuguese: "remoções".
5. In this area, on the eve of the mega-sport events (2014–2017) many squats were evicted, although they were located in an "Area of Special Social Interest", an urban area earmarked for popular dwellings (Bogado, 2017).
6. Municipal Enterprise of Housing and Land.
7. Institute of Housing of Madrid.
8. Further information: http://afectadosporlahipoteca.com/wp-content/uploads/2016/06/GreenBook-PAH-21juny.pdf
9. Management Society of Funds from bank restructuring processes.
10. In Portuguese: Movimento Nacional de Luta pela Moradía.
11. In Portuguese: Movimento dos Trabalhadores Sem Teto (MTST).

Rights Begin in the Small Places Closest to Home: A Story from Constitution Street

Jemma Neville

I live on Constitution Street in the Leith area of Edinburgh, northeast Scotland, United Kingdom. Maybe you know the street, maybe you don't. That doesn't particularly matter for the purpose of the story I want to share with you. For certain, you will know another street well. Maybe it's the street where you live or work in your part of the world. Your street too will likely have a beginning, middle, and an end, like all streets and all stories do. One street among many streets in the city. A wee story within another wee story, as we would say here in Scotland. Hear me to the end of the road.

Where to begin the story? Stories are about hospitality, about the giving and receiving of experience, so I'll begin with a welcome. Make yourself right at home. We've heard a lot on this street and streets up and down Scotland, and the UK, about our differences of late. The Yes and the No. The Leave and the Remain. The them and the us. Binary positions in referendums. Some neighbours displayed posters in their windows. Others closed the curtains. Some sang protest songs or wrote plays. Some felt anxious. Some felt excited. It is time for new conversations and new ways of considering the distribution of power, land and resources.

If it sounds a revolutionary sort of a place that's because it is. Or it once was, what with a name like Constitution Street, built in the late eighteenth century amidst the radical thinking of the Scottish Enlightenment and the overthrow of monarchies elsewhere in the world. You may know though that the UK doesn't have a written constitution. Rather, there are constitutional conventions and principles based on case law developed over centuries. There is an ongoing debate amongst legal scholars about whether or not it is time to write a constitution to better safeguard the country against excessive executive power, particularly in light of the UK leaving the European Union and its safeguards regards employment, social security and environmental law. Some consider whether Scotland, as a devolved nation within the UK, or perhaps as an independent country of its own one day, could draft a written constitution based on a human rights framework.

The Universal Declaration of Human Rights, adopted in 1948, is the most revolutionary document of the international human rights framework. It is hard to imagine the international community of nations in the present day agreeing to respect, promote and protect social, economic and cultural rights along with civil and political rights. Head of the drafting committee for the Declaration, Eleanor Roosevelt, famously remarked that human rights begin in the small places closest to home. So small and so close that they cannot be seen from any world map. They are the farmyard, the factory, the playground and the community garden. Like the neighbours living side by side as a neighbourhood community on a street, human rights are universal, indivisible, interdependent and must be interpreted for the context of the times in which we are living.

The economic, human and environmental wreckage in the world we live in today has shaped an age of anxiety in this, a liminal land. Liminal times and places are those that are in-between, in transition, on a threshold of change. And the anxiety resulting from liminal times and places can make us sensitive and curious about ourselves, making us want to search out new ways of being and doing in the world. In search of these new ways, I set out on a long walk along my street in the city of Edinburgh. I wanted to find the common ground that overrides division and difference.

I began the long walk by interviewing some of my neighbours and local business owners about their lived experiences of the rights to health, housing, education, culture, food, the environment and so on. My "methodology" began with recorded conversations with those neighbours I know well and then I asked each of them to recommend someone new that I should speak to. In this way, the conversations rippled outward in concentric circles like everyday human contact does, rather than following any linear structure like the chronological addresses of a street. My interview consent forms were approved by an Edinburgh University research ethics committee, but fundamentally the exploration relies on trust and it was really important to me that participants—my neighbours—were kept informed about the Constitution Street learning. I have invited everyone who took part to a communal meal to say thank you.

People were not shy in the conversations and talked to me for hours about local history and neighbourhood gossip. We laughed and cried. There were confessions about how and why people voted in the recent referenda. I then asked my neighbours to imagine that, as residents of one street in one city, we could draft a new written constitution by, for, and with ourselves as rights holders. I asked them to imagine what rights we should include. People said nothing. Their faces were blank. I elaborated with props like a parchment scroll and quotes from other constitutions and human rights declarations around the world. Still nothing. Neighbours complained that it all sounded like legalese. It seemed a bit dry and boring. I needed to reframe the question. I needed to go in close and local and ask about how we want to live together in common, about how we practice the old saying of *love thy neighbour*. This is love in its true meaning, with acceptance of vulnerability and flaws, and as a verb, a doing-word.

I love my next door neighbour, Flora. She is ten years old. An in-between, liminal sort of an age. Not quite an adult and no longer a young child. She has lived her whole life on Constitution Street. Her mother, a Scotswoman, voted No to Scottish independence. Her father, an Englishman, voted Yes.

These are the ambiguities and complexities of our many identities shaped by life experience and the people we meet.

Come with me and Flora to an Autumn day in our community garden next to Constitution Street. The garden is called the Community Croft and is organised by a group of local volunteers. *Croft* is an interesting old Scots word. It comes from traditional settlements or smallholdings where people kept enough animals and grew a few crops to feed their own family. Crofts have a little bit of everything. Enough and no more. No fences, no walls. Traditional crofting was hard, physical work in a harsh climate and shouldn't be overly romanticised, but the principle of growing and sharing still holds true.

Right now, it's a Sunday morning in the first quarter of the twenty-first century in postmodern, post-referendum Scotland. Flora is blowing the seeds from a dandelion flower. These are the wispy stems made up of small circular flowers. The number of puffs it takes to scatter all the petals is a game said to be a way to tell the time. We both have our backs pressed flat onto picnic table benches and we are blinking up at the big, shuffling sky. An upside down kaleidoscope of kinetic colour and shape. The season is only hinting at the changes to follow. The green foliage of chestnut trees shows glimpses of racy yellow and orange at their corners—frayed, delicate edges where leaves will soon disintegrate, fall and land at our feet and in our laps like garments made of antique lace that have shrunk in the wash.

We have been daydreaming for some time when I ask Flora if she has any homework before school the next day. She tells me about a recent school trip to the devolved Scottish Parliament to learn about the separation of powers and about the social contract. She and her classmates have been tasked with preparing a short presentation about power. I ask her what she thinks about the commons.

You mean the House of Commons?

No. The Commons. As in community. Sharing. Common land and participation and food. Establishing a pattern of active participation and assembly. It's quite a hard thing to articulate, but you know it when you see it. It's when a group of people share resources or goods for a common purpose, for the benefit of all.

A resource?

A thing. Like, like—the slide over there in this garden that we're sitting in is a thing. It's a play thing.

My brother got a climbing frame last Christmas and because it was a much bigger present than the one I got, Mum and Dad say that he has to let me have a go on it sometimes.

Well, good luck with that! Imagine that the climbing frame has a slide and swings and that you share it equally with the other children of the street.

Who gets to go down the slide first?

That's for you two or more to negotiate and agree upon.

Who else is here playing?

Erm. It's just a metaphor. Imagine there are all your childhood friends and neighbours, including some that you don't know well but would like to know. If someone gets tired or is unwell, you can help one another stay safe on the climbing frame. A team game! Home ground. Common ground. Cooperation rather than competition. The city and the world itself are round, a sphere that looks like a circle when drawn, so all the streets eventually join up. There is no gain in always being first on the slide and leaving others behind.

It sounds fancy. Can we sell it to spend the money on other things?

No. You don't actually own the climbing frame in that sense.

But I thought you said that it was ours?

Yes, it is. Until you want to pass it onto other children when you get bigger or while you're not using it. It's a public amenity, not a private wealth.

Ok. Is it a rusty old thing or brand new?

It could be either but you'll take good care of it so that it lasts a long time. One of you can oil the bolts. Another paint the frame. And so on. Making use of different skill sets and materials. A dynamic mix.

I'm still not sure if my brother and I could share that well together.

You'll probably fall out. Siblings usually do because of how you know and love one another so much that it can hurt. You must agree between you how to resolve any disputes and if one of you should damage the climbing frame deliberately or steal part of it or something so that other children can't play on it, there will be graduated sanctions that you've agreed to abide by in advance. It's one of Ostrom's principles for commoning.

Ostrom?

Nobel Prize Winner for Economics. A smart woman.

Seems common sense.

Exactly.

But will it be safe to play alone in the park and what about when it gets dark?

Ok. Good points. All of you that are playing together, and with the support of the city authorities, will agree safe lighting and maybe restrict car parking nearby. It's your right to play. And when you're hungry, maybe you can organise a picnic together. Did you know that the word companionship comes from the Latin to eat bread? Eating is best done in company.

And when you're out playing on the climbing frame in the park, you will see birds and animals and plants. Everything is involved and interconnected. Without the plants, the trees, the grass, the seeds and so on, there would be no soft ground on which to land from a jump, no water to drink when you get thirsty after playing. No sound of birds singing to make your heart soar and to guide you home! But you know this stuff. It's empirical naturalism.

What?

Trust me. You already know it. You're doing it. Here, now, in the garden, having this conversation with me, your neighbour. It's social ecology. People in nature. Bookchin. Read some Murray Bookchin. I've got a book from a conference in Greece. Have I told you all about that? Inspiring people. I'll pass the book on when you're a bit older. And then I want you to pass it onto another neighbour. So, you see, commoning, social contracts, power, constitutions. We have lots in common already. And the power to find out more.

End of conversation, back to the street garden and the quiet observation in community. Small children are heard stamping out an angry path behind us in the far edges of the Community Croft. Mini street gods, they test the boundaries by wrestling then embracing one another and quarrelling once more, flinging large handfuls of what Aristotle referred to as organic matter at one another.

There is a fresco hanging in the Vatican by the Italian Renaissance artist Raphael. The fresco is called the School of Athens and depicts Plato and Aristotle in conversation at the centre of a semi-circle filled with other ancient Greek philosophers. Plato is concerned with matters spiritual and looks up towards the Heavens while Aristotle casts his gaze down to Earth. Sitting apart from the others and appearing to daydream with his head resting in his hands is Heraclitus. He is best known among contemporary environmentalists for his insistence that no one ever steps into the same river twice and that the path up and the path down are one and the same because of the ever-present flow of nature.

The Raphael fresco also depicts a paradoxical tension: humans are intrinsically part of the natural world—we breathe the same air and eat the same plants and animals as our fellow creatures, but humans have also developed the reasoning and technological skills with which to debate with one another in a semicircle. Humans are both natural and social beings. This is what Murray Bookchin referred to as our second nature.

The Croft here is common ground, hard-fought by the young families of the neighbourhood. Unlike other areas of Edinburgh, few of our flats have communal back gardens; such was the pressure on available land for housing during the overcrowding of the Leith area of Edinburgh in its seafaring heyday when the Port was the busiest in Scotland and Constitution Street was first laid out in 1790. Old maps from the archives of the National Library of Scotland hint at market gardens extending from the back of the original dwellings, but traces of these have long since been replaced by car parks and budget supermarket chains. More on that another time.

Here ends one wee story within another wee story. You are welcome to visit our street anytime, but you probably have your own street in your own city to be getting back to. Our streets and our cities could even link up and become more streetwise! Meanwhile, I will be having more conversations about the lived experience of human rights in practice on Constitution Street. Right here, right now.

I have told this long, sort of circular, conversation to bring to mind my learning from the TRISE conference in Thessaloniki, 2017. I learnt that the commons in the city might provide a way through the wreckage of nation-state politics at a time when national borders and realpolitik is limiting our full potential as human beings to live in peaceful, sustainable communities with full rights to housing, health, the environment, and so on. I learnt that local, active participation is where democracy and the meaningful distribution of power can most flourish. Conversations with activists and researchers from around the world, who are passionate about this and more, felt, to me, like coming home.

Back home in the city of Edinburgh, I will continue to walk up and down Constitution Street every day, paying attention to the extraordinary detail in our ordinary places and encounters so that I might come to know the street, my neighbours, and indeed myself better. To be in conversation like this—constantly negotiating our boundaries and realising our human rights—is a form of living constitution.

NOTES ON THE CONTRIBUTORS

Ercan Ayboga is an environmental engineer and co-founder of the Tatort Kurdistan Campaign in Germany for which he co-wrote the book *Revolution in Rojava*, published in several languages. While living in North Kurdistan he co-founded the Initiative to Keep Hasankeyf Alive in 2006, a long-term campaign against the destructive Mega Dam Ilisu on the Tigris River. Ercan is also engaged in the Mesopotamian Ecology Movement, a social movement in North Kurdistan.

Diana Bogado is architect and urbanist activist, and has researched rights to housing from an activist experience in occupations and squats in Brazil and Spain. She completed her doctoral thesis at Seville University (2012–2017), while her professional work ranges from teaching to scientific research. She has coordinated community participatory projects in Brazil, especially the construction of the Evictions Museum in the favela Vila Autódromo, in Rio de Janeiro, and has been engaged in the social movement "Stop Despejos" in Portugal. She has recently embarked on post-doctoral research on the right to housing and the Right to the City in Centro de Estudos Sociais da Universidade de Coimbra, (CES-UC), 2018–2019.

Daniel Chodorkoff is the co-founder and former executive director of the Institute for Social Ecology in Vermont. For fifty years now, he has been actively committed to progressive urban and ecological movements. Chodorkoff has a Ph.D. in cultural anthropology from the New School for Social Research, and was a long-time faculty member at Goddard College. He is a life-long activist living in Northern Vermont with his wife and two daughters where he gardens, writes, plays harmonica, and works on environmental justice issues. His essays on social ecology and community development have been published under the title *The Anthropology of Utopia*, and he is also author of the novel *Loisaida*.

Emet Değirmenci is a long-term social ecologist, an independent researcher in women and ecology, a writer, speaker, teacher, and forager, a re-indigenizing and rewilding enthusiast, and an ecological farm designer.

Eleanor Finley is a writer, speaker, activist, and organizer. Former Board Member at the Institute for Social Ecology (ISE), she participates in various popular education and organizing projects about libertarian municipalism. Eleanor is also a Ph.D. Student in anthropology at the University of Massachusetts, Amherst. Her research focuses on social movements for popular assemblies in a comparative and transnational perspective.

Magali Fricaudet is a French activist involved in anti-globalization and Right to the City movements. Professionally, she is a civil servant in charge of local democracy in a municipality in northern Paris. She lived in Barcelona for three years, in charge of coordinating an international network of cities for the Right to the City, UCLG Committee of Social Inclusion, Participatory Democracy, and Human Rights.

Havin Guneser is a Kurdish writer, journalist, women's rights activist, and a spokesperson for the International Initiative Freedom for Abdullah Öcalan—Peace in Kurdistan. She is also a translator and publisher of the works of Abdullah Öcalan – the leading figure of the Kurdish liberation struggle imprisoned by the Turkish state on İmralı Island since 1999.

Metin Guven has, since the 1980s, been involved in social ecology groups and other libertarian organizations in Turkey, Australia, New Zealand, and the US. Metin was on the editorial board of the Turkish social ecology journal *Toplumsal Ekoloji*, and has also written for newspapers, magazines, and other journals.

Theodoros Karyotis is an independent researcher, translator and social activist based in Thessaloniki, Greece. Trained in sociology and social anthropology, he is active in grassroots movements practicing direct democracy, solidarity economy, and the defence and self-management of the commons. He has translated many relevant books and articles, and he is a regular op-ed contributor to roarmag.org in English and diagonalperiodico.net in Spanish. He is the coordinator of workerscontrol.net, a multilingual resource on workers' self-management, and sits on the Advisory Council of the Transnational Institute of Social Ecology.

Noel Manzano studied architecture in Spain, sociology in France, and now urban planning in Germany for his Ph.D. in the European Joint Doctorate program "UrbanHist". As an architect, he has worked on urban planning and social housing projects in Paris, Rio de Janeiro, and Barcelona. As a researcher, he has studied the conflicts over public space and urban renewal programs on the periphery of Paris, the social housing privatisation and squatting dynamics of Madrid, and, currently, the history of European informal urbanisation. Between 2014 and 2015, he studied in LeMetro, Laboratory of Metropolitan Ethnography of Rio de Janeiro. He has participated in social movements as the PAH (the Platform for Victims of Mortgages) and recently he collaborated in the birth of the Sindicat de Llogaters (Tenants' Union) of Barcelona.

Inés Morales is a forest engineer, a specialist in agroecology and organic farming, and holds a Ph.D. in Natural Resources and Sustainable Management. Her most recent research interests are social reproduction, food politics and urban struggles with case studies in Madrid, Athens, Lisbon and Naples. Currently she collaborates with 'Surcos Urbanos', a professional initiative that works on sustainable urbanism. As an activist, she has been involved in autonomous and anarchists movements across Europe.

Brian Morris is emeritus professor of anthropology at Goldsmiths College at the University of London. He is a specialist on folk taxonomy, ethnobotany and ethnozoology, and on religion and symbolism. He has carried out fieldwork among South Asian hunter-gatherers and in Malawi. His writings include the books *Bakunin: The Philosophy of Freedom* (1993), *The Anarchist Geographer: An Introduction to the Life of Peter Kropotkin* (2012), and *Pioneers of Ecological Humanism* (2012).

Jemma Neville has a background in human rights law and outreach. Her first book, *Constitution Street*, explores a year in the life of one street during constitutional change and an age of anxiety in Scotland and the UK. Jemma is Director of Voluntary Arts Scotland, the national development agency for community-led arts. She was the inaugural Community Fellow at the Institute of Advanced Studies in Humanities, University of Edinburgh, and was shortlisted for the Guardian International Development Journalism Award.

Egit Pale spent his childhood in North Kurdistan, and is now a survey engineer. He was, for more than three years, on the editorial team of the Istanbul magazine *Toplum ve Kuram*. For several years Egit has been involved in the Mesopotamia Ecology Movement and, since 2016, he has also been strongly engaged in the Initiative to Keep Hasankeyf Alive, a campaign against the destructive Mega Dam Ilisu on the Tigris River.

Alexandros Schismenos earned his Ph.D. in Philosophy from the University of Ioannina in 2017. He is a member of the editorial team of *Babylonia* political magazine and has been an active participant in social movements since 2000. He is the author of three books and several articles published in Greece regarding contemporary social issues and political philosophy.

Marta Solanas Domínguez works as a teacher in Secondary Education, responsible for Coeducation, at Instituto Diamantino García Acosta, Sevilla. She studied architecture at Universidad de Sevilla, Spain, and finished her Ph.D. in Environmental Studies, with a thesis on cooperative housing in Uruguay as a way of self-managing neighbourhoods (2016, UPO, Sevilla). She is a member of the research group *Estructuras y Sistemas Territoriales* (GIEST), Universidad de Sevilla. She participates as a housing rights activist at APDH–Andalucía (Human Rights) and is on the editorial board of the local journal *El Topo tabernario*.

Olli Tammilehto is an independent researcher, writer and activist. He has published ten books about global social-ecological issues including, most recently, *Stop the Progress of Devastation—The Societal Phase Shift* (Into Publishers, Helsinki 2017), in Finnish. He is a frequent contributor to various Finnish magazines and journals on global ecology, on war and peace, and on social movements and radical social change. In his lectures on environmental philosophy in the University of Helsinki during the years 1990–2001 he emphasized the approach of social ecology. For decades he has been active in various environmental movements, especially the anti-nuclear movement.

Federico Venturini is an independent activist-researcher. In 2016, he earned his Ph.D. at the University of Leeds on the relations between contemporary cities and urban social movements. He holds an M.Phil. from the University of Trieste, as well as a master's degree in History and European Culture from the University of Udine, Italy. He has been a member of the Advisory Board of the Transnational Institute of Social Ecology since 2013, and the International İmralı Peace Delegation, organized by the EU–Turkey Civic Commission, since 2016.

ALSO FROM BLACK ROSE BOOKS

Political Ecology:
System Change Not Climage Change
Dimitrios Roussopoulos

Ecologists, Roussopoulos argues, aim for more than simply protecting the environment—they call for new communities, new lifestyles, and a new way of doing politics.

"A useful and timely history of the environmental movement and its philosophical bases."
– BOOKS IN CANADA

Paperback ISBN 978-1-55164-634-3 $22.99

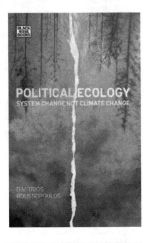

The Politics of Social Ecology:
Libertarian Municipalism
Janet Biehl

Best known for introducing the idea of ecology to the Left, and for first positing that a liberatory society would also have to be an ecological society, Murray Bookchin, over the course of several decades, developed the basic components of "libertarian municipalism" - how to create free cities.

Written in short, to-the-point chapters, the book presents an introductory overview and sketches the historical and philosophical context in which these ideas are grounded.

Paperback ISBN: 978-1-55164-100-3 $19.99

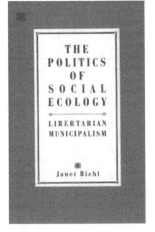

Villages in Cities: Community Land Ownership, Cooperative Housing, and the Milton Parc Story
Dimitrios Roussopoulos and Josh Hawley

"There were so many rules in the way of what you could do and what you could not do, and this is a great lesson that if you really believe in something and really fight for it, it happens. I've ordered 25 copies of the book to give to people. That tells you how much I think about it."
– PHYLLIS LAMBERT, founder of the Canadian Center for Architecture and Heritage Montreal

Paperback ISBN: 978-1-55164-687-9 $22.99

ALSO FROM BLACK ROSE BOOKS

Participatory Democracy:
Prospects for Democratizing Democracy
George Benello, Dimitrios Roussopoulos, eds.

A completely revised edition of the classic and widely consulted 1970 version

First published as a testament to the legacy of the concept made popular by the New Left of the 1960s, and with the perspective of the intervening decades, this book opens up the way for re-examining just what is involved in democratizing democracy.

With its emphasis on citizen participation, here, presented in one volume are the best arguments for participatory democracy written by some of the most relevant contributors to the debate, both in an historic, and in a contemporary, sense.

This wide-ranging collection probes the historical roots of participatory democracy in our political culture, analyzes its application to the problems of modern society, and explores the possible forms it might take on every level of society from the work place, to the community, to the nation at large. Part II, "The Politics of Participatory Democracy," covers Porto Alegre, Montreal, the new urban ecology, and direct democracy.

"The book is, by all odds, the most encompassing one so far in revealing the practical actual subversions that the New Left wishes to visit upon us.
– WASHINGTON POST

"It is good to be reminded of the origins of this yeasty rebelliousness...and to that end, editors Dimitrios Roussopoulos and the late C.George Benello have produced...a volume that is part inspiration and part reference work for a generation of earnest social reformers...Our democracy desperately needs more democracy, and a reflection upon these essays is a credible place to start the process"
– COLLEGE QUARTERLY

Apart from the editors, contributors include: George Woodcock, Murray Bookchin, Don Calhoun, Stewart Perry, Rosabeth Moss Kanter, James Gillespie, Gerry Hunnius, John McEwan, Arthur Chickering, Christian Bay, Martin Oppenheimer, Colin Ward, Sergio Baierle, Anne Latendresse, Bartha Rodin, and C.L.R. James.

Paperback ISBN 1-55164-224-7 $24.99

ALSO FROM BLACK ROSE BOOKS

Green Politics, Green Economics:
The Basics of Ecology
M. Athena Palaeologu

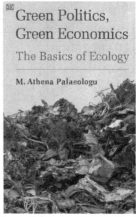

Given the world-wide ecological crisis, to what extent do the current economic systems of production and consumption need to change? To make substantial changes to the dominant economic system as the author proposes, area new politics required? What are the relations between economic and political changes? M. Athena Palaeologu's lucid and engaging analysis offers concrete proposals for moving beyond our current social and environmental impasse.

In market-driven economies around the world ecological crises are creating major problems of supply and distribution. The inability of governments to manage these environmental problems both domestically and internationally has led to widespread contradictions between public rhetoric and political practice. A growing number of contemporary publications respond to these crises by advocating a successful marriage of the corporate marketplace with the goals of environmentalism, in a marketing landscape where large and small corporations are tripping over each other to present their "green"credentials. M. Athena Palaeologu's timely work *Green Politics, Green Economics* examines these apologetic responses to broach an uncomfortable but fundamental question–is long-term and sustainable development really possible under market capitalism?

Palaeologu develops two alternative approaches to these environmental challenges: (i) a"green politics"that places major importance on achieving ecological goals through grassroots participatory citizen involvement, drawing heavily on values shared with feminist and social movements, and; (ii) a"green economics"that address the dynamic and spatial interdependence between human economies and the natural ecosystems which sustain them.

M. Athena Palaeologu is a long-time researcher and activist. An organiser of alternative movements for social change, she is editor of *The Sixties in Canada: A Turbulent and Creative Decade* (Black Rose Books). She holds a PhD in politics and economics, exploring political and economic alternatives through social ecological movements.

Paperback ISBN 978-1-55164-332-8 $19.99